Democracy and Institutions

Democracy and Institutions

The Life Work of Arend Lijphart

Edited by
Markus M. L. Crepaz, Thomas A. Koelble,
and David Wilsford

Ann Arbor

THE UNIVERSITY OF MICHIGAN PRESS

Copyright © by the University of Michigan 2000
All rights reserved
Published in the United States of America by
The University of Michigan Press
Manufactured in the United States of America
⊗ Printed on Acid Free Paper

2003   2002   2001   2000   4   3   2   1

A CIP catalog record for this book is available from the British Library.

Library of Congress Cataloging-in-Publication Data

Democracy and institutions : the life and work of Arend Lijphart / edited
   by Markus M.L. Crepaz, Thomas A. Koelble, and David Wilsford.
      p.   cm.
   Includes bibliographical references and index.
   ISBN 0-472-11126-4 (cloth : alk. paper)
   1. Democracy.   2. Lijphart, Arend—Contributions in democracy.   I. Crepaz,
Markus M. L., 1959–   II. Koelble, Thomas A., 1957–   III. Wilsford, David.

   JC423 .D439793   2000
   321.8—dc21   00-020166

Contents

Studying Democracy and Putting It into Practice: The Contributions of Arend Lijphart to Democratic Theory and to Actual Democracy

David Wilsford

Distinguished contributions by distinguished scholars comprise this book's timely reassessment of the seminal and pathbreaking work in political science by Arend Lijphart, one of the most influential political scientists of our time. The task of an introduction to such a volume is to provide a framework for the reader's subsequent exploration and appreciation of the scholarship here, without unduly getting in the way or distracting from the main issues at play.

And the issues at play in this book are among the most important in all of political science: What are the conditions that underlie successful democracy? How can different forms of democracy respond to widely varying social and economic conditions in the world? Can democracy be engineered where it does not currently exist?

With the remaking of a whole world order upon the advent of a post-Cold War era, these issues obviously assume ever-heightened importance.

Arend Lijphart has made critical contributions to three important areas of democratic theory. The first is *consociationalism*, initially laid out in an early book, *The Politics of Accommodation* (Lijphart 1968), based on a case study of the Netherlands, his native country. He extended and developed his thinking about how democracy can work in divided societies in a later pathbreaking book, *Democracy in Plural Societies* (Lijphart 1977), in which his scholarship took on an explicit, highly rigorous comparative approach. In that book, Lijphart induced the conditions that could support a stable democratic political system in societies not usually thought of as conducive to democracy—those characterized by many deep cleavages—economic, social, linguistic, cultural, religious, ethnic.

Lijphart's work on consociationalism has been criticized by some scholars on both practical and normative grounds. Practically, some argue, consociationalism hinges on the cooperation of elites representing different segments of a divided society. Yet, engineering elite cooperation is precisely the problem that characterizes most divided societies. I, myself, argued this point in the first seminar paper I ever did for Arend in graduate school (although I was neither the first, nor the best, proponent of this criticism).

Other scholars have criticized consociationalism on normative grounds because it requires a certain autonomy of the elites from their constituencies. Consociationalism is thus not very "democratic" after all, for it is divorced from the segmented mass publics. Or at the very least, it constitutes a very distant democracy indeed.

In response to these critiques, Lijphart gradually developed his second major contribution to democratic theory, the elaboration of typologies of democratic systems, which led to his specification of two *different* non-majoritarian alternatives to majoritarian democracy: consociationalism *and* consensus democracy. This work culminated in his book, *Democracies* (Lijphart 1984), wherein he classified the world's set of stable democracies on a two-dimensional conceptual map and then examined the impact of system differences on actual politics. Lijphart describes the history of this exercise in his concluding chapter to this volume.

The most notable conclusion, perhaps, of *Democracies* is that, contrary to the prevailing view at the time, there is no special reason to believe that the majoritarian model—as seen in the United Kingdom, Canada, Australia, and other countries—is inherently more "democratic" or more fair than the consociational counterpart. Indeed, Lijphart argued, perhaps it is consociational systems that are much better at safeguarding the rights of minorities. Therefore, *they,* in fact, may be more democratic than majoritarian systems.

Indeed, in subsequently extending the analysis of *Democracies* to an additional 15 countries (bringing the total set to 36), Lijphart's current work is establishing that consensus democracies *are* more egalitarian and participatory and offer better representation of women and minorities. They are also more welfare-oriented, more environment-friendly, and less punitive in their criminal justice systems. These conclusions have tremendous practical implications for countries designing their first democratic constitutions or contemplating democratic reform.

Lijphart's third major contribution to democratic theory has been to help refocus the comparative political science lens back onto the impact of electoral laws on politics and policy outcomes, a field largely fallow since *Political Consequences of Electoral Laws* (Douglas Rae 1967). Lijphart and some of the collaborators in this volume have mounted a sustained comparative effort to assess the impact of electoral laws on a wide-ranging set of countries from

Japan to Spain and points in between. These studies have played a substantial role in specifying the various consequences of diverse electoral systems and have therefore been of major importance to the design of electoral institutions in newly emerging democracies, a critical variable.

Deliberately, the editors of this volume have chosen to concentrate on these triple themes of Lijphart's contributions to democratic theory. However, Lijphart is known equally well for his far-reaching contributions to our understanding and practice of the comparative method in the social sciences. He has done as much as any scholar in comparative political science to delineate the characteristics of social science comparison and to emphasize the importance of scientific rigor and research design in the social sciences.

All of his work is imbued with concern about adequate specification of the dependent variable, appropriate case selection (his early work on the "politics of accommodation" was based upon a deviant case, the Netherlands), and the proper operationalization and measurement of variables. His concluding essay to this book, among other things, contains a fascinating account of the scientific design, and then modification, of his book, *Democracies*. For example, he recounts a revealing anecdote about a meeting with Gerhard Lehmbruch and their discussion regarding where Lijphart had placed Austria on his two-dimensional conceptual map of democracies. Lehmbruch told him bluntly that he was totally wrong. The methodological lesson: "Since then, I have come to the conclusion that, when this kind of discrepancy between expert judgment and 'hard' measurements occurs, it is necessary to take a second look at one's measurements."

Lijphart's methodological approach has had great impact on comparative political science and has influenced many hosts of self-aware researchers and teachers in the following areas:

- The importance of the dependent variable
- The systematic search for independent variables as explanations for the dependent variable
- Careful case selection
- Careful specification and measurement of variables
- An awareness of the limitations of the social scientific enterprise
- Above all, the science in political science is about the science of comparison

This last point is made with great force by Russell Dalton (1996, 4; quoted by Bernard Grofman in his essay here): "Even if we are interested only in a single nation [as Lijphart first was with the Netherlands], comparative research is a useful approach. An old Hebrew riddle expresses this idea: 'Question: Who first discovered water? Answer: I don't know, but it sure wasn't a fish.'" The point being that "immersing oneself in a single environment renders the characteristics of that environment unobtrusive and unnoticed." Put a different way, without comparison it is simply impossible to appreciate both the distinctiveness of a single case and the common patterns characterizing many cases.

Finally, Lijphart's scholarship has always been characterized by two important traits: First, in linking empirical investigation to theory building, he has tended to proceed inductively rather than deductively, seeking to specify the social scientific patterns that emerge from the data rather than deducing propositions first, then testing them later. Second, his theory building, because it is so empirically grounded, has had great impact on the design and redesign of political systems undergoing reform and transformation. He has been deeply engaged as an adviser to governments and nongovernmental political actors as they grapple with democratic reforms, many times in less than ideal circumstances. Moreover, the diligent interaction between theory and practice at the highest levels of the design and redesign of political systems has always been a hallmark of Lijphart's scholarship.

Taking *Democracies* and *Power Sharing in South Africa* as companion works, for example, illustrates the compelling force of Lijphart's work. In the first, he demonstrated convincingly that there is more than one way to run a stable democracy. As Bingham Powell has noted, "Too often citizens and scholars who know only particular systems think that stable democracy cannot be sustained in other ways. [*Democracies*] is a powerful refutation of that assumption." Then, in *Power Sharing in South Africa*, Lijphart proceeded to use the theory built in *Democracies* to prescribe the most optimal institutions for reform in South Africa given the deeply and distinctly contextualized environment of that case. In other words, he proceeds to use inductive theory to engineer answers to very difficult real-world problems.

In so doing, he also definitively refuted the long-ago criticism made about consociationalism by that audacious graduate student, namely that the dependence on elite cooperation in a deeply divided society put the problem the wrong way, that it was precisely the existence and stability of that cooperation that was so problematic. Lijphart's answer in *Power Sharing in South Africa* was to stress the importance of self-determination of the segments in a consociational system, as opposed to predetermination of them. The two methods for accomplishing this, which he suggested in the South African case, were proportional representation and segmental autonomy on a voluntary basis. Self-determination does not presume that merely putting segmental elites together will lead to cooperation, as predetermination does. Self-determination, to the contrary, facilitates the emergence of the segmental elites that both matter and have at least a basic interest in the concept of cooperation.

Organization of the Book

A short note on the history of this volume: All three editors of this book were graduate students of Arend Lijphart at the University of California, San Diego, more or less at the same time during the 1980s. To us, Lijphart was (and is) a towering intellectual figure, while personally and consistently giving new definition to that old description of "the gentleman and the scholar." We were honored, each of us, that he agreed to direct our Ph.D. dissertations. We were also probably a little more than scared that we would not be able to rise to his expectations.

Arend also believed that, in his own words, "institutions ought to exist to serve the individuals within them, rather than the other way around." He made this remarkable statement to me when, in 1980, just after beginning graduate school at UCSD, I asked him whether or not it would be advisable to accept an unexpected opportunity to study history for a year at the Ecole des Hautes Etudes in Paris. Taking his advice to go was one of the best decisions of my professional and personal life.

The project for this book became concrete when the conjuncture of Arend's 60th birthday and his term as president of the American Political Science Association led us to organize a panel of scholars to assess his work at the 1996 Annual Meeting of the Association in San Francisco. This early group formed the core to which other contributors were subsequently added.

The present volume divides itself fairly naturally into four sections: Grouping theoretical essays together, we open with Bingham Powell's analysis of a fundamental question of representation, the intersection of political responsiveness with constitutional design. Bernard Grofman then provides a penetrating overview of Lijphart's influence on and guidance of a whole school or approach that we might call "comparative institutionalism." Rein Taagepera explores Lijphart's work in significantly expanding our notions of democratic institutions, both in terms of qualitative concepts and quantitative measurement to back them up. And Milton Esman builds on Lijphart's work on power sharing by universalizing it to include nondemocratic divided societies, as well, providing a counterintuitive but powerful extension to "the politics of accommodation."

We next turn to three country-oriented essays. Jack Nagel uses New Zealand to illustrate how, on the one hand, Lijphart's work has significantly shaped specific reform efforts, while on the other hand, the effects of those reforms suggest modifications to theory. Thomas Koelble examines the unfolding drama of South African constitution building in order to ask the question: Will South Africa implement institutions and political structures that point to a consensus democracy, this in the face of formidable obstacles that remain in the path of democratic development? And Andrew Reynolds develops a typology of democratic regimes ranging from full majoritarianism to qualified majoritarianism to integrative majoritarianism to consensus democracy and consociational democracy. In the Southern African cases that underpin his analysis, experiments with majoritarianism have led to dictatorship or disaster, and so Reynolds pleads for the introduction of consensus systems.

The essay by Markus Crepaz and Vicki Birchfield assesses the viability of consensual political institutions in this purported age of "globalization," asking what effects economic globalization has on local politics compared to how local political institutions mediate the effects of globalization. Their important contention is that consensus democracies more actively mediate the effects of globalization on their societies, seeking to cushion losers as well as encourage winners. Their argument reaffirms the "primacy of the political," and in so doing, links empirical economic forces firmly to strong political theoretical grounds.

Finally, we conclude this volume with Arend Lijphart's own summation of his life's work and his analysis of our contributors' essays. During the 1980s, the late Henry W. Ehrmann and his wife Claire would come to La Jolla every winter, and Henry would teach at UCSD. Henry was a mentor to many of us in graduate school and was a very close friend to Arend. When a Festschrift in his honor was published in 1983, Henry told us that he was following the German tradition of showing his appreciation to the Festschrift contributors by writing extensive commentaries on each of the essays and sending these to each of the authors. We liked this tradition very much, and it gave us the idea of adapting it by asking Arend Lijphart to write such a commentary before the publication of this book and including it in the volume itself.

Overall, as Lijphart notes in his own conclusion, the book's essays point to the conclusion that nonmajoritarian democracy in its various forms and shapes is clearly preferable to the majoritarian or pluralitarian alternatives. We, the editors, also conclude that Arend's person and his work personify the expression "a gentleman and a scholar," demonstrating it to be neither a cliché nor extinct.

References

Dalton, Russell. 1996. *Citizen Politics: Public Opinion and Political Parties in Advanced Industrial Democracies, 2nd edition.* Chatham: Chatham House Publishers.

Lijphart, Arend. 1968. *The Politics of Accommodation: Pluralism and Democracy in the Netherlands.* Berkeley and Los Angeles: University of California Press.

Lijphart, Arend. 1977. *Democracy in Plural Societies: A Comparative Exploration.* New Haven: Yale University Press.

Lijphart, Arend. 1984. *Democracies: Patterns of Majoritarian and Consensus Government in Twenty-One Democracies.* New Haven: Yale University Press.

Lijphart, Arend. 1985. *Powersharing in Africa.* Berkeley: Institute for International Studies.

Rae, Douglas W. 1967. *The Political Consequences of Electoral Laws.* New Haven: Yale University Press.

CHAPTER 2

Political Responsiveness and Constitutional Design

G. Bingham Powell Jr.

Political responsiveness is used here to mean a close connection between the choices that citizens express in elections and the formation of governments or policymaker coalitions.[1] Responsiveness in this sense is not, in my view, the only democratic virtue. At best it captures only a part of the broad democratic claim to connect citizen preferences and government policies.[2] Yet the failure of responsiveness, even in this narrow sense, is clearly a point of concern for citizens and democratic theorists. Several examples can illustrate.

First, the mere presence of elections by no means guarantees a strong connection between citizens' electoral choices and the installation of policymakers. The election outcomes may be irrelevant to selection of policymakers, as in the rigged elections typical of many one-party states. Yet more perversely, an election may trigger intervention by the armed forces who explicitly exclude the citizens' choice, as it did in Greece in 1967 or Nigeria in 1993.

Second, even with competitive elections and all parties adhering to the rules of the constitutional game, the connections between election outcomes and forming governing coalitions can be frayed or severed by the operation of the election laws on the distribution of citizen votes across districts and parties. In New Zealand in 1978, for example, the Labour Party increased its vote share to nearly 40 percent, while support for its arch rival, the National Party, declined 8 points, dropping it to second place. Yet, thanks to the election rules and the distribution of the votes for these two parties and the third-place Social Credit Party, the "losing" National Party easily achieved a strong absolute majority in the legislature and formed a majority government that had no place for the Labour vote "winners." A majoritarian system created a majority government—but not one endorsed by even a plurality of voters.

Third, in a very different kind of setting—the "proportional world" of the Netherlands in the mid-1960s—a new party, D66, was formed explicitly

9

to protest a series of government formations in which citizen votes seemed irrelevant to the make-up of subsequent governing coalitions. Between the 1963 and 1967 general elections there were three Dutch governments, headed by three different prime ministers (from two different parties), and composed of three different coalition combinations: three religious parties and a right-wing party, two religious parties and a left-wing party, and two religious parties alone. The voters were not consulted about the government changes. Although all three Dutch government formations, like that in New Zealand, were constitutional and explicable (perhaps even justifiable) in the context of the rules and party configurations of the time, the turnovers illustrate a tenuous connection between citizen voter choices and selection of policymakers. They seem to lessen the responsiveness of democracy.

Of course, much of the time the selection of policymakers in contemporary democracies *is* responsive to election outcomes: Citizens' voting choices provide critical resources of office to some parties or candidates and not others; those who receive citizen's support use these resources to shape policy. Table 2.1 shows some simple evidence of this. In 141 elections in 18 parliamentary democracies across a quarter of a century, there was a clear relationship between government parties' gain or loss of votes and their being retained or replaced in office. When the incumbent parties gained or broke even in votes, they were retained in office 68 percent of the time, partially replaced 22 percent, and fully evicted only 11 percent. When the incumbent parties lost over 5 percent of their voting support, they were retained in office only 33 percent, partially replaced 19 percent, and fully evicted 49 percent of the time. Clearly, the elections do make a difference; there is a responsiveness connection.

My goal in this paper is to develop the "responsiveness" concept more precisely and to illuminate the conditions under which it operates. I shall also investigate whether the institutions of majoritarian or proportional constitutional design are in fact more successful in creating close connections between voters' choices and the formation of governments and policymaker coalitions.

TABLE 2.1.   Incumbent Vote Losses and Subsequent Government Changes (in percentage)

	Change in Government Parties After Election				
Incumbent Vote Change	None	Some Change	All New Parties	Total Percent	Cases
Losses over 5%	32.6	18.6	48.8	100	(43)
Losses 1–5%	47.5	30.5	22.0	100	(61)
None or Gain	67.6	21.6	10.8	100	(37)

Total Cases: 141 elections in 18 parliamentary democracies, from 1969 through 1994. Statistics: $r = .33$ **; Kendall's Tau-B = .29; Gamma = .44.

In all this analysis I shall assume that the major unit for assessing responsiveness will be the political party. The political party is one piece of information given formally and explicitly to voters in most parliamentary systems to connect their choice of any specific candidate in the election to a collective group of national policymakers. The political party or, in some cases, a less formal equivalent, is essential for assessing responsiveness to elections unless a single individual wields policy-making power. I shall not be exploring differences in the meaning and cohesion of the party bond, although I shall make a few comments on pre-election party coalitions.

Constitutional Designs in Parliamentary Democracies: Majoritarian and Proportional

In his influential 1984 book *Democracies,* Arend Lijphart suggests that the two great approaches to representative democracy offer two different answers to the question: "to whose interests should the government be responsive when the people are in disagreement?" The answer proposed by the Westminster or majoritarian approach is that the government should be responsive to "the majority of the people." The answer proposed by the consensual approach is "that the government should be responsive to "as many people as possible" (Lijphart 1984, 4). Later in the book and in many other works (especially Lijphart 1994) Lijphart has identified various connections between constitutional designs and democratic practices that realize these alternative answers. (Also see Powell 1989; Huber and Powell 1994.)

In this analysis I shall discuss directly only the constitutional designs, not such partially related features as party systems. By *constitutional design* I mean the rules that govern the selection of policymakers and the making of policy, whether these are in a formal constitution, or simply ordinary law, or even internal institutional rules. I shall focus particularly on two dimensions of those designs—the election rules and the legislative policy making rules—which should, theoretically, shape the connections between voters and policymakers, particularly in parliamentary systems. Table 2.2 sketches more concretely critical aspects of these two dimensions: the rules for converting votes to seats in legislative elections (the vertical dimension) and the potential offered by the committee system for influence by opposition parties (the horizontal dimension).

In the lower left-hand part of the table we see political systems whose election rules frequently have the effect of producing single-party majority governments, and whose internal policy-making rules feature domination of the legislature by the government. Our theories and previous research on the consequences of election laws, in particular (see Duverger 1954, Rae 1967, Riker 1982, Lijphart 1994, and Cox 1997), lead us to expect that this combination of

TABLE 2.2. Two Dimensions of Constitutional Rules

Legislative Election Rules[a] (Effective Threshold)	Legislative Committee Rules[b]		
	Government Domination of Weak Committees	Mixed: Weak Committees with Shared Chairs or Vice Versa	Opposition Influence: Strong Committees and Shared Chairs
Pure Proportional Representation	Greece 1989–1990 (3.3)	Finland (5.4) Italy (2.3)	Austria (2.6) Belgium (4.8) Denmark (1.6) Netherlands (.7) Norway 89ff (4.0) Sweden (4.0)
Pure PR Plus Coalition Encouragement	Ireland (17)	—	Germany[c] (5.0) Switzerland (8.5)
PR with Majority Distortion	Greece (17)	Japan (16.4)	Norway pre89 (8.9) Spain (10.2)
Single Member Districts	Australia[c] (35) France[c] (32) New Zealand (35) United Kingdom (35)	(USA 35)[c] Canada (35)	—

Note: Numbers in parentheses are Lijphart's Effective Legislative Threshold from Lijphart 1994. France averages different rules.

[a] Pure proportional representation rules include 1986 France, 1989–1990 Greece, post 1985 Norway, as well as all elections in countries shown above. (Italy 1994 ff is not included.) See text and Lijphart 1994.

[b] Committee rules from Interparliamentary Union (1976, 1986); Doering 1994.

[c] The upper houses in Australia and Germany and the Presidency in France and the USA occasionally provide possibilities for dispersed power in policy making also.

rules will frequently lead to single-party governments, generally linked to electoral pluralities. The internal policy-making rules lead to domination of the legislature by the government, thus furthering the concentration of political power. In the top right of the table we see political systems whose election rules encourage more exact representation of citizen voter preferences into the legislature. Moreover, in the systems in this part of the table, strong and shared committee powers are designed to provide influence to opposition parties as well as the government.[3] (We know from various studies that the formal properties of the committee system are also linked to other rules and procedures constraining government domination. See Strom 1990 and the contributions in Doering 1994.) Thus, we expect the constitutional forms in the upper right to seek to engender policy making that is responsive to "as many people as possible," in proportion to their electoral voice.

The other levels and categories show various mixtures and/or special features of electoral and committee systems. In parentheses after the name of each system is the "effective threshold" measure proposed by Arend Lijphart (1994) on the basis of his careful analysis of various features of the election rules. This variable provides a continuous, rather than nominal measure for the electoral dimension. On the other dimension, the table also notes the presence of powerful upper houses chosen by different electorates in Germany, Australia, and the United States, and the presence of the directly elected, significantly powerful presidents in France and the United States, which can, under the right electoral circumstances, further disperse political power. In the concluding section of the analysis I examine correlations between responsiveness, the continuous Lijphart measure, and the three-level committee measure, as a check on the results from the classification of constitutional designs.

In exploring the consequences of these constitutional designs for responsiveness in the following sections, initially I classify the political systems into three groups, based on majoritarian, mixed, or proportional designs. The majoritarian designs are, of course, those in the lower left-hand corner: Australia, France, New Zealand, and the United Kingdom, plus Canada with single-member district election rules and a slightly more mixed committee system. The proportional designs feature the top-right systems (Austria, Belgium, Denmark, Netherlands, pre-1989 Norway, and Sweden), plus those in the adjacent cells (Finland and Italy, with slightly less formal committee systems, and Germany, with a slightly less pure form of PR). To these I add pre-1989 Norway, despite some electoral distortion because of inequitable representation of districts and somewhat larger average effective threshold (8.9). The electoral system is still on the verge of pure proportional representation (PR) and the Norwegian policy-making system emphasizes opposition influence in policy making to such an extreme degree (see Strom 1990, Chapter 6) that even a mixed categorization seems inappropriate. The remaining systems of Ireland, Greece, Japan, and Spain fall into a mixed category in their combination of electoral and policy making rules. Greece is especially interesting as it experienced four elections (1977, 1981, 1985, 1993) under reinforced PR with an effective threshold of about 17—it is virtually a majoritarian system in this period—but three elections (1989, 1989, 1990) under much purer PR.

Because of the heterogeneous nature of the mixed category, I am reluctant to draw many conclusions about it, and subsequent discussion focuses on the systems that better approximate the pure types. Similarly, I am postponing the analysis of responsiveness in the United States and Switzerland, where the executive is not responsible to the legislature; although they are shown (in parentheses) in the table, they are not included in any subsequent analysis.

It is worth emphasizing that the classification is based purely on the system's constitutional designs at this stage, and not on its expected performance. Thus, the number of political parties, which we would expect to have some partially independent impact on the concentration of political power and its connection to the voters, is not a basis of the classification. Two-party Austria and Germany are classified as PR designs, and multiparty France is classified as a majoritarian design, based on the election rules and the legislative policymaking rules. This follows my interest in this paper purely in the consequences of constitutional design.

Representative Legislatures, Governments, and Policymakers

Before turning directly to the concept of responsiveness, it is useful to take a moment to consider the effectiveness of the constitutional designs in creating electoral representation at the three critical parliamentary stages: legislature formation, government formation, and policymaker formation.

Of course, the literature on representativeness of the legislature in relationship to the votes cast is very large. Lijphart (1994) summarizes the various measures of (dis)proportionality and their advantages and disadvantages. Fortunately, all the measures give roughly similar results at the present crude level of analysis. The measure chosen here is designed to highlight conceptually the comparative representation of voters at the three stages. It is simply the proportion of voters who voted for parties in the government, plus the *lessor* of the proportion of votes or seats received by parties not in the government. The conceptual idea is that voters for government parties are always fully represented in the legislature, but that voters for opposition parties are represented only to the extent that they hold proportionate seats. Thus in Britain in 1983, the 42 percent of the electorate who voted for the Conservatives are fully represented (regardless of their 61 percent of the seats); the 28 percent who voted Labor are also fully represented (32 percent of the seats); but the 25 percent who voted for the Alliance received only 3.5 percent of the seats and are considered represented only to that extent; another 2.5 percent comes from the lessor of votes/seats for various small parties, giving a total legislative representation score of 76. As expected from the various analyses of disproportionality in Lijphart, Rae, and others, average representation in the legislature drops from 96 percent in the proportional design systems (71 elections in 9 countries) to 84 in the majoritarian systems (41 elections in 5 countries).

A second stage is the selection of governments after the legislature meets. Here, we think of the representation of only voters who supported the (eventual) governing parties. In contrast to the legislative representation scores, average representation among those who vote for the governing parties drops off only slightly from 50 percent in the PR systems to 44 percent in the majoritarian systems. It is the opposition parties who are underrepresented, naturally enough, in the latter. In fact, the majoritarian systems' governments often achieve single-party majority status on the basis of many fewer votes than some of the large post-election coalitions in, say, Austria, the Netherlands, and Belgium. However, it is rare for even the proportional influence systems to include all the parties in the government. Moreover, some of the proportional design systems produced frequent minority governments (e.g., all the governments in Norway and Denmark during this period) that also have a small electoral base. For this reason, the proportional design advantage is slight.

Of course, the third stage is the most significant. It is also the hardest to measure. How much policy impact do opposition parties have in the various political systems? My approach is explained at more length elsewhere (see Powell, 1989, and Powell, forthcoming, Chapter 5), but can be sketched briefly. I assume voters for government parties receive full (100 percent) effective representation in the policy-making process between elections. Voters for parties in formal support agreements with the governments—but *not* holding cabinet portfolios—receive 75 percent of their legislative representation, reflecting somewhat less influence on the formation and implementation of policies. Voters for opposition parties receive representation by multiplying their relative legislative representation by a two-component weight. One component reflects the degree to which the committee system guarantees influence to the opposition; the second component reflects the ability of the opposition to threaten the stability of the government. The *committee* component gives opposition representatives in the legislature a weight of 0 if the system is in the first column in table 2.1; 12 percent if it is in the second column; 25 percent if it is in the third column. The *bargaining* component depends primarily on the control of the legislature by the government. If the government commands a majority of seats, the opposition gets only a 10 percent bargaining weight; if the government is a supported minority, the opposition gets a 20 percent bargaining weight; if the government is a pure minority, the opposition gets 50 percent. (Control of a special outside institution, such as the German upper house is treated as equivalent to facing a supported minority.) So the weight to the opposition voters can range from 10 percent of their legislative representation in a situation with a majority government and government-dominated committees to 75 percent in a situation of a pure minority government and strong committees with shared chairs.[4]

This measure captures, I think, the real differences in distributions of party influence, despite some arbitrariness in the specific weights given. In situations of helpful committees and especially minority governments, being in opposition is not such a severe impediment to effective representation of voters in policy making. It would be a mistake to ignore this fact. Using this measure, the representation of the total electorate in policy-making declines sharply from the proportional design systems (72 percent of the voters) to the majoritarian designs (52 percent of the voters).

The first three data rows of table 2.3 compare the representation of party voters in legislatures, governments, and policy making after elections in the countries with majoritarian versus proportional influence constitutional designs.

Note that representation of voters in policy making, as opposed to government only, increases much more in the proportional influence systems than in the majoritarian ones. Opposition voters in a system such as Norway, where the governments commanded only a minority of legislative seats and where power in the legislature was widely dispersed, received a high percentage of possible representation in policy making—although never as high as voters for parties gaining a role in government, of course. As we might expect, a regression analysis (not

TABLE 2.3.   Comparing Majoritarian and Proportional Influence Constitutional Designs: Alternative Measures of Responsiveness to Elections

Alternative Measures of Responsiveness to Elections	"Majoritarian" Constitutional Designs (41 Elections)	Proportional Influence Constitutional Designs (72 Elections)
REPRESENTATION OF PARTY VOTERS		
Legislature	84%	96%
Government	44%	50%
Policy making	52%	75%
MINIMALLY RESPONSIVE GOVERNMENTS		
Duration of initial gov.	93%	81%
Plural governments (pty or pec)	79%	89%
Duration X Plural	74%	71%
IDEALLY RESPONSIVE GOVERNMENTS		
Majoritarian Criteria	69%	34%
Proportional Criteria	41%	41%
IDEALLY RESPONSIVE POLICYMAKERS		
Majoritarian Criteria	67%	1%
Proportional Criteria	49%	60%

shown) using effective threshold and the nominal committee categories suggests electoral rules have the most impact on legislative representation, but both are important for policy making representation, with the committee effects actually somewhat more powerful. These results strongly suggest that the constitutional designs are doing their expected job, with the proportional designs providing effective representation for more voters in the policy making process itself, as well as in the legislature.

Electoral Responsiveness: Concepts and Hypotheses

Each of the two great vision of elections as instruments of democracy implies a hypothesis about the democratic connections between elections and the selection of policymakers. The majoritarian vision relies on elections featuring few competitors and identifiable future governments during the election, and majority governments that thoroughly control policy making after the election. Such conditions should create tight, almost mechanical, connections between election outcomes and the authorization of policymakers. A single party wins the election, controls the legislature, and makes policy. Governments can claim voter mandates for their election promises[5] and are clearly responsible for their actions. In selecting policymakers, little needs to be left to the discretion of the elected representatives. The connections between elections and the composition of policymakers should be both strong and highly visible.

On the other hand, the proportional influence vision implies its own hypothesis about responsiveness. This vision would stress the superiority of multiparty electoral competition and rules that directly reflect the choices of citizens into the composition of the legislature, fairly and without the distortions that so frequently accompany majoritarian arrangements. The legislature suffers from neither over-weighting some parties at the expense of others nor forced cohabitation within individual parties or pre-election coalitions that can freeze bargaining opportunities. Authorization of policymakers will be dependent on this fairly and equitably reflective body, and thus dependent on the expressed preferences of the voters themselves. Parties that have gained substantial voter support will be indispensable in forming governments and policy making coalitions; those that have done badly will play a proportionately lessor role.

The hypotheses of the alternative visions thus counterpose alternative strengths and weaknesses. The putative strength of the majoritarian vision is a strong and direct connection between votes, legislative seats, and governments; its potential weakness is the distortion in representation of voter preferences that is often necessary to create pre-election identifiability and/or post-election majorities. The putative strength of the representational vision is the multiplicity of choices and their fair reflection in legislative representation; its weakness is the dependence of policymaker coalition formation on elite bargaining.

Expressed this way, it would seem a simple and straightforward matter to examine empirically and comparatively the successes and failures of each vision in creating responsiveness connections in our 18 democracies. But such analysis proves a harder task than it might appear. It is difficult to test the predictions of the two hypotheses against each other because of the differences in the fundamental conceptualizations of to whom policy making should be responsive. The majoritarian vision seeks connections between voter choices and concentrated political power, so that voters' choices will provide effective mandates for *the citizen majority* and so that the voting majority can hold incumbents clearly accountable for their performance. The proportionate influence vision seeks equitably dispersed political power, so that the composition of a majority can change flexibly across different issues and so that *the preferences of all citizens*, not just majorities, will be taken into account in all policies.

We can sharpen our understanding of the implications of these different expectations by considering a simple ideal case. Suppose we have only two political parties, proportional election rules, and one party holding office on the basis of 55 percent of the vote. Suppose the incumbents lose 10 percent, which—with only two parties—will imply that the opposition gains 10 percent. After such an election the ideal responsiveness outcome in the majoritarian vision is for policy-making control to shift completely from the former incumbents to the opposition. Both the previous and new situation will allow for clear accountability; the incoming government will clearly represent a majority of the voters and be authorized to put into practice the policies promised in the election campaign. But for the proportional influence vision, the ideal responsiveness outcome in these circumstances would be for the former incumbents to have 45 percent of the new policy-making influence and the former opposition to have 55 percent of the influence. In both situations parties representing the choices, and presumably the preferences, of large minorities of the electorate should be taken into account in making policies. Electoral responsiveness here means to weight the relative importance of the parties in the policy making in proportion to their electoral support. It should not be an all or nothing proposition unless the voters completely desert one party for the other. This difference in expectations about how the composition of policymakers should respond to election outcomes is shown in figure 2.1. For simplicity, I show the share in government that a party would receive as the consequence of voting support in each theoretical vision. The proportional influence outcomes are shown by the dashed 45 degree line—as a party gets more voter support, it should steadily gain in its share of the policy making. The majoritarian control outcomes are shown by the solid line that is first flat, indicating the party has no influence when it has support from less than

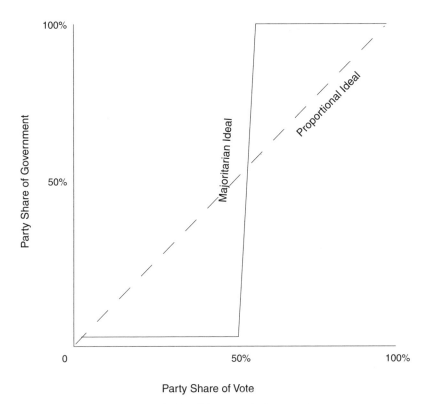

Fig. 2.1.   Two Ideals of Democratic Responsiveness

half the electorate, then a steep slope as its support crosses the 50 percent mark, than flat again as it has complete control in all cases where it has greater than majority support.

The expectations from the two visions of democracy are not, of course, completely different. We can envision downward sloping lines that would be considered unresponsive according to either vision. (The situation of military intervention just as a party becomes large enough to have real influence exemplifies this kind of negative outcome in extreme form.) Or, we can imagine flat lines that indicate complete irrelevance of voter support for a party's participation in government. Nonetheless, their specific expectations are dissimilar. The reflection of these normative differences in political science work is nicely illustrated by studies of legislative representation: In the United States such studies usually define greater responsiveness as the steeper slope at the 50 percent crossover point, so that a shift in a few percent of votes will result in a shift in a much *greater* percent of seats (see Gelman and King 1995, and the references therein). In Europe, with its strong proportional representation tradition, a one-for-one shift of seats for votes is usually defined as ideal responsiveness, and high American responsiveness would be a form of distortion.

If we consider the change in vote for the incumbents from table 2.1 separately for the majoritarian and proportional constitutional systems, we find some reflection of these different normative views. Figure 2.2 shows the average change in government on a 0 to 100 scale, where no change is 0, partial change is 50, and full change is 100, for increasingly improved government vote. The dark bars are for elections in the majoritarian systems. We can see that there is some correspondence to the ideal of all or nothing change, with lots of change in governments that lose a good deal and no change for vote winners. But there is also a lot of "jaggedness" on the government loser side, some of it caused by distortions in seat-vote relationship, but more of it reflecting different margins of government support at the time of the election; some governments can lose 5 percent and still be the largest party, whereas others can lose 3 percent and fall behind.

On the other hand, the proportional systems (the light bars) show a rather gradual, linear decline in government change as the governing parties do better. Interestingly, single statistical measures of the tables like those in table 2.1, are often rather similar for the two kinds of systems. (Tau-b and Tau-c are

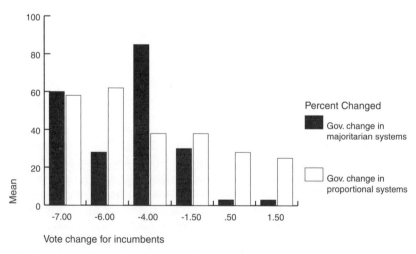

Fig. 2.2.   Impact of Vote on Government Change

both around .33.) But summary statistics of these tables are not really satisfactory for comparison, especially for the majoritarian systems, because so much depends on the current position of the government and there are so few parties (in either kind of system) with real voter majorities, and because the percentages in the vote loss categories hide a mixture of no and total change in the majoritarian systems, in contrast to many partial changes in the proportional ones (as shown in table 2.1). These kinds of changes are, of course, consistent with expectations of the visions themselves.

If we run a regression equation predicting government change from incumbent government vote change, we find, of course, a significant relationship. The slope is −2.55 for the 140 cases, implying that a 5 percent loss in the government incumbent parties' votes means a 13 percent less likelihood of being retained in power. If we add an interaction term, multiplying vote change by a dummy variable for PR constitutional arrangements, the slope for the majoritarian and mixed cases is −3.1, and the net slope (subtracting the interaction term of +1.4) for the proportional constitutional systems is only −1.7. The *difference* between the slopes has a T of 1.3, significant only at .20 level, but certainly about what we might expect theoretically and from figure 2.1. A loss of 5 percent in the majoritarian and mixed systems implies 15.5 percent difference in the likelihood of government change, whereas the same loss in a proportional system implies only an 8 percent probability of change in government. As we might expect from figure 2.1, the effect of a given vote loss is on average half as great in the PR systems. However, there are various technical difficulties, especially because the majoritarian cases almost all have the government either entirely retained or entirely changed, and 42 percent of the elections in the proportional systems involve partial change. Thus (as we expect from the broken line pattern in figure 2.1), relationships in the majoritarian systems are nonlinear, violating the technical assumptions of regression models. The configurations are fundamentally different. Quite aside from the technical difficulties here, though, it is important to keep in mind that the lesser slope in the proportional systems is consistent with what we might expect normatively from the assumptions of those systems as suggested in figure 2.1. This difference does not necessarily imply superior performance in the majoritarian systems.

With such divergent expectations, as well as the different configurations of support, how are we to compare the relative successes and failures of the two visions? The answer is that we can do so only partially. I shall first suggest some minimal criteria of responsiveness, which seem appropriate given the common assumptions of both visions, and examine the frequency with which these are achieved under the conditions of each vision and the reasons for failure. Then I shall provide parallel analyses of the success of each vision in creating responsiveness in its own terms.

Minimal Criteria for Responsiveness to Elections in Forming Governments

Here I want to create measures that will discriminate between elections followed by governments that meet criteria of minimal responsiveness to voter's choices and elections that do not. (I shall focus first on government formation, then turn to policymakers.) These criteria will be minimal in the sense that they eliminate outcomes whose responsiveness is unacceptable under the logic of *either* vision of citizen influence. There seem to be two relevant dimensions: the proximity of a government's formation to the elections and the nature of the parties included in it.

Criteria

First, it seems to me that electoral responsiveness can be understood as implying the formation immediately after the election of a government that will endure until the next election (see Strom 1990, 72–74). This was the complaint of the Dutch voters in the 1960s and a perpetual complaint of Italian voters: government turnover unrelated to voter action. Whatever reasons may be given for a government breaking up and then being replaced, reshuffled, or even renewed before the next election, it seems to me hard to argue that the second (or later) government formation can be responsive to choices of voters expressed in the previous election. To make this argument we would need some substantive information about the preferences of voters and the positions of the governments. (For work along these lines, see Powell and Huber 1994 and Powell, forthcoming, Chapter 9.) Without such information, multiple government formation between elections seems to be *prima facia* evidence that government formation is responding to something other than the choices of voters, even if some or all of the specific governments seem appropriate in their composition. As a measure of this connection between election and government, I shall use the *percent of the period between elections that the first government is in office*. Thus, a government receives a full score of minimal responsiveness either if it endures the full period between ordinarily scheduled elections or its premature demise immediately leads to consultation with the voters.

Although this concept of proximity between election and government formation is a simple one, several readers have been troubled by the general characterization of low proximity as unresponsive. One suggestion is that a new government might be responding to new conditions, perhaps ones that have made new issues salient, and thus be responsive to what the citizens would wish, even though they have not had opportunity to vote. This is, of course, possible (and an interesting topic to investigate through survey research). I doubt that the frustrated Dutch voters of 1966, or the frustrated

Italian voters through most of the post-war period, thought this was true. But even if it were, this kind of reading of public opinion polls would be something different than government formation responding to *the choices citizens express in elections*, which is the target of my interest here.

Nor should we confuse concern about multiple government formation between elections as dismissing Juan Linz's argument that an advantage of parliamentary systems is that they, unlike presidential systems, can reform governments when public confidence in the executive has been undermined by scandal or policy failure. Most parliamentary systems are not locked into long, fixed electoral terms as are presidential systems. (Only Norway seems to have a fixed parliamentary term written into its constitutional arrangements.) When governments fail, they generally have the option of consulting the electorate if changing conditions make likely a new configuration of voter support. Failure to do so usually means that the members of the current legislature see no advantage in bringing voters into the bargaining; it does not imply responsiveness, but the contrary.[6]

In my view, it is the composition of new governments, rather than the proximity of their formation to the election, that is the harder issue. It is hard precisely because of the differing logic of government formation just discussed. Of course, if a single party wins a majority of votes, any government formation that excluded that party would clearly fail to be minimally responsive under either vision. Although the two visions differ in whether the ideal government after such an election should include only that party (majoritarian) or also other parties winning significant support (proportional influence), excluding from policy making a party winning support of a majority of voters seems unacceptable to each. However, empirically, in only a handful of cases do we find a single party winning a majority of votes (three in Austria, one each in Canada (perhaps), Ireland, and Sweden). In these cases the party did come to power and the government endured until the next election. But this information does not take us very far in analyzing responsiveness. I should note at this point, however, that the failure of the majoritarian systems to provide majority votes for any single party means that one important assumption of its hypothesis is not met—subsequent discussion of responsiveness has already made a serious compromise with the majoritarian ideal. I follow the standard practice of defenders of the Westminster systems in shifting from majority to plurality party, but the compromise should be noted.

I want to suggest, however, that there is a strong case for requiring the inclusion of the party winning the largest number of votes—the *plurality party*—as a condition for a government to be considered minimally responsive. The arguments are slightly different for the two visions. For the majoritarian vision, I note first the undesirability of coalition (or minority) governments as blurring both accountability and mandates. But if we are to have single-party governments, *there can be no basis in democratic theory for subjecting the party with more citizen voting support to domination by a party with less citizen support* (e.g., Dahl 1989, Chapter 10). Single party governments by a nonplurality party seem unresponsive on their face. Coalition governments of any kind are of doubtful responsiveness under this vision, but if we are to have them, then excluding the plurality party again seems dubious (with a special exception for announced pre-election coalitions as noted later). For the proportional influence vision, there is, of course, no bias against coalition governments. But one would surely always want the largest (electoral) party in such a government. That is the party that received the largest proportion of the electorate's endorsement; excluding it from policy-making influence is more unjust than excluding any other single party. This criterion, is, however, perhaps less crucial from the proportional influence point of view than from the majoritarian one; if the first and second largest parties are not very far apart in size, the proportional vision would not distinguish so significantly between them. The proportional ideal, after all, includes both of them. I offer the plurality criterion here as minimal with some hesitation. Indeed, we can see that the all or nothing character of the majoritarian or Westminster model makes it easier to argue minimal criteria (for both proximity and inclusion) than do the proportional expectations of its great rival.

A critical factor that must be considered at this point is the presence of *pre-election* coalitions between political parties. If two or more parties clearly announce their intention of forming a government together after the election, and subsequently win a majority of the vote, it seems essential to treat them as a single unit in assessing the tightness of connection between voters' choices and government formation. In such a case the voters, if informed about the parties' intentions, have given their support to the collective enterprise and responsiveness implies honoring the commitment.

We could, of course, complicate the analysis by considering the precise nature of the pre-election commitment and the degree to which the parties' intentions were known to the electorate. Pre-election coalitions in fact vary greatly in their commitments, ranging from a general expectation that parties close on the ideological spectrum will form governments together, as in much of Scandinavia (but not in Finland), to explicit commitments to govern together and carry out a common program of policies. The situation is underlined where the parties agree to withdraw candidates in each other's favor (as in France) so that the electorate does not even have a choice between members of the coalition. These varying arrangements have varying claims to be considered jointly authorized by the electorates to form a government. Here I shall simply assume that where it is widely expected, as best I can infer from accounts of the election (largely as reported in *Keesing's Archives*, supplemented by other sources, such as Laver and Budge, 1992 and various country studies), specific parties will govern together if they jointly win legislative control, it is appropriate to treat the coalition as a single unit.[7]

Thus, post election government formation will be considered minimally responsive to the extent that the first government formed after the election includes the party (or recognized pre-election coalition) that wins more votes than any other contender and endures until the next election.

Theoretical Expectations

Having developed two criteria for minimal responsiveness, we can briefly reconsider our theoretical expectations about the likelihood that each of the two types of systems, majoritarian and proportional, will create governments that will meet these. Here we can draw upon the substantial literature on governments and coalitions.

The proximity of governments to the elections can be seen to depend on two factors, the durability of the government formed immediately after the election and the propensity to call new elections if a government fails. There is a large amount of literature on government durability (e.g., Powell 1982, Chapter 7, and Warwick, 1992). It proposes that, by and large, single-party majority governments will be the most durable. Majority coalition governments can be durable if their internal policy range is not too great—a factor especially shaped by the presence of extremist parties in the legislature. Minority governments as a general type are the least durable, although lasting minority governments certainly appear, especially if consistent "outside" can be arranged and/or if the legislative opposition is badly split (Martin and Stevenson 1995). One tricky problem for our expectations about durability in the different types of systems is the frequency of minority governments in majoritarian systems (see Powell, 1982, Chapter 7), especially as these minority governments are less likely to face a badly divided opposition. (But in fact there are not many such cases in the present data set.) Still, as extremist parties are more likely to achieve legislative representation in more fractionalized systems, and to cause fractionalization when they appear, our general expectations would be for more durable governments in majoritarian systems.

Moreover, we expect elites in majoritarian systems to be more likely to consult the electorate when governments fall, because elections are more likely to resolve the problem. If it is hard to arrange a stable government because of multiparty, multi-issue complexity and extremist support, calling for new elections is likely merely to reflect the same problems into the legislature. Elections in Denmark in the 1970s and 1980s illustrate both that elites can create proximity by frequently calling for new elections when governments fall—and that such elections frequently reproduced the same deadlocks. In systems with plurality election laws a new election will more often change the legislative configuration and/or create a majority, as in Britain in 1974 and Canada in 1979. Thus, theory and previous research both lead us to expect greater proximity in the majoritarian settings; the first government is likely to endure the entire period between the elections.

Theoretical expectations are not so clear about inclusion of the plurality party or plurality pre-election coalition. In the majoritarian systems, as previously noted, much depends on the working of the election laws. In systems with relatively few parties and/or majority-producing election laws, the plurality party will frequently gain a legislative majority, and thus a durable and responsive government. On the other hand, interactions between party support distributions and election rules can produce famously distorted results. If the party with the voter plurality is not the party with the legislative plurality, then responsiveness clearly fails.

In proportional influence systems, the counterpart to distorted legislative representation would usually be elite bargaining that fails to bring the plurality party into the government. Naturally, it will be easier to form and sustain a government if its largest party commands a lot of legislative seats, and in proportional systems the plurality vote gainer will have the most seats in the legislature. Moreover, formal rules either of constitution or law (and well-established custom elsewhere) frequently stipulate that the largest party be asked first to attempt to form a government, which can confer a strategic advantage. If the largest party also happens to occupy the strategic center position on a unidimensional political spectrum, then it may often be virtually impossible to deny it a position in government. But because of the complexity of election competition in multiparty systems, the largest party may well not be at the electoral center (Denmark, Finland, France, Japan, Norway, and Sweden, for example), or such a center may effectively fail to exist because of the multiplicity of issue dimensions and party preferences. In such cases the coalition formation process may result in the exclusion of the plurality party, despite claims that it may make. (There are some nice examples of such claims and their rejections in Belgium and Netherlands, reported in *Keesing's Archives*.) On the basis of the current literature, I can see no *a priori* empirical reason to expect either type of system to have the advantage in inclusion of the plurality party in the government, although the concept is probably closer to Westminster expectations.

Empirical Results

The proximity score is the average duration (as a proportion of the time between elections) of the first government formed after the elections. A score of 100 percent proximity means that the government formed after the election lasted until the next election. A score of 33 percent means that the government lasted only one third of the way into the interelectoral period.[8] The average score for the 114 elections in our two sets of pure design types (for which proximity could be estimated because the next election had occurred or was immediately at hand) was 85, meaning that the first government lasted 85 percent of the time until the next election, which seems reasonably responsive performance by this criterion. As theoretically expected, proximity is a more serious problem for responsiveness in the proportional countries, which averaged only 81 percent, compared to 93 percent for the majoritarian designs. In Italy the first government lasted on average only 38 percent of the interelection period in the eight elections between 1972 and 1992. Belgium, Finland, and Norway also had proximity scores below 80 percent. An alteration or restructuring of the parties in government without consulting the electorate occasionally occurs elsewhere also, as in France (e.g., when the PCF left the Communist/Socialist coalition that took office after the 1981 election), New Zealand after 1993, and even in the United Kingdom in the late 1970s, when the Labour government lost its majority and temporarily took on the Liberals as a support party. But it is primarily a problem for proportional systems, especially where the presence of extremist parties greatly complicated the process of building sustainable government coalitions. Although some multiparty, proportional systems did well either in sustaining stable governments (the Netherlands in this period) or in frequently consulting the electorate when they failed (Denmark), the proximity advantage is clearly to the majoritarian designs.

The empirical results are reversed when we consider the party or pre-election coalition included in the government. Considering only the single party winning the most votes, the two types of systems had nearly identical scores: 76 percent of the first post-election governments contained the plurality party. It is especially notable that Belgium, Finland, and Italy, despite their poor proximity scores, do well by this measure of the composition of the governments that were formed. In Italy, for example, the largest vote winner, the Christian Democrats throughout this period, is always included in the governments until the collapse of the party system and formation of a nonparty government in 1993. There are also, of course, cases where post-election bargaining excluded the plurality winner, as in Denmark in 1973 and the Netherlands in 1977. The majoritarian systems, on the other hand, were particularly hurt by instances where the plurality vote winner was deprived of a legislative plurality by vote-seat distortions of the election laws, as in Australia in 1969, Canada in 1979, New Zealand in 1978 and 1981, and the United Kingdom in February 1974; thus, the similar overall averages for the two types of systems.

However, such results can be normatively and empirically misleading in some countries, where the voters were usually offered clearly identified pre-election coalitions of parties committed to governing together (e.g., Australian plurality "failures" in 1972, 1975, 1980). It is clear from examining the individual countries and elections that in countries such as Australia, Denmark, France, Germany, Ireland, and Sweden, the pre-election coalitions played a critical role in government formation. The largest single party may have been outvoted by a pre-election coalition and the latter took office. Considering pre-election coalitions as if they were single parties raises the overall average to nearly 85 percent.

Although considering the pre-election coalitions corrects Australian plurality "failures" of 1972, 1975, and 1980, on average it is the proportional influence systems that are helped more by considering the pre-election coalitions (e.g., Sweden 1976 and 1979; Germany 1972–1994). The first government included the plurality party or pre-election coalition after 79 percent of the elections in the majoritarian systems and after an impressive 86 percent of the elections in the proportional influence systems.

If we combine the two minimal conditions, we find that the majoritarian advantage of proximity and the proportional advantage of plurality/pec inclusion roughly cancel each other. I constructed a single minimal responsiveness measure that scores the election in the following way: 0 if the first government does not contain the plurality party or pre-election coalition; if it does contain that party (coalition), then the score is the percent of the term it endured. Across the 114 elections considered here, the average score was 72. This is consistent with the general responsiveness of government change to votes that we saw in table 2.1 and figure 2.2. Elections do matter, if somewhat imperfectly, in all kinds of democracies. The averages for the two types of systems are quite similar, with only a slight advantage for the majority systems (74 percent) over the proportional influence systems (71 percent). (See table 2.3.)

Government Responsiveness to Elections under Majoritarian and Proportional Criteria

We have already identified minimal criteria for responsiveness under majoritarian criteria: a government should be formed immediately after the election and should contain the single party or pre-election coalition receiving the most votes. But are these criteria sufficient for majoritarians to consider a government fully responsive? Probably not.

From the majoritarian point of view there can be two kinds of problems with governments, even if they meet the minimal criteria. They may be too small or they may be too large. A government is clearly too small if it does not possess a legislative majority. Such a government cannot control the policy process. It must bargain with other parties, either on a rotating basis or with single-party outside support. It must exist at the sufferance of other parties that can depose it at any time. In any of these situations both accountability and mandates are badly blurred. Even if a minority government attains *de facto* policy control through subtle manipulation of a divided opposition (e.g., see Huber's account of France 1988 in Huber 1996, Chapter 4), such arrangements are difficult for the voter to assess and majority control is surely diluted.

On the other hand, from the majoritarian perspective a government clearly is too large if it contains additional political parties (not part of an explicit pre-election coalition ratified by the voters), even though the plurality party has won a legislative majority. Inclusion of parties beyond the minimum needed for legislative control dilutes both the current mandate and future accountability. Such inclusion may be justified by national emergency conditions (as in wartime Grand Coalitions), or because of the complex configuration of policy preferences, or by special policy-making rules, or by desire to maintain durable government and proximity. But however laudable such a government, it is not ideally electorally responsive according to the majoritarian vision unless the parties were explicitly in alliance at the time of the election.[9]

In fact, governments in the majoritarian systems met the additional criteria quite well. Only a handful of governments (Canada 1972, 1979; France 1988, and UK February 1974) failed to gain legislative majorities through the election. (Note that two of these were wrong-party legislative pluralities that already failed the minimum criteria.) The initial government formed never contained superfluous parties not included in a pre-election coalition. Thus, nearly 70 percent of the post-election government formation in the majoritarian systems fit the ideal criteria as well as the minimal ones. On the other hand, only about a third of the elections in the proportional design systems were followed by such governments (see table 2.3.). It is less than 20 percent if we excluded governments created by post-election bargaining. Governments in the proportional design systems were, on average, quite successful in meeting the minimal criteria, but very far from the majoritarian ideal.

We can think about the responsive formation of majority governments this way: either voters and election laws must create them automatically, or the process of party bargaining (before or after the election) must construct them. If the election creates legislative majorities for the plurality party or coalition, elite bargaining seldom alters the outcome. But if there is no majority outcome, the bargaining may fail to create one that includes the plurality winner. Less party fractionalization and/or election laws designed to create majorities will indeed tend toward mechanically predictable outcomes. These will be initially responsive about 75 percent of the time, failing in nearly 20 percent of the cases to give the legislative plurality or majority to the party (pre-election coalition) with the vote plurality, and failing in an additional 5 percent to give any majority at all. All but a few will endure unchanged until the next election. On the other hand, proportional election laws and, typically, fractionalized party representation usually leave it up to the party leaders in their pre- and/or post-election bargaining. These governments usually do include the plurality vote winner. But the bargaining efforts seldom succeed in meeting the additional majoritarian responsiveness criteria. Lack of proximate governments, oversize governments, and above all, minority governments (which were the norm in Denmark, Norway, and Sweden) contribute to failures of this constitutional design to create governments responsive by majoritarian criteria.

What about the proportional vision? We have already identified minimal criteria for responsiveness under proportionate influence criteria: A government should be formed immediately after the election and should contain the single-party or pre-election coalition receiving the most votes. These are necessary criteria for a government to be responsive under either vision. But they are not sufficient for a government to be considered fully responsive according to the proportional influence vision. As with the majoritarian vision, additional criteria are needed—and they are fundamentally different from those of the majoritarian vision.

The critical property of this vision, of course, is that all the voters should be represented fairly in the policy-making process. For governments, the implication is that the ideal government would be the government of all political parties, a true Grand Coalition, and that these should be included in proportion to their voting strength. Full Grand Coalitions are rare, but a good approximation of concept is simply the vote received by the parties participating in the government (which would, of course, be 100 percent in a Grand Coalition). Such parties usually share cabinet seats in proportion to their relative legislative representation, but we shall bypass this additional refinement at the moment. I think that it would not change the current analysis greatly.

Of course, by considering the proportion of votes won by the governing party, we are already giving a higher score if the plurality party/coalition is in the government. But we do need to multiply that score by the duration of the first government.

Interestingly enough, the proportional influence systems do not fare exceptionally well as approximations of Grand Coalitions, even before we take account of the duration problem. There are a few very large coalitions in Austria, but in most of the proportional influence systems governments are likely to be based on parties supported by no more than 50–60 percent of the electorate. The average government in Austria, Belgium, Finland, Netherlands, and Germany was in this range, with Italy just at 49 percent. The majority governments in these systems are usually closer to simple majoritarian than to grand coalitions of all parties. Governments can be sustained and (except in Finland) most policies enacted with no more than a bare legislative majority and government coalition formation reflects that fact. As we have seen, frequent minority governments in Sweden, Norway, and Denmark pulled their voter support averages much lower.

What is perhaps most surprising about considering the bases of government support is that overall the proportional influence systems do not greatly outscore their majoritarian counterparts. The average vote for the governing parties is about 44 percent in the majoritarian systems and about 50 percent in the proportional ones (with the latter divided into two quite different groups), as we already saw in the representation discussion. Each is, of course, rather far from its own ideal. If we multiply these scores by the respective percentages of the term the proximate government was in office (93 percent for majoritarian systems and 81 percent for plurality systems), we find identical scores of 41 percent in each type of system. However, there is much greater range in the proportional systems; high durability plus large governments in Austria and the Netherlands yielded government averages of 59 and 58, whereas the reverse combination yielded only 18, 24, and 31 in Italy, Norway, and Denmark, respectively.

Yet, we must recall that many of the proportional influence systems depend on continuing bargaining in the legislature, not government dominance. Minority governments, with their fairly low percent of vote for the governing parties, tend to provide such bargaining opportunities. Moreover, most of these systems offered very strong and proportionally divided committee systems and related institutional opportunities for the opposition. To treat the proportional logic fairly, we must consider policymakers, not merely governments.

Responsiveness in Forming Policymaker Coalitions

I have already discussed the difficulties in assessing the weighting of parties' influence in policymaker coalitions. The influence weights discussed in the preceding representation analysis are the most reasonable estimates I can provide at this time, although the weighting details are certainly debatable. Analysis of the connections between elections and policymaker coalitions is troubled both by doubts about the appropriate weighting of party influence and, as usual, by the differences in ideal responsiveness between the two visions themselves.

Nonetheless, we can rely on a critical, but extremely plausible, assumption to help us here. Whatever other factors are taken into account, it almost certainly remains true that the parties in the government—holding cabinet portfolios—have greater influence on government policies than parties outside the government. The degree of difference in influence of governing and nongoverning parties changes with majority control, decentralized committee systems, influence through second houses, party discipline, and the like. But it is highly likely that the governing parties will have more influence than nongoverning parties.

This assumption immediately leads us to reassert from the majoritarian perspective the critical minimal conditions developed in the analysis of government formation. Responsive policymaker coalitions should give more influence to the party or pre-election coalition winning the most votes from the electorate than to other parties. Moreover, although we cannot observe all the changes in influence across issues and over time, we can infer that a change in government does signify some change in the patterns of influence. Plurality and proximity of governments remain, then, minimal conditions for responsiveness in the formation of policymaker coalitions as well as in the formation of governments themselves. Plurality is already taken directly into account, proportionally, in the policymaker representation analysis, so it does not need to be reintroduced for the ideal proportional vision, but proximity remains (at least somewhat) relevant.

Beyond this minimum, the visions diverge, familiarly, in their ideal criteria. The majority control vision views any diminution of the influence of the electorate's plurality party or coalition as undesirable. Thus, its ideal responsiveness would involve the same measures of responsiveness we discussed for governments, but *diminished* if the policy-making arrangements enhance the importance of the opposition. On the other hand, the proportional influence vision argues for influence to all parties in proportion to their electoral support. Its closest approximation that we can estimate is the "Representation of Party Voters in Policy-Making" measure itself.

I have calculated the average number of governments that: (a) are at least minimally responsive, (b) are minimally majority, and (c) exercise unchecked control of the legislature. Control is considered checked, and thus the policymaker coalition is not considered ideally responsive from a majoritarian point of view, if power was shared through committee systems, opposition control of the upper house, or lack of party discipline in the governing party.[10] Not surprisingly, by these strong, ideal majoritarian criteria the majoritarian design systems perform the best by far. (Indeed, as the classification of systems depending in part on the legislative arrangements, this relationship is to some extent stipulated, yet of interest in filling out the full picture.) By this measure of majoritarian ideal policymaker responsiveness, the majoritarian systems still score a strong 67 percent. The primary reason for departure from the ideal is, as usual, the one-fifth of the cases where the wrong party wins government control, further diluted by minority governments and (slightly) by limited opposition influence. The policymakers in the proportional influence systems, on the other hand, look very different from this ideal for all of the reasons already discussed—plus the presence of checking opposition committee power, yielding an average score of only about 1. (See table 2.3.)

What is interesting in the policymaker analysis, of course, is the approximation to the proportional ideal. As we have already seen, the duration problems and governments that seldom include parties representing all the voters pull these policymaker representatives quite a ways below the ideal. But the much greater weight given to opposition parties in policy making in these systems makes them significantly better performers by these criteria than their majoritarian counterparts. The majoritarian systems score 49 by the ideal proportional policymaker standards (their policymaker representation score multiplied by the .93 average duration measure). The proportional influence systems score a respectable 60 percent of their own ideal (their policymaker representation score of 75 multiplied by the .81 duration average). Here we see the return to the expected pattern of each type of system performing better according to its own preferred criteria. However, the contrast is not as pronounced as when comparing the two types according to the majoritarian ideal. (See table 2.3.)

Concluding Comments

The concept of responsiveness to citizen's choices in elections is attractive and interesting as a measure of democratic performance. But its apparent simplicity conceals subtle problems.

1. There is, across the parliamentary democracies, a general relationship between *change* in voter support of government parties and the retention or replacement of governments (table 2.1). However, because of the differences in levels and configurations of support, it is not clear that the relationship should be the same in all cases (e.g., a government whose support falls from 58 percent to 53 percent of the voters should not be replaced, while the situation may be different if support falls from 52 percent to 47 percent).[11]

2. Moreover, careful consideration of the nature of the relationship between voters and policymakers assumed by the majoritarian and proportionate influence approaches to democracy suggests substantial divergence in their ideals of responsiveness. Majoritarian democracy assumes an all or nothing relationship, but the proportional influence approach does not (figure 2.1).

3. Both approaches seem to imply that responsiveness to elections would minimally require that the party or pre-election coalition winning the largest number of votes would be part of a government immediately after the election and continue in office until the next election.

   (a) The constitutional designs based on the two approaches are about equal in their probability of forming governments containing the single party winning a plurality of votes, but the proportional designs did better when we allow plurality pre-election coalitions to count as the equivalent of parties. In the majoritarian designs, failures appeared in 15–20 percent of the elections and at least once in each majoritarian country, because distortions in the vote-seat relationship caused the vote plurality party to fail to be the legislative plurality party (pre-election coalition). In the proportional designs the failures—in 10–15 percent of cases—were caused by the failure of the plurality party/pre-election coalition to win a place in the cabinet in post-election negotiation.

(b) The majoritarian systems were significantly more successful in forming governments that endured the full period between elections (proximate governments). This success reflected both the greater average durability of governments in these systems and their greater tendency to call new elections when governments fell.

(c) The majoritarian designs were only slightly (and insignificantly) more successful (74 percent to 71 percent) in creating governments that met both minimum responsiveness criteria. Both types of systems performed reasonably well, with somewhat different types and causes of failures, by the joint criteria.

4. Additional criteria for responsiveness suggested by the majoritarian and proportional visions were sharply divergent.

(a) Not surprisingly, the majoritarian designs were much more likely than proportional designs to create governments with minimally winning legislative majorities. Similarly, they were much more likely to provide such governments with unchecked policy powers (majoritarian policy coalitions) that endured the entire post-election period. This was a very unlikely outcome in the proportional influence systems.

(b) The proportional designs were more likely to create policy maker coalitions that offered some influence to representatives of all voters, with, typically, greatest influence to the party (or coalition) winning the most support. The relative success of the proportional designs systems in this respect was somewhat lessened by failure in some countries to create coalitions that endured the entire period between elections. They still retained a significantly superior performance edge (60 to 49).

These results are summarized from a slightly different point of view in table 2.4, which shows the simple correlation coefficients between the two main constitutional features and the measures of representation and responsiveness for the 141 elections in the 18 parliamentary democracies between 1969 and the mid-1990s. Because the comparisons summarized in table 2.3 show averages for only the two pure groups, and because there may be some doubt about classification or exclusion of some countries, the correlations serve usefully to confirm the previous results. The electoral variable here is

Lijphart's 1994 *Effective Threshold* for legislative representation; the committee variable is the three-level classification from table 2.2.

It is clear that the higher thresholds of representation (a majoritarian feature) are associated with less accurate and complete representation of party voters in the legislature, in governments (to a much lessor extent), and in policy making.[12] However, the higher effective threshold is related to greater proximity between elections and government formation (i.e., durability of the first government formed after the election, nearly significant at .05) and very strongly related to the majoritarian ideal governments: proximate minimal majorities, unchecked by legislative power sharing. Such higher electoral thresholds are strongly and significantly less likely to provide proportional influence for all parties in policy making.

The committee variable relationships largely mirror these. As the electoral and committee variables are themselves correlated at −.82 in this set of countries, they tend to go together in the opposite directions. A supplementary regression analysis (not shown here) strongly suggests, as common sense would indicate, that the electoral law variable dominates the legislative and government results, with committee variable correlations just going along for the ride. But the policymaker measures are significantly shaped by both constitutional factors: electoral rules and committee rules.

TABLE 2.4. **Pearson Correlations Between Constitutional Features and Electoral Responsiveness in 137 Parliamentary Elections**

Alternative Measures of Responsiveness to Elections	Effective Electoral Threshold (Lijphart 1994)	Committee Influence in Legislature (Table 2.2)
REPRESENTATION OF PARTY VOTERS		
Legislature	−.76**	+.56**
Government	−.28**	+.14
Policy making	−.79**	+.73**
MINIMALLY RESPONSIVE GOVERNMENTS		
Duration of Initial Gov.	+.16	−.06
Plural Governments (pty or pec)	−.10	+.01
Duration X Plural	+.02	−.02
IDEALLY RESPONSIVE GOVERNMENTS		
Majoritarian Criteria	+.30**	−.21*
Proportional Criteria	−.04	+.05
IDEALLY RESPONSIVE POLICY MAKERS		
Majoritarian Criteria	+.61**	−.58**
Proportional Criteria	−.28**	+.33**

** Significant at .01.   pec = Pre-election coalition

Overall, we should first note that although each approach has significant weaknesses, they each do reasonably well in creating minimal responsiveness. In about three elections out of four the party or pre-election coalition winning the most votes forms a government that endures most of the period between elections. Moreover, there is clearly a significant relationship between government electoral losses and the likelihood it will be replaced. From any point of view there is meaningful responsiveness in most of the democracies most of the time. Beyond this minimum, however, successes and failures of responsiveness depend largely on the values and assumptions of the beholder.

Any analysis that accepts the plurality (not pure majority) vote criterion and considers as clearly responsive only unchecked majority governments of the plurality party (or explicit pre-election coalition) will find much more responsiveness in the majoritarian designs.[13] Moreover, as Lijphart has suggested (Lijphart 1994, pp. 146–48), majoritarian designs could be made even more satisfactory by using some form of two-tier districting, with a national tier to correct extreme disproportionality and guarantee that the plurality vote winner won a legislative plurality or even majority. Through such means the troubling and not uncommon creation of a legislative plurality or majority for a party that did not win a plurality of votes could largely be avoided. This design flaw in the majoritarian constitutional approach seems clearly correctable if we use election rules other than simple single-member districts.

It is less easy to see how to engineer the bargaining problems of the proportional systems, reflected in the proximity difficulties as well as in the occasional failure to put the plurality party/coalition in the government. However, analysts that seek responsiveness to as many voters as possible will find much to like in the proportional designs. Although Grand Coalition governments are quite rare, a variety of bargaining and structural arrangements enhance the role of opposition parties. From this point of view, the proximity considerations merely weigh against the advantages of the proportional approach. Thus, although our analysis helps to illuminate the issues of responsiveness to elections, it cannot claim a definitive solution to the divergent normative expectations.

Notes

[1]Sometimes the term is equated simply with correspondence between actions of government and the preferences of citizens, or even with democracy itself (e.g., Lijphart, 1984, 1; also see Pennock, 1979, pp. 260–63). For usage more comparable to mine, see Strom's (1990) discussion of electoral decisiveness, pp. 72–78.

[2]On one side the concept assumes that voter's choices do reflect their preferences in a meaningful way, avoiding various problems of information and,

perhaps more importantly, the substantive alternatives presented to them by political parties. (I shall touch somewhat on this later, however.) On the other side, I shall not be exploring what parties actually do in office once they achieve influence in policy making, nor the important role of elections, at least under some circumstances, in holding them to their commitments. (On this theme, see Powell 1989).

[3]For a more complete discussion of internal legislative rules, see Powell, forthcoming, Chapter 2 (table 2.2 and the various sources referenced there, especially Doering 1994).

[4]It is somewhat reassuring to check my measure of Representation of Party Voters in Policy Making with the data on the reputed influence of the opposition among journalists and political scientists reported in Laver and Hunt (1992, Appendix B). Of course, the question asked by Laver and Hunt is not quite specific enough to get at the same concept; we cannot be sure whether the respondents are taking account of various structural and political factors and exactly what opposition they have in mind. Yet, using only the 18 parliamentary systems and the 27 elections held in 1990 or later (to fit roughly the Laver and Hunt time frame), there is a correlation of .75 between their reputed "Influence of the Opposition" and the combined "probability of opposition influence" used to calculate my Representation of Party Voters in Policy Making measure and a correlation of .49 with the latter score itself. Given the very different operationalizations, these correlations seem rather encouraging.

[5]Of course, there are many difficulties with such claims, both because of the lack of information on the part of voters and the problems of multidimensionality of issue preferences. See Riker 1982, on populism.

[6]However, some proponents of the proportional vision may still find post-election government formation responsive if multiple governments between elections sequentially bring different parties into government for time periods proportional to their electoral strength. Such readers will find the proximity criterion excessively "majoritarian."

[7]This criterion is easy to document in cases of more explicit coalitions, such as those between Gaullists and UDF in France, National and Liberal parties in Australia, and the CDU/CSU (itself a coalition) and FDP (since 1983) in Germany. Some of the more implicit Scandinavian cases are trickier, especially where the expectations have changed over time, and one must avoid the temptation to characterize a coalition as "pre-electoral" or not depending on the post-election behavior.

[8]In some previous analyses I have used a proximity measure that counts the number of governments between elections. But upon reflection it seems to me

that the duration of the first government is more conceptually appropriate than the number of additional governments forming between elections.

[9]A final issue is what to do about a government whose size is "just right," in the sense of being the smallest size necessary to control the legislature (and including the plurality party), but still the product of (proximate) post-election bargaining. This is, I think, the hardest case for the majoritarian vision to evaluate. On one hand, multiparty governments can still cloud their accountability by campaign arguments and the plurality winner must negotiate its mandate. On the other hand, there is at least collective responsibility and the plurality party usually will be the larger partner with putatively the upper hand in negotiations. There seems no easy resolution of this argument; the government seems more than minimal in its responsiveness status, but short of fully responsive under the majoritarian vision. In tables 2.3 and 2.4 they are counted as responsive.

[10]On lack of discipline in the governing party, see the discussion in Powell and Whitten 1993. Among the 18 countries considered here, only Italy and Japan experienced such lack of discipline on a regular basis; the United States and Switzerland are also identified in the larger set of countries. On opposition influence through the upper house, cases here appear only in Australia and Germany; such dispersed influence also occurs in the cohabitation periods in France.

[11]A measure that I do not explore in the main text is the average vote gains or losses for the parties in the government taking office after the election. It turns out that incoming governments are more often vote gainers in the majoritarian systems than proportional ones. In the majoritarian designs the average incoming government gained 1 percent (in the mixed systems this figure was +1.9 percent). But in the proportional designs the average incoming government was composed of parties who actually *lost* .75 percent. Intuitively, this difference seems to speak to greater responsiveness to elections in the majoritarian design systems. I have frequently treated it that way in discussions of these issues.

But on close analysis, the apparent advantage of the majoritarian designs seems to be a consequence of the ways vote losses of plurality parties can be distributed in two-party versus multiparty systems. In two-party systems, when a government loses votes (which most do), all those votes go to the main opposition party; if the incumbent loses very many votes, there will be a new majority party, which usually becomes the government—showing up as a vote gain for the new government. However, in multiparty systems, vote losses of plurality parties in government can go to all kinds of parties, not necessarily or primarily to the largest opposition. This lack of constraint means less frequent change of plurality party when that party loses votes and, hence, more frequent formation of governments made up of vote losers as much as winners. As these mechanical dynamics do not seem to fit well into the normative bases of responsiveness, I have not included these vote gain measures here.

[12]The Effective Threshold also has a correlation of −.39 (significant at .05) with the Laver and Hunts (1992) reputed influence of the opposition (using the 27 elections held in the early 1990s in the 18 parliamentary democracies). The committee influence variable has a positive correlation of .24 with the Laver and Hunt measure (significant at only .2). These results are roughly consistent with expectations, keeping in mind that it is a bit unclear what the Laver and Hunt respondents had in mind, but that influence of the opposition is probably a desirable feature for responsiveness in the proportional vision and an undesirable one in majoritarian approaches.

[13]This in effect is also what happens in a responsiveness measure such as that proposed by Strom (1990, 73–74), which assigns full responsiveness to single-party governments with legislative majorities, and responsiveness proportional to the number of parties who are vote gainers where there is no single-party majority. Almost all the single-party governments with majorities will be in the majoritarian design systems. The other governments will largely be composed of a mixture of vote winners and losers, leaving a strong relationship between majoritarian design and his responsiveness measure. Of course, Strom designed his measure for predictive, rather than normative purposes, so the connection to normative majoritarian assumptions is not a problem for his purposes. But it explains why I do not offer it as a norm-neutral measure here.

References

Cox, Gary. 1997. *Making Votes Count: Strategic Coordination in the World's Electoral Systems*. New York: Cambridge University Press.

Dahl, Robert A. 1989. *Democracy and Its Critics*. New Haven: Yale University Press.

Doering, Herbert. 1994. *Parliaments and Majority Rule in Western Europe*. New York: St. Martin's Press.

Duverger, Maurice. 1954. *Political Parties: Their Organization and Activity in the Modern State*, B. North and R. North, trans. New York: John Wiley.

Gelman, Andrew, and Gary King. 1994. "Enhancing Democracy through Legislative Redistricting." *American Political Science Review*, 88:541–59.

Huber, John D. 1996. *Rationalizing Parliament: Legislative Institutions and Party Politics in France*. New York: Cambridge University Press.

Huber, John D. and G. Bingham Powell Jr. 1994. "Congruence between Citizens and Policy Makers in Two Visions of Liberal Democracy." *World Politics* 46:291–326.

Inter-Parliamentary Union. 1976, 1986. *Parliaments of the World: A Comparative Reference*. New York: Facts on File Publications.

Laver, Michael, and W. Ben Hunt. 1992. *Policy and Party Competition*. New York: Routledge.

Laver, Michael J., and Ian Budge, eds. 1992. *Party Policy and Government Coalitions*. New York: St. Martin's Press.

Lijphart, Arend. 1984. *Democracies: Patterns of Majoritarian and Consensus Government*. New Haven: Yale University Press.

Lijphart, Arend. 1994. *Electoral Systems and Party Systems: A Study of Twenty-Seven Democracies, 1945–1990*. New York: Oxford University Press.

Martin, Lanny, and Randolph Stevenson. "Explaining Formation and Durability of Minority Governments." Unpublished manuscript, 1997.

Pennock, J. Roland. 1979. *Democratic Political Theory*. Princeton: Princeton University Press.

Powell, G. Bingham, Jr. 1989. "Constitutional Design and Citizen Electoral Control." *Journal of Theoretical Politics* 1:107–30.

Powell, G. Bingham, Jr. 1982. *Contemporary Democracies: Participation, Stability and Violence*. Cambridge: Harvard University Press.

Powell, G. Bingham, Jr. Forthcoming. *Elections as Instruments of Democracy*. New Haven: Yale University Press.

Powell, G. Bingham, Jr. and Guy D. Whitten. 1993. "A Cross-National Analysis of Economic Voting: Taking Account of the Political Context." *American Journal of Political Science*, 37: 391–414.

Rae, Douglas. 1967. *The Political Consequences of Electoral Laws*. New Haven: Yale University Press.

Riker, William H. 1982a. *Liberalism against Populism*. San Francisco: W. H. Freeman.

Riker, William H. 1982b. "The Two-party System and Duverger's Law: An Essay on the History of Political Science." *American Political Science Review*, 76:753–66.

Strom, Kaare. 1990. *Minority Government and Majority Rule*. Cambridge: Cambridge University Press.

Warwick, Paul. 1992. "Economic Trends and Government Survival in West European Parliamentary Democracies." *American Political Science Review* 86:875–87.

CHAPTER 3

Arend Lijphart and
the New Institutionalism

Bernard Grofman

March and Olsen (1984: 734) characterize a new institutionalist approach to
politics that "emphasizes relative autonomy of political institutions, possibilities for inefficiency in history, and the importance of symbolic action to an
understanding of politics." Among the other points they assert to be characteristic of this "new institutionalism" are the recognition that processes may
be as important as outcomes (or even more important), and the recognition
that preferences are not fixed and exogenous but may change as a function of
political learning in a given institutional and historical context. However, in
my view, there are three key problems with the March and Olsen synthesis.

First, in looking for a common ground of belief among those who use the
label "new institutionalism" for their work, March and Olsen are seeking to
impose a unity of perspective on a set of figures who actually have little in
common. March and Olsen (1984) lump together apples, oranges, and arti-
chokes: neo-Marxists, symbolic interactionists, and learning theorists, all
under their new institutionalist umbrella. They recognize that the ideas they
ascribe to the new institutionalists are "not all mutually consistent. Indeed
some of them seem mutually inconsistent" (March and Olsen, 1984: 738), but
they slough over this paradox for the sake of typological neatness.

Second, March and Olsen (1984) completely neglect another set of figures, those associated with positive political theory in political science and
with game theoretic and/or Public Choice approaches in economics, who
surely also deserve the label new institutionalists.[1]

Third, and most important for present purposes, March and Olsen (1984)
completely neglect the revival of interest in institutions in comparative politics

An earlier version of this paper was given at the Annual Meeting of the American Political
Science Association, San Francisco, August 29–September 1, 1996. I am indebted to Dorothy
Green for library assistance.

that was already underway in political science long before the term new institutionalism became popular—especially that in the area of electoral systems research (e.g., Rae 1967, 1971) and in constitutional design.[2] In both these areas Lijphart's work had already played (e.g., Lijphart 1975, 1977a,b) and would continue to play a major role (e.g., Lijphart and Grofman 1984; Grofman and Lijphart 1986; Lijphart 1992; Lijphart 1994). Though some might say this research was merely a continuation of the old institutionalism, a style of approach that had never really gone away[3] even though it was supplanted in importance by other approaches such as that of the Michigan School (with its strong emphasis on public opinion), in my view there are sufficiently many distinctive aspects of the institutionalist focus that has become associated with Lijphart (and now his students) that it deserves separate recognition as an important and separate strain of the new institutionalism.[4]

My argument for the claims to recognition of a distinctively Lijphartian approach to institutional analysis is strengthened by the fact that March and Olsen's (1984) own claims for the novelty of the ideas they attribute to the new institutionalist strains they talk about are based on a "potted" history of political science that bears little resemblance to anything I can recognize.

In contrast to the insights of the new institutionalist ideas they discuss, March and Olsen (1984: 738) see post-1950s political science as emphasizing the aggregating of individual behavior motivated by utilitarian and instrumental concerns. They also view political science of this period as by and large seeing politics as subordinated to other features of the social environment such as class, ethnicity, economics, and religion; and they assert that political scientists have been functionalist, by which they mean that political scientists have tended to view politics as the outcome of a generally beneficent process of historical adaptation.

Clearly, any attempt to paint with a broad brush tendencies allegedly characteristic of all of modern political science can be challenged. For any generalization, we can find large bodies of literature that seem to refute it. March and Olsen's (1984) characterization of the salient features of post–World War II political science as contextual, reductionist, utilitarian, functionalist, and instrumentalist, however, seems particularly ill-conceived, since it lumps together orientations that in fact were mutually antagonistic rather than mutually complementary.

In particular, I am extremely skeptical that modern political science, for the most part, has described political events as the consequences of calculated decisions, as March and Olsen (1984) claim. I do not read the *American Voter* that way, nor most of the subsequent literature of the Michigan school. Downsian views may now be *de rigueur*, but political socialization, party identification, citizen duty, and ideas of that sort are far from dead even today—and certainly were alive and well and the dominant leitmotifs in the study of voter choice for most of the post–World War II period.[5] Similarly, in comparative politics, I would hardly describe leading contributors in the 1960s and 1970s such as Gabriel Almond, Harry Eckstein, or Lucian Pye, say, as rational choice modelers.

I do not wish to try to fight with March and Olsen (1984) about the history of the discipline. Rather, my limited aim here is to set the record straight in one limited domain by arguing that there were many different revivals of interest in institutions after World War II, all of which have legitimate claims to being called new institutionalism,[6] and by pointing out that at least two of these new institutionalisms, associated with Bill Riker and his students and colleagues, and associated with Arend Lijphart and his students and colleagues, simply do not fit into the new institutionalist mold poured by March and Olsen (1984).[7] It is the Lijphartian strain of new institutionalism, however, that will be the principal focus of this essay.

Arend Lijphart is the author of seminal work on the political consequences of electoral systems and on the logic of constitutional design, whose work on mechanisms for power-sharing has world-wide visibility and an influence that has extended far beyond academic circles (particularly in South Africa). The concern for institutional structure and its effects that underpins almost all of his books and articles entitles Lijphart to a central place among the set of rather diverse folks who identify themselves with the new institutionalism in political science. Moreover, when the history of the discipline is written, say in the year 2020, looking back not just at Lijphart's own work but also that of the students and colleagues that he has influenced—as with Bill Riker and the "Rochester School of positive political theory," or Phil Converse and Warren Miller and the "Michigan School of survey research"—we[8] will be able to identify a distinctive methodological stance and set of central questions that future political scientists will come to label Arend Lijphart and the "UCSD/UCI School[9] of comparative institutional analysis."[10]

Even without the advantages of 20-20 hindsight, there are some things to be said about what I believe will come to be identified as seven common elements of the approach of the UCSD/UCI School of comparative institutional analysis:[11]

1. There is the cross-national scope of analysis and the emphasis on comparisons.
2. There is a blending of concern for taxonomic conceptualization and a concern for measurement, in the form both of a search for plausible operationalizations and in terms of really knowing the data.
3. There is an emphasis on the need to identify variables that can be shown to have explanatory power.

4. There is an absence of dogmatism; that is, a strong belief that institutions can matter, without a view that they are in any way the whole story.
5. There is the view that a necessary ingredient in important research is important questions.[12]
6. There is the belief that institutions are not just constraints on the feasible choice set, or reifications of existing power relationships; they are also often solutions to important societal problems, for example, to the problem of creating political stability in an ethnically divided society within a democratic framework.
7. There is a desire to keep things as simple as the reality will allow, and to write to be understood.

Although no single one of these features is any way distinctive, the package as a whole is—albeit in a refreshingly commonsensical way.

Lijphartian Perspectives on Comparative Institutional Analysis

Lijphart's work can be distinguished from the positive political theory approach with its emphasis on institutions as game-theoretic equilibria and ways of avoiding preference cycling; from that of the sociological approach to organizational theory, with its emphasis on nonsystematic and unanticipated consequences of organizational choice and/or insistence that preferences are shaped by institutions as well as shaping them; and from the narrative historical approach, with its emphasis on institutions as organic growths whose understanding requires "thick description." Lijphart's work also may be contrasted with authors who focus so tightly on formal rules and constitutional jurisprudence as to exhibit relative disregard for empirical evidence about the extent to which rules do matter.

Emphasis on Cross-National Analysis

Although necessarily relying heavily on secondary sources and aggregate data, a single scholar with great knowledge and theoretical insights of his/her own can produce important work, even when trying to understand more than one polity; but authors who fall prey to misunderstandings of local political realities or lack a rich theoretical framework with which to organize their data all too often produce comparative work that is pedestrian at best or misleading at worst. In like manner, although examining only a single case, a scholar of perception can make of that case a fount of insight and even a direct test of theory (Eckstein, 1975, 1992), or do work that is so dragged down by detail and proper names that its theoretical usefulness is zilch.

There is a Scylla of theoretical elegance but empirical irrelevance, and a Charybdis of atheoretical hyperfactualism, each of which must be avoided. Lijphart's own work (e.g., Lijphart 1977a, 1984, 1994) exhibits exactly that remarkable feat of steersmanship. Perhaps Lijphart's greatest gift is his ability to integrate vast masses of cross-national data (especially aggregate data) into a theoretically meaningful whole, as shown in Lijphart (1984) and Lijphart (1994).[13]

Conceptualization and Measurement

Without variables (both dependent and independent) to consider, generalizations are impossible and we are lost in a forest of facts. But concern for taxonomy and conceptualization, like concern for mathematical modeling, can easily degenerate into scholasticism of the worst sort if it becomes divorced from the development of *testable* theory and the continual cross-check of empirical validation. To do analysis (especially cross-national analysis) well, we must be able to find the forest, without losing sight of the trees. Before we can begin to explain, it is necessary to classify.

The two conceptual frameworks with which Arend Lijphart is most closely identified are the approach to consociationalism found in his early work using the Netherlands as a prime exemplar, and the polarity between majoritarian (Westminster) and consensual forms of governance laid out in *Democracies* (1984). Neither of these ideas sprang *de novo* from Arend's brow, but in each case he provided something significantly new (e.g., the specification of four criteria used to determine the presence of consociationalism, in the case of the former, and the empirically grounded linking of seemingly different institutional arrangements into a common continuum, in the case of the latter).

Concern for Explanatory Power

If we look at the work of students of comparative politics (such as Gary Cox) who fully integrate formal modeling and hypothesis testing, it becomes impossible to draw hard and fast contrasts between Lijphart's approach and those of scholars like Cox associated with positive political theory. The differences are primarily ones of emphasis and preferred techniques of analysis. Still, not all those in the positive theory camp of institutionalist analysis are like Cox; some act as if mathematical theorems are what social science is all about. In contrast, Lijphart and his students are constantly seeking to develop testable theory and are eager to examine data in the process.

If we compare Lijphart's work with those who study institutions from a more traditional historical perspective (e.g., various essays in Steinmo, Thelen, and Longstreth, 1992), again we would not wish to draw too sharp a line of difference. In particular, Lijphart is a highly knowledgeable observer, whose research has often included considerable historical background. Moreover, even when working with highly aggregated data at the cross-national data, he is often able to bring to that data the expertise of a country specialist. It is only with respect to extreme points of view that contrasts stand out. A few of those doing narrative history of institutions, with an emphasis on institutions as organic growths, have so stressed the importance of detailed historical explanations and the quiddity of cases as to leave doubt about the possibility of meaningful generalization. In my own view, Lijphart's work puts the lie to any claim that each polity (or each institution) is so unique and so in need of thick description that there is little to be learned from comparative analysis.[14]

Nondogmatism

In general, Lijphart's view of the explanatory power of institutions is certainly more positive than what we get from, say, March and Cohen's garbage-can model of organizational theory, with its emphasis on nonsystematic and unanticipated consequences of organizational choice. Nonetheless, in the debate about institutions as strong forces or paper tigers (Koelble, 1995), Lijphart tends to be both pragmatic and "from Missouri;" that is, for him the proof is in the empirical evidence—that institution X has been shown to be important in context R does not prove that institution Y will be found to be important in other contexts. Moreover, like the mountains, even the strongest institutions may crumble (or tumble) with time.

Lijphart's work on institutions is also far less dogmatic than that of the really hard-core rational choice modelers with respect to methodology. First, the latter often write as though formal models are the only way to derive insights into social phenomena. Some of Lijphart's colleagues (Taagepera and myself, for example) often make use of mathematical modeling, but others do not. Second, unlike some of the game theory folks who appear obsessed with the idea of equilibrium, Lijphart is willing to recognize the possibility of institutional flux. Third, while Lijphart certainly looks at the role of individual actors and especially that of entities such as political parties that can often usefully (for certain purposes at least) be treated as unitary actors, he is far from the kind of radical methodological individualism espoused by some scholars associated with Public Choice.

Concern for Important Questions

Although Lijphart occasionally has written on relatively narrow topics, such as comparisons of different types of thresholds in PR systems (Lijphart,

1977b), almost all of his work has dealt with questions that are part of a bigger picture; for example, having to do with the roots of stability in multiethnic polities, or the fundamental institutional choices that affect the inclusiveness, responsiveness, and durability of political regimes.

Institutions as Objects of Choice Chosen to Solve Problems on the One Hand, and Determinants of Outputs on the Other

As suggested previously, if we wish to generalize, we must have both dependent and independent variables. Institutions may be thought of as midlevel entities; sometimes used to explain and sometimes themselves in need of explanation (e.g., as to origins and continued existence).[15] Lijphart's work has used institutions in both ways.[16] On the one hand, Lijphart has treated institutions as, in part at least, solutions to problems (e.g., the problem of religious or ethnic conflict in a divided society),[17] and thus institutional choice and institutional maintenance can be linked to the nature and importance of the problem being solved. On the other hand, Lijphart has also viewed institutions primarily as constraints on outcomes, as in his work on the effects of electoral system on party proliferation and on political inclusion,[18] and, in his most recent work, he has begun to look more closely at the policy consequences of various types of institutional choices.[19]

My own ideas on how to think about comparative institutional explanations have been very much influenced by Lijphart's work, although my perspective also reflects the early work of David Easton,[20] as well as my commitment to what I have called "reasonable choice theory."[21] The first four columns in Table 3.1 may be thought of as factors that affect/condition societal institutional preferences (however, I would emphasize that the causality may also go in the other direction as well), the next four columns refer to important institutional features (especially those signaled out for special attention by Lijphart, 1984), and the last two columns identify various types of outcomes/outputs that can be linked directly or indirectly to governmental decision-making.[22]

Table 3.1 is set up to reflect what I view as the intermediate role of institutions in comparative analysis.[23]

The two sets of items in the table that have a border around them correspond to the two dimensions in the factor-analytic dimensional analysis in the last chapter in Lijphart (1984). The numbers in parentheses refer to the various categories of institutional arrangements discussed in Lijphart (1984).

Writing To Be Understood

Unlike some rational choice modelers who eschew English language explanations of their results and seem to think that if its not obscure it can't be profound, and unlike the "if it's incomprehensible in translation it must be awesome in the

TABLE 3.1 Typology of Variables for Comparative Research

POLITICAL CULTURE	SOCIAL AND DEMOGRAPHIC STRUCTURE	SOCIALIZATION MECHANISMS	PUBLIC OPINION	CONSTITUTIONAL PROVISIONS	ELECTORAL SYSTEM
participant vs. allegiant vs. apathetic civil culture	racial heterogeneity	structure of media/media ownership	ideological breakdown of public opinion	*fused powers/cabinet or executive dominance vs. separation of powers (L2)*	*basic electoral system type (majoritarian vs. proportional (L6a)*
moralistic vs. traditional vs. individualist vs. fatalistic culture	religious heterogeneity	media consumption patterns in the electorate	stability of public opinion	provisions for judicial review	mean district magnitude
guilt vs. shame culture	ethnic heterogeneity	structure of education		*written vs. unwritten constitution (L8a)*	special electoral system features such as representation threshold, tiering, bonus seats
shared sense of past vs. divisive sense of past	membership in groups such as unions			*supermajorities required to amend constitution/minority veto (L8b)*	party centered vs. candidate centered electoral rules
	class and occupational structure/share of pop. engaged in agriculture			*unitary vs. federal arrangements (L7)*	provisions affecting voting (e.g., registration requirements, compulsory voting, weekend voting)
	foreign-born share of citizen population			*(balanced) bicameral vs. unicameral legislature (L3)*	campaign finance rules (e.g. matching funds, campaign spending limits)
	age distribution			*provisions for direct democracy (L9)*	
	population density			bill of rights with negative liberties	
	proportion urban			bill of rights with positive liberties	
				special treatment constitutionally mandated for certain ethnic/religious groups	
				option to become naturalized citizen is available	

TABLE 3.1 (Continued)

PARTY SYSTEM	REGIMEN/ GOVERNANCE STRUCTURE	DIRECT GOVERNMENTAL OUTPUT	OUTPUTS INDIRECTLY RELATED TO GOVERNMENT ACTION	EMBEDDEDNESS IN GLOBAL SYSTEM
effective number of parties in the legislature (or electorate) ($L4$)	*majority/near majority cabinets vs. power sharing vs. minority governments* ($L1$)	taxes (amount/share of GDP)	growth in GDP	treaty obligations
number of issue/cleavage dimensions underpinning the party system (one dimensional vs. multidimensional) ($L5$)	*proportionality of votes to seats conversion* ($L6b$)	taxes (type)	employment	participation in intl. organizations
	low vs. high cabinet duration	spending (amount/ share of GDP	inflation	imports as share of GDP
turnout	degree of corporatism	spending (type)	income inequality	exports as share of GDP
social and interest group base of cleavage structure underpinning the party system	degree of consociationalism	deficits/surpluses in government accounts	longevity	balance of trade
embedding of party organization in social life (e.g., party bowling leagues, insurance plans)	ideological/ethnic/ sectional makeup of governing party(ies)	national debt	infant mortality rates	share of GDP devoted to foreign aid
strength of party organizations		prime lending rate	worker safety	foreign tourists who visit
degree of centralization of party organizations		interest rate on government securities	demonstrations/ riots/work stoppages	capital investments abroad
party tactionalism			crime rate	commitment of troops abroad
vote share and seat share volatility/ degree of party loyalty				foreign investment in the domestic economy
reelection rate of incumbents				

original" worshippers of what my colleague, A Wuffle,[24] refers to as "pre-post-erous obscurantism," Lijphart writes clearly and presents his data (and the tests of hypotheses) in the simplest and most direct form that he can.

Critiques and Extensions of Lijphart's Majoritarian vs. Consensus Continuum

In this section of the paper I will focus on one of the two conceptual frame-works for which Lijphart is best known: that between majoritarian (Westminster) and consensus-oriented forms of governance.

First, drawing on what Arend himself says in the concluding chapter of *Democracies* (and anticipating what Arend will be saying in the next edition of *Democracies*), I will suggest that the nine variables he singles out for special attention do not really give rise to a single continuum, but rather appear, empir-ically, as constituents of three different dimensions of institutional choice.

Second, rather than thinking about social institutions as naturally either falling into one of the two polar ends of the majoritarian-consensus contin-uum, it is useful to consider deviations from the pure majoritarian or pure con-sensus model as being deliberate attempts to reach a particular tradeoff between two competing goals: the ability of governments to reach decisions and the avoidance of negative consequences of those decisions for some mem-bers of a society. That leads me to contrast the approach to governmental insti-tutions taken in *Democracies* with the approach to constitutional design taken in Buchanan and Tullock's equally classic (and much older) *The Calculus of Consent: The Logic of Constitutional Design*.

Third, again following Arend's own recent lead (Lijphart, personal com-munication, 1995), and that of John Stuart Mill as interpreted by Duff Spafford (1985), and picking up on a similar argument in Buchanan and Tullock (1962), I will argue that PR is a more truly majoritarian institution than plurality. To support such a seemingly implausible claim, it is necessary to distinguish the rules used to assure the inclusiveness of representative institutions with the nature of the rules used for legislative decision-making as to policy outputs.

Finally, I wish to elaborate further on ideas of institutions as solutions to problems, by briefly considering some additional types of political problems that institutions might be needed to cope with in addition to inclusiveness, responsiveness, or stability.

Multiple Dimensions of Institutional Choice re Governance

In chapter 1 of *Democracies* (and again in chapter 13), Lijphart identifies nine key variables. Although the discussion in the early part of *Democracies* seems to suggest that all nine fall into a single governance dimension, which can be labeled majoritarian (Westminster) vs consensus, the more detailed analysis in chapter 13 (see table 13.1) shows that there is really at least one more distinct dimension. The majoritarian vs consensus dimension is associated with five of these nine variables, and a federalism vs unitary dimension is made up of three of the four remaining variables.[25] Moreover, when I replicated Lijphart's factor analysis (see table 13.1 in Lijphart 1984), the remaining single variable, use of direct elections, does not fit with either of the first two dimensions. What we find is that this last variable defines a direct versus indirect democracy dimension that is essentially orthogonal to the first two. Thus, empirically, there are really *three* different sets of governmental design questions, not just one.

Table 3.1 is an inventory of types of variables that may be useful in macro-level cross-national research.[26] The three different clusters of institutional choice variables that we have identified from *Democracies* are each captured by the black borders around various groups of cells in the middle four columns of table 3.1, with the numbering attached to the variables matched to that found in chapter 13 of *Democracies*.[27] As shown in table 3.1, Lijphart's analysis finds three distinct questions of institutional choice:

1. How much consensualism?[28]
2. How much regionalism?
3. How much direct democracy?

These three questions (especially the first two) are clearly distinguished in the next edition of *Democracies* (1999, forthcoming).

To these three questions I would add three more, questions that I believe are equally important for the structuring of political institutions:[29]

4. Shall the legislative and the judicial powers be separated; in particular shall there be one or more courts that can override legislative decisions in the name of the fundamental constitutional order?[30]
5. What is the nature of citizenship; in particular, can citizenship be acquired or is it only by descent?[31]
6. Are the laws set up to operate solely on individuals qua individuals or (also) to distinguish among individuals on the basis of their membership in particular segmented groups?[32]

Comparisons with Buchanan and Tullock (1962)

The Calculus of Consent is rich in ideas about institutional design, but despite the fame of the book, a number of these ideas have largely been lost sight of in subsequent research. In my discussion I draw primarily on chapters 15–17 in *Calculus*, in my view the most neglected section of the book.[33]

Buchanan and Tullock identify four basic features of the rules under which representation takes place. Let N be the total number of voters; let n be the number of voters in a given constituency; let k ($= N/n$) be the size of the legislature. For convenience we let N, n, and k be odd.

> X_1, *the degree of agreement required to elect a representative*, generally ranging from plurality to n/n (unanimity).[34]
>
> X_2, *the degree of randomness in the specification of the constituencies from which representatives are to be chosen*, ranging from maximally homogeneous constituencies (e.g., a functional form of representation such as election from within occupational groupings, as the late Senator Paul Douglas once proposed in the 1920s) to a purely random assignment process.
>
> X_3, *the degree of democracy*, ranging from 1/N (dictatorship) to N/N (direct democracy).
>
> X_4, *the decision rule for internal legislative decision-making*, ranging from 1/k to k/k (unanimity).[35]

For Buchanan and Tullock, the anticipated consequence of a given mode of representation on the magnitude of the sum of external costs plus decision-making costs is what determines an individual's preferences among alternative forms of representation, where external costs are the costs imposed on the individual by having choices made that affect him negatively, and decision costs are the costs imposed (transaction costs, perhaps also side-payments) as part of the process of reaching agreement. Each of these variables can be thought of in terms of its consequences for these two types of costs. For example, if we look at x_2, as we move toward unanimity then we raise transaction costs and lower external costs. Similarly, if we have more than one parliamentary chamber, each with different modes of selection, then we increase the heterogeneity of the selection process and increase decision costs if the agreement of the two chambers is needed to pass legislation, while lowering external costs by making changes from the status quo less likely.[36]

For Buchanan and Tullock, the optimal set of rules is simply that in which the sum of external costs plus decision-making costs is minimized. Because choices that lower one of these two forms of cost tend to raise the other kind, Buchanan and Tullock emphasize tradeoffs between the two kinds of costs and complementarity across these variables; that is, we need to look at the costs consequences of each choice in the context of the full institutional specification—we need to look at partial derivatives. Hence, the costs and benefits of a particular institutional choice can only be properly weighed in the light of the total institutional package.[37] Another potentially important implication of the Buchanan and Tullock approach is that it suggests extreme solutions (i.e., those in which all institutions are "of a piece" in terms of which type of costs they are most concerned with minimizing) are probably unlikely to be minimizing of total cost (and thus optimal from the Buchanan and Tullock perspective) in that the gains to be achieved by bringing down one type of cost are likely to be paid for by raising the other type of cost to a very high level. Thus, hybrid sets of institutions may well prove more desirable than ones whose motivation is singularly in terms of minimizing one of the two types of institutional costs.

Two Kinds of Majoritarianism

If we wish to assure that the majority will of the electorate will be reflected in the choices made by the legislature in its name, then we want the set of legislators to be representative of that electorate, since a majority vote of an unrepresentative group is unlikely to be faithfully representative of the broader polity.[38] As numerous authors have pointed out, even with fairly apportioned constituencies, plurality-based elections have the potential for a minority of voters to elect a majority of representatives. Assuming fairly apportioned districts, this is virtually impossible under PR. For example, Buchanan and Tullock (1962: 222) say about PR systems that "(a)ll voters, not just the majority of each constituency, are represented in the legislature. Consequently, a majority of the legislature represents a majority of the voters, not just 1/4+ as may be the case in a logrolling or party coalition when the members are elected from single-member constituencies."[39] Thus, PR for legislative elections, coupled with majority rule decisions in the legislature arguably give rises to outcomes that are more faithfully majoritarian in nature than does the combination of plurality (or majority) for legislative elections and majority rule in legislative voting.

Inclusiveness, as fostered by PR, which is fully compatible with majoritarian decision-making about governmental policies, should not be confused with nonmajoritarian procedures such as power-sharing or legislative supramajoritarian requirements, or arrangements that permit certain groups to veto decisions affecting their fundamental interests (à la Calhoun), or rules/norms that require proportional division of most governmental outputs among members of some set of cognizable groups (à la Lani Guinier (1994) and some versions of consociationalism). This is true even if, as a matter of observation, such arrangements are much more likely to be found together with PR than with first-past-the-post legislative elections. This is an important point, often blurred or misunderstood by writers discussing the plurality versus proportionality debate.

Institutions as Problem-Solvers: Athenian, Madisonian, Downsian, and Lijphartian Perspectives

There are, in my view, important parallels between Lijphart and the tradition of Madison, Hamilton, and Jay.[40] In the *Federalist*, we see the notion that institutions can be the solutions to important problems: for example, harnessing self-interest, preventing factionalism, assuring that choices reflect long-term perspectives that resist the passions of the moment.[41] So too, with Lijphart. Like the *Federalist's* assertion of the importance of political institutions and the notion that political institutions can be viewed as matters of explicit choices and tradeoffs, Lijphart treats institutions as rules of the game whose partly predictable consequences may contribute to the solving of important societal problems; for example, facilitating political stability within a democratic framework in an ethnically divided society.[42]

Democratic theorists/reformers of an institutionalist bent can usefully be distinguished in terms of the problems they see institutions as being needed to solve. Table 3.2 is my very preliminary attempt to distinguish in these terms three important institutionalist traditions concerned with the design of democratic institutions: that of the framers of Athenian democracy, that of James Madison, the principal author of the *Federalist Papers*, and that of Anthony Downs. I identify seven needs to be met—to assure popular sovereignty, to prevent the rise of tyranny, to improve the competence of decision-making, to prevent corruption, to foster participation, to protect liberty, to strengthen the power of the polity to act collectively—and I match these problems with institutional solutions offered by these different schools.[43]

The list in table 3.2 is in no way exhaustive either in terms of problems or in terms of solutions, nor is it meant to be. In particular, it omits a central concern of Lijphart's work, the problem of ethnic accommodation. Similarly, though I discuss Downsian perspectives on institutional design, table 3.2 neglects the views of important democratic theorists of the Public Choice School such as James Buchanan, Kenneth Arrow, Gordon Tullock, or Macur Olson; for example, controlling Leviathan, avoiding cycles, eliciting honest preferences about public goods from voters (the literature on demand revelation), or minimizing free riding.[44] Other recent work in positive political theory has dealt with other important types of problems that institutions might be used to solve; for example, how to design electoral rules to inhibit political corruption (Myerson, 1993). An important implicit point in table 3.2 (shown by the blank spaces in the table) is that different institutional theorists focus on different problems.[45]

Lijphart as Teacher and Colleague

Let me conclude this essay with somewhat more personal comments.

TABLE 3.2.   Institutions as Problem-Solving Devices: Comparisons of Athenian, Madisonian and Downsian Perspectives

	ATHENIAN DEMOCRACY	MADISONIAN DEMOCRACY	DOWNSIAN DEMOCRACY
To Assure Popular Sovereignty	Universal male citizen suffrage; selection of assembly, council, juries and most other offices by lot from entire age-qualified citizen pool (but wealth requirements for some offices, e.g. *STRATEGOS*; and women and slaves ineligible to vote).	Popular election of representatives; Eligibility for office of age-qualified white males (but race and gender limits on eligibility for suffrage; initial property requirements for suffrage in many states).	Popular election of representatives; partisan competition for office (two-party competition intended to lead to centrist politics).
To Prevent the Rise of Tyranny	Only a plural and largely ceremonial executive; frequent rotation in office; use of lottery availability of ostracism.	Divided and limited government with complex system of checks and balances; extended territory; patents of nobility prohibited; no ex post facto laws; frequent elections.	
To Improve Decision Making	Public deliberation in assembly and council; preparation of bills by council; experienced slave deputies to oversee work; small number of elected officials for vital offices (e.g., that of *strategos*) chosen in large part on basis of merit.	Separation of powers: bicameral legislature (whose upper chamber has a longer term of office); judiciary with life service; single executive who can act with energy, secrecy, and despatch.	

(Continued)

TABLE 3.2   Institutions as Problem-Solving Devices: Comparisons of Athenian, Madisonian and Downsian Perspectives (Continued)

	ATHENIAN DEMOCRACY	MADISONIAN DEMOCRACY	DOWNSIAN DEMOCRACY
To Improve Accountability and to Prevent Corruption	Formal review of background of potential office-holders (*dokimasia*); periodic public scrutiny of accounts (*euthynai*); lawsuits against those who recommend policies that prove unwise or unconstitutional (*graphe paranoumon*); large juries whose members cannot be predicted in advance of their selection.	For elected offices, voter ability to deny reelection; (eligibility for reelection intended to spur continued concern for public approbation). For appointed offices, potential for impeachment by legislature.	Party platforms; voter ability to deny reelection to public officials.
To Foster Participation	Civic culture that fosters view that public service is citizen duty; payment for office holding.	Payment for office holding.	
To Protect Liberty	No lawyers; short trials; no appeal to precedent; citizen brought lawsuits with no state prosecutor, but with punishment for frivolous lawsuits; oaths of office containing explicit limits on official actions (e.g., protection of property rights).	Bill of Rights; no bills of attainder; judicial review; limitations on scope of governmental activities.	
To Strengthen Power of the Polity to Act Collectively		Ability to tax the people directly; federal law supreme (to be enforced by state as well as by federal judges).	

Scientists can make their mark both by what they do and what they inspire others to do. Most scholars succeed at neither; Arend has been one of the few to succeed at both. Here let me praise Arend for the quality of his students. I see Arend's importance in political science in the 1990s and in the next century as parallel to Bill Riker's importance in the 1970s and 1980s:[46] nurturing a cadre of scholars who will continue the style of research of which Arend has been a premier exponent, as will their students after them.[47] Arend has been able to impart to his best students a taste for comparisons, and to inspire a willingness to dig deep to generate the data necessary for them, along with an uncompromising commitment to try to make sense of the world and to try to find answers to questions that matter. His successes inspire in me a strong feeling of envy, as well as one of deep respect.

Lastly, let me note for the record that I first met Arend as a result of my unsuccessful efforts to recruit him to UCI (not long after I arrived there myself, over 16 years ago). Since then, I have had the pleasure of coediting three books with him, have recently cotaught a graduate course with him, have run a conference with him (on the historical origins of electoral and party systems in the Nordic countries) that will probably become yet another coedited book, and continue to nourish the fond hope that, not long after the century expires, Arend and I will actually coauthor (and not merely coedit) a book together, on the United States in comparative perspective. May you all have such luck in finding true collegueship and lifelong friendship with the job candidates you didn't get to hire.

Notes

[1] Among this latter set are scholars such as James Buchanan, Geoffrey Brennan, and Gordon Tullock (Buchanan and Tullock, 1962; Brennan and Buchanan, 1985), Elinor Ostrom (1986), Ken Shepsle (Shepsle, 1979a, 1979b, 1989), Andrew Schotter (1981, 1986), Barry Weingast (Shepsle and Weingast, 1989; Weingast and Marshall, 1988), Oliver Williamson (1981) and Donald Wittman (1985, 1995; see also Grofman and Wittman, 1989), to name but a few. Of the authors working in this tradition, only Downs (1957) and one article by Shepsle and Weingast are found in the March and Olsen (1984) bibliography. However, the contributions of Shepsle and Weingast are not actually discussed in this article, and the discussion of Downs is not in the context of his contributions to new institutionalist thought.

[2] Within American politics, in the area of representation there was also a major revival of interest in institutions that was taking place in the 1970s and 1980s and that continues to the present—occurring largely or entirely independently of work in positive political theory. Consider, for example, the work on the

consequences for racial and gender representation of at-large versus single-member districts (e.g., Engstrom and McDonald, 1981, 1982; Heilig and Mundt, 1981; Karnig and Welch, 1979; Grofman, Migalski, and Noviello, 1986; Davidson and Grofman, 1994), or on the political consequences of the internal rules of representation within U.S. political parties (e.g., Lengle, 1981; Polsby, 1983), or consider recent interest in reform of electoral institutions such as the movements for direct elections of the president, term limits, or a balanced budget amendment.

[3]As Koelble (1995: 231) aptly notes, "the study of institutions has been central to political science since its inception."

[4]Still, if we wish to claim an historical progenitor for Lijphart's style of research, a plausible candidate is the Aristotle of "The Constitution of Athens," who set his students to collect constitutions and who is the inventor of that most long-lasting of all political conceptualizations, the distinction between aristocratic, oligarchic, and democratic forms of government; that is, rule by the one, the few, or the many. Later in this paper I will also briefly allude to parallels between Lijphart and another early important institutionalist thinker, James Madison.

[5]Indeed, Ordeshook (1987: 19–20) suggests that this new [public choice] institutionalism is a response to the implicit determinism of the behaviorists, whose revolution after World War II is seen as response to the nearly atheoretical, descriptive mode of political science then dominant. But that earlier mode focused also on political institutions—the structure of legislatures, electoral rules, constitutional provisions, and the like—which is a disciplinary emphasis that somehow was lost in the definition, measurement, and correlation of social class, partisan identification, attitudes, childhood socialization, norms, socio-economic status, and the like.

[6]A similar point about the actual diversity of perspectives all going under the name "new institutionalism" is made in Koelble (1995).

[7]As a member in good standing of the California Drive-in Church of the Incorrigibly Eclectic (founded by my colleague, A Wuffle), I do not object to March and Olsen (1984, 1989) espousing a set of disparate (or even contradictory) insights (cf. Walt Whitman, 1885: "Do I contradict myself? Very well, then, I contradict myself. I am large—I contain multitudes.") especially when, as in this case, many of the insights are important ones. I do object to their attributing the new institutionalism they describe to that rather heroic assemblage of strange bedfellows they cite in their bibliography, since no *one* of the authors they discuss ever advocated *all* (or even most of) the ideas claimed to be the thrust of the new institutionalism. Furthermore, the connection among

the different schools of thought (who do not, by and large, read or cite each other's work) exists only because March and Olsen are themselves catholic in their taste and discerning in their ability to pick out theoretically significant resemblances.

As with countries that used to call themselves "democracies," it is remarkable what disparate activities pass under the rubric of "new institutionalism" (cf. Smith, 1988; Levi, 1987; Powell and diMaggio, 1991; Steinmo and Thelen, 1992; Crawford and Ostrom, 1995; see also review in Koelble, 1995). Indeed, even when we confine ourselves to the political economy literature, the term "new institutionalism" still covers a motley set of disparate perspectives, ranging from, Marxist, historical, and evolutionary ideas (e.g., Langlois, 1986b) to the work of the Public Choice school and closely related approaches (e.g., North, 1981, 1986; Levi, 1988).

[8]I am an incorrigible optimist (as well as an incorrigible methodological eclectic).

[9]I prefer this label to another narrower label that has already been applied: "the Southern California electoral systems mafia." On the one hand, Lijphart's work is far wider than the study of electoral systems and, on the other hand, a number of Arend's students are no longer in southern California. Also, I have chosen to call it the "UCSD/UCI School" rather than just the "UCSD School" because of the ways my own work and that of Rein Taagepera (e.g., Taagepera, 1986; Taagepera and Shugart, 1989; Taagepera and Grofman, 1985) have been influenced by Lijphart, and because there are some students we already share in common (especially Matthew Shugart, who worked with both Rein and Arend, and Andy Reynolds, who worked with both Arend and myself) and others who will come to fall into that category because of the joint UCSD/UCI graduate course "The United States in Comparative Perspective" that Arend and I have started teaching (taught for the first time in Winter 1996). Of course, not all who would identify with the seven points set out here have direct links to Lijphart as student or colleague; for others (e.g., Powell, 1982) the linkage is purely an intellectual one.

[10]I have used the term institutional rather than constitutional (which was the term used in the title of an earlier draft of this essay) both because I wish to place Lijphart's work in the context of work that uses the label "new institutionalism," and because not all important institutional choices are embedded in constitutions; for example, electoral system choices are often matters of legislative decision. My reasons for adding the adjective "comparative" are obvious to anyone familiar with Lijphart's work.

[11]Although, in a number of his books and articles Arend Lijphart has laid out his ideas about how to study particular institutions, the central features of his

general approach to institutional design and to the study of institutional effects have not, as far as I am aware, ever clearly been fully articulated either by Lijphart or his students.

[12]In Isaiah Berlin's metaphor, Arend Lijphart has been a hedgehog, not a fox—there is a unity to virtually all of his work in that certain basic questions about political stability and democratic governance are at the heart of it, along with a relative handful of key variable and key ideas that have been elaborated and extended over the past three decades.

[13] In the latter, he is aided by an international team of scholars who collaborated on the database for the book.

[14]I was taught by David Easton that all political analysis is ultimately necessarily comparative, either across Time, across Nations, or across Types (e.g., types of institutional settings). (This point is referred to as the TNT principle by another colleague of mine, A Wuffle (personal communication, April 1, 1992).) Indeed, I would go further. I also believe quite strongly that we can *best* understand any single case by seeing it in comparative context. Russ Dalton (1996: 4) has made related points in a very elegant way that deserves quoting at length: "Even if we are interested only in a single nation, comparative research is a useful approach. An old Hebrew riddle expresses this idea: '*Question:* Who first discovered water? Answer: I don't know, but it wasn't a fish.' Immersing oneself in a single environment renders the characteristics of the environment unobtrusive and unnoticed." I would add to Dalton's comments only that it is important not to treat rarity or even uniqueness as synonymous with inexplicability. For example, that some polity's institutions are often found located at an extreme on some set of continua may make it easier rather than harder to make sense of its politics in comparative perspective (e.g., although U.S. turnout is very low by international standards, models predicting national turnout levels can fit the U.S. quite well—because U.S. registration rules, electoral institutions, and party systems differ from those of other countries in ways that predictably lower turnout; cf. Crepaz, 1990). It is our strong and very similar views as to these and related points that led Professor Lijphart and myself to organize a jointly taught course on the U.S. in comparative perspective, and eventually (the fates willing), to turn that course into a book (Lijphart and Grofman, 2001??). See further discussion in Grofman (1996a, 1999a, b, c, forthcoming).

[15]I take this point from discussions with Edwin Winckler. See Grofman (1999a) for further elaboration.

[16]This dual view of the role of institutions in explanations argues, in my view, against any attempt to pose a sharp dichotomy between institutionalist and

cultural explanations of social phenomena (cf. Koelble, 1995). Culture may shape institutions, but there will usually be an independent effect of institutions even after we hold culture constant. For my own views of the notion of "contextually embedded institutions" see Grofman (1999a, c, forthcoming).

[17]See, e.g., Lijphart (1975, 1977a).

[18]See, e.g., Lijphart (1977b, 1982, 1992, 1994). See also various of the other essays in the volume edited by Grofman, Lijphart, McKay, and Scarrow (1982), and those in the other two volumes coedited by Lijphart and Grofman: Lijphart and Grofman (1984) and Grofman and Lijphart (1986).

[19]Some of this work has been jointly with his former student, Markus Crepaz (e.g., Lijphart and Crepaz, 1991, 1995). See also Crepaz (1992, 1994, 1996).

[20]Long before I became David Easton's colleague at UCI, as a graduate student at the University of Chicago I was his research assistant. His influence on me is unlikely to wear off.

[21]See especially Grofman (1993a, 1993b, 1997); Wuffle (1999).

[22]This table should be very much viewed as a preliminary effort; there is certainly no claim that it identified all of the critical variables in comparative institutional analysis. I should also note that I am indebted to Russell Dalton for helpful suggestions as to variables to be included in columns 3, 4, and 7 of Table 3.1.

[23]Note that this three-fold classification parallels the early form of Easton's black-box model of government (Easton 1966), with its inputs on one end and outputs on the other. In Table 3.1 (many of) what are supposed to be the most internal important elements of that black box are now being specified. For more details on my own approach to comparative institutional analysis, see especially (1999a, b, c, forthcoming), and the various of my articles that emphasize the importance of natural experiments as a methodological tool (e.g., Niemi, Hill, and Grofman, 1985; Grofman, Migalski, and Noviello, 1986; Grofman, Griffin, and Glazer, 1990; Grofman and Davidson, 1994; Grofman, Griffin, and Berry, 1995).

[24]A Wuffle (personal communication, April 1, 1996).

[25]See also discussion in Taagepera (1996).

[26]This table was developed for my first lecture in the joint course with Arend Lijphart on "The U.S. in Comparative Perspective," taught in Winter 1996 (www.democ.uci.edu/democ/nsf.htm). It should be thought of a work in progress; I make no claims as to its inclusiveness.

[27]Other aspects of this table are discussed later.

[28]Interestingly, as a matter of empirical connectedness, the choice of a presidential or parliamentary system, like the choice of an electoral system, is associated with the majoritarian vs consensual dimension.

[29]Space constraints do not permit me to do more than identify these important aspects of the political order.

[30]Although this fourth question is associated with the presence of a federal dimension as a matter of empirical fact (Lijphart, 1984), there is nothing that constrains it to be so limited. In particular, even if there are not conflicts between competing claims of federal and provincial authorities there can still be competing claims of individual (or group) versus government that need to be resolved, and courts are one way to do so.

[31]Here, it is sometimes claimed that citizenship by descent is inherently incompatible with democracy. I disagree, but space does not permit me to pursue this issue here. (My views on this matter owe much to discussions about Estonia with my colleague Rein Taagepera.)

[32]Questions like the last have been the focus of much of Arend Lijphart's early work (e.g., Lijphart, 1977). The answers to these questions (and related ones like the extent of power sharing and supramajoritarianism) are empirically correlated with the majoritarian versus consensus dimension identified in Lijphart (1984). However, in theory at least, they need not be.

[33]Most of these chapters heavily reflect the ideas of Gordon Tullock.

[34]Although Buchanan and Tullock suggest this variable can take on values as low as l/n, such a value would only seem possible in a society in which not all individuals have votes that count, or in some lottery process.

[35]In Grofman (1988) I suggest that four variables, not directly considered by Buchanan and Tullock in *Calculus*, are especially good candidates for addition to their select list of key representational variables: equality of treatment of voters, committee structure within the legislature, ease of constitutional amendment, and degree of legislator/legislative accountability. In addition, the domain of governmental action, a central concern of the early chapters in *Calculus* in my view, ought, I think, to be explicitly identified as one of the key variables in determining an optimal form of representation.

[36]The exact link between the two types of costs and the values of the various variables is far from obvious, and I am far from happy with Buchanan and Tullock's treatment of this question, especially since they emphasize the costs of unfavorable decisions and tend to neglect the potential gains from agree-

ment on mutually beneficial collective action—but these are matters that must be left to another essay. For my initial thoughts on these and related topics see Grofman (1988).

[37]A closely related but more narrowly focused point has been made in the literature on presidentialism, where it has been argued that presidential systems are particularly pernicious in their potential for conflict when coupled with systems that create rival centers of power.

[38]Cf. Feld and Grofman (1986).

[39]The number 'one quarter' comes from imagining that, in first-past-the-post two-party elections, exactly half of the voters in exactly half of the constituencies determine the winning majority coalition in the legislature.

[40]Lijphart (1992) contains excerpts from the *Federalist Papers*.

[41]The founding fathers, among the greatest political engineers, were believers in a "new science of politics" (Ranney, 1976). Indeed, according to Daniel Moynihan (1987: 22), the fundamental question in the *Federalist Papers* was not about the merits or demerits of ratification but about political science: "Could a government be founded on scientific principles?"

[42]This role of institutions as problem-solving devices is neglected if we look at institutions as a set of norms or as a synonym for a set of game rules, or if we view institutions as primarily naturally evolving entities rather than objects of choice. Quite surpassingly, given Ostrom's own work, the Crawford and Ostrom (1995) essay on institutions slights the problem-solving aspect of what an institution is all about.

[43]Albeit not every problem is addressed by the institutions offered by each of these three institutionalist traditions.

[44]Elsewhere (Grofman, 1989) I have suggested that scholars such as James Buchanan, Gordon Tullock, and William Riker could also be regarded as natural heirs of the Madisonian tradition. Riker was, of course, a leading student of federalism even before he found religion in the form of rational choice, and the appendix in Buchanan and Tullock (1962) makes explicit reference to the *Federalist Papers*—although few political scientists seem aware of the connection. Other scholars in public choice and positive political theory have also rediscovered the *Federalist Papers* as a source of inspiration. For example, Hammond and Miller (1987) reexamine bicameralism from the perspective of its contributions to stability. Their analysis is similar in spirit (albeit not in language) to *Federalist* No. 63, which they cite. Keech (1986) links contemporary rules of political business cycle to arguments about the proper term length for

legislators. Points of departure for his essay are *Federalist* Nos. 52 and 62. Brams (1989) addresses the relative power of the two chambers of Congress, in the context of *Federalist* Nos. 58 and 63. Other essays in Grofman and Wittman (1989) also explicitly take their point of departure from the *Federalist Papers* (see also various essays in Grofman, 1996b). Many of the themes of institutional design in contemporary public choice theory can be found in the *Federalist Papers*, even though the absence of present-day technical jargon may mask the identity.

[45]Of course, as suggested in table 3.2, a question central to Downs (1957) and the literature that springs from him—how to solve the problem of assuring legislator responsibility to public opinion—is also a central question in many other research traditions. Still the peculiarly Downsian way of framing the problem, where public opinion is treated as tantamount to the views of the median voter, remains distinctive.

[46]It is important to acknowledge that, just as other Rochester faculty shared with Riker the training of students such as Ken Shepsle and Peter Ordeshook, especially with respect to methodology, other UCSD faculty (especially Gary Cox, and more recently Kaare Strom, Matt Shugart, Matt McCubbins, and Arthur ("Skip") Lupia) have also played a key role in training the students who have worked with Arend who are taking a comparative institutionalist approach.

[47]See, e.g., (Matt) Shugart out of Taagepera/Lijphart (see Taagepera and Shugart, 1986 and numerous Shugart publications thereafter), followed by (John) Carey out of Shugart/Lijphart (see Shugart and Carey, 1992; Carey, 1996) and most recently, (Andy) Reynolds out of Lijphart/Shugart/Grofman (see Reynolds, 1993, 1994, 1995, 1996; Grofman and Reynolds, 1996). Other Lijphart students include Dave Wilsford, Thomas Koelble, and Marcus Crepaz.

References

Brams, Steven J. 1984. "Are The Two Houses of Congress Really Co-Equal?" In B. Grofman and D. Wittman, eds., *The Federalist Papers and The New Institutionalism*. New York: Agathon Press.

Brennan, Geoffrey, and James M. Buchanan. 1985. *The Reason of Rules: Constitutional Political Economy*. New York and London: Cambridge University Press.

Buchanan, James, and Gordon Tullock. 1962. *The Calculus of Consent: The Logical Foundations of Constitutional Democracy*. Ann Arbor: University of Michigan Press.

Carey, John. 1996. *Term Limits and Legislative Representation*. New York and London: Cambridge University Press.

Crawford, Sue E. S. and Elinor Ostrom. 1995. "A Grammar of Institutions." *American Political Science Review*, 89, No. 3: 582–600.

Crepaz, Markus. 1996. "Constitutional Structures and Regime Performance in 18 Industrialized Democracies—A Test Of Olson's Hypothesis." *European Journal of Political Research,* 29, No. 1 (January): 87–104.

Crepaz, Markus. 1996. "Consensus Versus Majoritarian Democracy—Political Institutions and Their Impact on Macroeconomic Performance and Industrial Disputes." *Comparative Political Studies,* 29 (February): 4–26.

Crepaz, Markus and Arend Lijphart. 1995. "Linking and Integrating Corporatism And Consensus Democracy—Theory, Concepts And Evidence." *British Journal Of Political Science*, 25 (April): 281–88.

Crepaz Markus. 1994. "From Semisovereignty To Sovereignty—The Decline of Corporatism and Rise of Parliament in Austria." *Comparative Politics*, 27, No. 1 (October): 45–65.

Crepaz, Markus. 1992. "Corporatism in Decline—An Empirical Analysis of the Impact of Corporatism on Macroeconomic Performance and Industrial Disputes in 18 Industrialized Democracies." *Comparative Political Studies*, 25, No. 2 (July): 139–68.

Crepaz, Markus. 1990. "The Impact of Party Polarization and Postmaterialism on Voter Turnout—A Comparative Study of 16 Industrial Democracies." *European Journal Of Political Research*, 18, No. 2 (March): 183–205.

Dalton, Russell. 1996. *Citizen Politics: Public Opinion and Political Parties in Advanced Industrial Democracies*, 2nd Edition. Chatham, NJ: Chatham House Publishers.

Downs, Anthony. 1957. *An Economic Theory of Democracy*. New York: Harper and Row.

Easton, David. 1966. *A Systems Analysis of Political Life*. New York: Wiley.

Eckstein, Harry. 1975. "Case Study and Theory in Political Science." In Fred I. Greenstein and Nelson W. Polsby, eds., *Political Science: Scope and Theory*

(Handbook of Political Science, Volume 1). Reading, MA: Addison-Wesley (reprinted in Eckstein. 1992, 117–78).

Eckstein, Harry. 1988. "A Cultural Theory of Political Change." In *American Political Science Review*, 82 (3) (September).

Eckstein, Harry. 1992. *Regarding Politics: Essays on Political Theory, Stability and Change*. Berkeley: University of California Press.

Engstrom, Richard L., and Michael D. McDonald. 1981. "The Election of Blacks to City Councils: Clarifying the Impact of Electoral Arrangements on the Seats/Population Relationship." *American Political Science Review*, 75: 344–54.

Engstrom, Richard L., and Michael D. McDonald. 1982. "The Underrepresentation of Blacks on City Councils: Comparing the Structural and Socioeconomic Explanations for South/Non-South Differences." *Journal of Politics*, 44: 1088–99.

Feld, Scott L. and Bernard Grofman. 1986. "On the Possibility of Faithfully Representative Committees." *American Political Science Review*, Vol. 80, No. 3, 863–79.

Grofman, Bernard. 1988. "Representation in the 'Calculus Of Consent'." Prepared for delivery at the "Liberty Fund Conference on 'The Calculus of Consent'," Santa Cruz, California, June 23–25.

Grofman, Bernard. 1989. "Introduction: The 'Federalist Papers' and the New Institutionalism." In Bernard Grofman and Donald Wittman, eds., *The 'Federalist Papers' and the New Institutionalism*. New York: Agathon Press.

Grofman, Bernard. 1993a. "Public Choice, Civic Republicanism, and American Politics: Perspectives of a 'Reasonable Choice' Modeler." *Texas Law Review*, Vol. 71, No. 7 (June), 1541–87.

Grofman, Bernard, ed. 1993b. *Information, Participation, and Choice: An Economic Theory of Democracy in Perspective*. Ann Arbor, Michigan: University of Michigan Press, 1–13.

Grofman, Bernard. 1993c. "On the Gentle Art of Rational Choice Bashing." In Bernard Grofman, ed., *Information, Participation, and Choice: An Economic Theory of Democracy in Perspective*. Ann Arbor: University of Michigan Press, 239–42.

Grofman, Bernard. 1996a. "Downsian Political Economy." In Robert Goodin and Hans-Dieter Klingemann, eds., *New Handbook of Political Science*. New York and London: Oxford University Press.

Grofman, Bernard, ed. 1996b. *Term Limits: Public Choice Perspectives*. Holland: Kluwer.

Grofman, Bernard. 1997. "Seven Durable Axes of Cleavage in Political Science." In Kristen Monroe, ed., *Contemporary Empirical Theory*. Berkeley: University of California Press.

Grofman, Bernard. 1999a, "Preface: Methodological Steps toward the Study of Embedded Institutions." In Bernard Grofman, Sung-Chull Lee, Edwin A. Winckler, and Brian Woodall, eds., *Elections in Japan, Korea, and Taiwan under the Single Non-Transferable Vote: The Comparative Study of an Embedded Institution*. Ann Arbor: University of Michigan Press.

Grofman, Bernard. 1999b. "SNTV, STV, and Single Member District Systems: Theoretical Comparisons and Contrasts." In Bernard Grofman, Sung-Chull Lee, Edwin Winckler, and Brian Woodall, eds., *Elections in Japan, Korea, and Taiwan under the Single Non-Transferable Vote: The Comparative Study of an Embedded Institution*. Ann Arbor: University of Michigan Press.

Grofman, Bernard. 1999c. "SNTV: An inventory of theoretically derived propositions and a brief review of the evidence from Japan, Korea, Taiwan and Alabama." In Bernard Grofman, Sung-Chull Lee, Edwin Winckler, and Brian Woodall, eds., *Elections in Japan, Korea and Taiwan under the Single Non-Transferable Vote: The Comparative Study of an Embedded Institution*. Ann Arbor: University of Michigan Press.

Grofman, Bernard and Chandler Davidson. 1994. "The Effect of Municipal Election Structure on Black Representation in Eight Southern States." In Davidson, Chandler and Bernard Grofman, eds., *Quiet Revolution in the South: The Impact of the Voting Rights Act, 1965-1990*. Princeton: Princeton University Press.

Grofman, Bernard, Robert Griffin, and Gregory Berry. 1995. "House Members Who Become Senators: Learning From a 'Natural Experiment' in Representation." *Legislative Studies Quarterly*, 20 (4) (November): 513–29.

Grofman, Bernard, Robert Griffin, and Amihai Glazer. 1990. "Identical geography, different party: A natural experiment on the magnitude of party differences in the U.S. Senate, 1960-84." In Johnston, R.J., F.M. Shelley and P.J. Taylor, eds., *Developments in Electoral Geography*. London: Routledge, 207–17.

Grofman, Bernard and Arend Lijphart, eds. 1986. *Electoral Laws and Their Political Consequences*. New York: Agathon Press.

Grofman, Bernard, Arend Lijphart, Robert McKay, and Howard Scarrow, eds. 1982. *Representation and Redistricting Issues*. Lexington, MA: Lexington Books.

Grofman, Bernard, Michael Migalski, and Nicholas Noviello. 1986. "Effects of Multimember Districts on Black Representation in State Legislatures." *Review of Black Political Economy*, Vol. 14, No. 4 (Spring), 65–78.

Grofman, Bernard and Andrew Reynolds. 1996. "Modeling the Drop-off Between Minority Population Share and the Size of the Minority Electorate in Situations of Differential Voter Eligibility Across Groups." *Electoral Studies*, 15 No. 2 (May): 255–61.

Grofman, Bernard and Donald Wittman, eds. 1989. *The 'Federalist Papers' and the New Institutionalism*. New York: Agathon Press.

Guinier, Lani. 1994. *The Tyranny of the Majority*. New York: Harper.

Hammond, Thomas H. and Gary J. Miller. 1987. "The Core of the Constitution." *American Political Science Review*, 81: 1155–74.

Heilig, Patty and Robert J. Mundt. 1981. "Do Districts Make a Difference?" *Urban Interest* (April) 62–75.

Karnig, Albert K. and Susan Welch. 1979. "Sex and Ethnicity in Municipal Representation." *Social Science Quarterly* (December) 69(3).

Keech, William R. 1986. "Thinking about the Length and Renewability of Electoral Terms." In Bernard Grofman and Arend Lijphart, eds., *Electoral Laws and Their Political Consequences*. New York: Agathon Press.

Koelble, Thomas A. 1995. "Review Article: The New Institutionalism in Political Science and Sociology." *Comparative Politics* (January): 231–43.

Langlois, Richard N. 1986. "The New Institutional Economics: An Introductory Essay." In R. N. Langlois, ed., *Economics as a Process*, Cambridge: Cambridge University Press, 1–39.

Lengle, James I. 1981. *Representation and Presidential Primaries: The Democratic Party in the Post-Reform Era*. Westport, CT: Greenwood.

Levi, Margaret. 1987. "Theories of Historical and Institutional Change." *PS* (Summer): 684–88.

Levi, Margaret. 1988. *Of Rule and Revenue*. Berkeley: University of California Press.

Lijphart, Arend. 1975. *Politics of Accommodation: Pluralism and Democracy in the Netherlands*. Berkeley: University of California Press, 2nd edition.

Lijphart, Arend. 1977a. *Democracy in Plural Societies: A Comparative Exploration*. New Haven: Yale University Press.

Lijphart, Arend. 1977b. "Thresholds and Payoffs in List Systems of Proportional Representation," *European Journal of Political Research*.

Lijphart, Arend. 1982. "Comparative Perspective on Fair Representation: The Plurality-Majority Rule, Geographical Districting, and Alternative Electoral Arrangements." In Grofman, Bernard, Arend Lijphart, Robert McKay and Howard Scarrow, eds., *Representation and Redistricting Issues*. Lexington, MA: Lexington Books, 143–60.

Lijphart, Arend. 1984. *Democracies: Patterns of Majoritarian and Consensus Government in Twenty-One Democracies*. New Haven: Yale University Press.

Lijphart, Arend, ed. 1992. *Parliamentary Versus Presidential Government*. Oxford and New York: Oxford University Press.

Lijphart, Arend. 1994. *Electoral Systems and Party Systems: A Study of Twenty-Seven Democracies, 1945–1990*. New York and London: Oxford University Press.

Lijphart, Arend and Markus Crepaz. 1991. "Corporatism And Consensus Democracy in 18 Countries—Conceptual and Empirical Linkages." *British Journal Of Political Science*, 21 (April): 235–46.

Lijphart, Arend and Bernard Grofman, eds. 1984. *Choosing an Electoral System*. New York: Praeger.

Lijphart, Arend and Bernard Grofman. 2001, forthcoming. *The United States in Comparative Perspective*. Book manuscript in very slow progress.

Madison, James, Alexander Hamilton, and John Jay. 1961. *The Federalist Papers*. New York: The New American Library (originally published 1787).

March, James G. and Johan P. Olsen. 1984. "The New Institutionalism: Organizational Factors in Political Life." *American Political Science Review*, 78: 734–49.

March, James G. and Johan P. Olsen. 1989. *Rediscovering Institutions: The Organizational Basis of Politics*. New York: Free Press.

Moynihan, Daniel Patrick. 1987. "The 'New Science of Politics' and the Old Art of Government." *Public Interest*, 86 (Winter): 22–35.

Myerson, Roger B. 1993. "Effectiveness of Electoral Systems for Reducing Government Corruption: A Game Theoretic Analysis." *Games and Economic Behavior*, 5: 118–32.

Niemi, Richard, Jeffrey Hill, and Bernard Grofman. 1985. "The Impact of Multimember Districts on Party Representation in U.S. State Legislatures." *Legislative Studies Quarterly*, Vol. 10, No. 4, 441–55.

North, Douglass. 1981. *Structure and Change in Economic History*. New York: W.W. Norton.

North, Douglass. 1986. "The New Institutional Economics." *Journal of Institutional and Theoretical Economics* (March).

Ordeshook, Peter C. 1987. "The Reintegration of Political Science and Economics and the Presumed Imperialism of Economic Theory." Social Sciences Working Paper 655 (September), California Institute of Technology.

Ostrom, Elinor. 1986. "An Agenda for the Study of Institutions." *Public Choice,* 48: 3–25.

Powell, G. Bingham. 1982. *Contemporary Democracies: Participation, Stability and Violence*. Cambridge, MA: Harvard University Press.

Powell, Walter W. and Paul DiMaggio, eds. 1991. *The New Institutionalism in Organizational Analysis*. Chicago: University of Chicago Press.

Rae, Douglas W. 1971. *The Political Consequences of Electoral Laws*. New Haven, CT: Yale University Press (1st Edition, 1967).

Ranney, Austin. 1976. "The Divine Science: Political Engineering in American Culture." *American Political Science Review,* 70: 140–48.

Reynolds, Andrew. 1993. *Voting for a New South Africa*. Capetown: Maskew Miller Longman.

Reynolds, Andrew, ed. 1994. *Election '94 South Africa: The Campaigns, Results and Future Prospects*. New York: St. Martin's Press.

Reynolds, Andrew. 1995. "The Case For Proportionality." *Journal of Democracy*, 6 (October): 117–24.

Reynolds, Andrew. 1996. Unpublished Ph.D. dissertation, Department of Political Science, University of California, San Diego, August.

Schotter, Andrew. 1981. *The Economic Theory of Social Institutions*. New York: Cambridge University Press.

Schotter, Andrew. 1986. "The Evolution of Rules." In Richard N. Langlois, ed., *Economics as a Process: Essays in the New Institutional Economics*. London and New York: Cambridge University Press, 117–33.

Shepsle, Kenneth A. 1979a. "The Role of Institutional Structure in the Creation of Policy Equilibrium." In Douglas W. Rae and Theodore J. Rismeir, eds., *Public Policy and Public Choice*, Vol. VI, Beverly Hills: Sage, 249–82.

Shepsle, Kenneth A. 1979b. "Institutional Arrangements and Equilibrium in Multidimensional Voting Models." *American Journal of Political Science,* 23: 27–59.

Shepsle, Kenneth A. 1989. "Studying Institutions: Some Lessons from the Rational Choice Approach." *Journal of Theoretical Politics*, 1: 131–48.

Shepsle, Kenneth A. and Barry Weingast. 1987. "The Institutional Foundations of Committee Power." *American Political Science Review,* 81: 85–104.

Shugart, Matthew and John Carey. 1992. *Presidents and Assemblies: Constitutional Design and Electoral Dynamics*. New York and London: Cambridge University Press.

Smith, Rogers M. 1988. "Political Jurisprudence, the 'New Institutionalism,' and the Future of American Law." *American Political Science Review*, 82: 89–108.

Spafford, Duff. 1985. "Mill's Majority Principle." *Canadian Journal of Political Science*, 18 No. 3 (September): 599–608.

Steinmo, Sven, Kathleen Thelen, and Frank Longstreth, eds. 1992. *Structuring Politics: Historical Institutionalism in Comparative Analysis*. New York and London: Cambridge University Press.

Taagepera, Rein. 1986. "Reformulating the Cube Law for Proportional Representation Elections." *American Political Science Review,* 80: 489–504.

Taagepera, Rein. August 29–September 2, 1996."Arend Lijphart and Dimensions of Democracy." Prepared for delivery at the Annual Meeting of the American Political Science Association, San Francisco, California.

Taagepera, Rein and Bernard Grofman. 1985. "Rethinking Duverger's Law: Predicting the effective number of parties in plurality and PR systems—parties minus issues equals one." *European Journal of Political Research*, Vol. 13: 341–52.

Taagepera, Rein and Matthew Shugart. 1989. *Seats and Votes*. New Haven: Yale University Press.

Thelen, Kathleen and Sven Steinmo. 1992. "Historical Institutionalism in Comparative Politics." In Sven Steinmo, Kathleen Thelen, and Frank Longstreth, eds., *Structuring Politics: Historical Institutionalism in Comparative Analysis*. New York and London: Cambridge University Press.

Weingast, Barry and William Marshall. 1988. "The Industrial Organization of Congress, or Why Legislatures, Like Firms, are Not Organized as Markets." *Journal of Political Economy,* 96: 132–64.

Williamson, Oliver. 1981. "The Economics of Organization: The Transaction Cost Approach." *American Journal of Sociology,* 87: 548–77.

Wittman, Donald. 1983. "Efficient Rules in Highway Safety and Sports Activity." *American Economic Review,* 72: 78–90.

Wittman, Donald A. 1995. *The Myth of Democratic Failure: Why Political Institutions are Efficient.* Chicago: University of Chicago Press.

Wuffle, A 1999. "Credo of a Reasonable Choice Modeler." *Journal of Theoretical Politics*, II No. 3: 203-06

CHAPTER 4

Arend Lijphart and Dimensions of Democracy

Rein Taagepera

What is the scope of political science? Institutional frameworks are not politics. Politics is a game, and like all games, it is played within certain rules and restrictions of which institutions are a part, but only a part, because there are also social taboos, psychological restrictions, and physical barriers. Many of these are givens that the political game cannot change. Political institutions are peculiar in that they restrict the game but also, with some time delay, can be changed by the game itself. Present institutions are products of past political games.

In this sense, politics consists of games and frames. Oh, it also involves claims, blames, fames—and some may add dames—but let us keep to the bare essentials. The study of these games and frames, both on micro and macro level, is the scope of political science—or politology, as they call it more elegantly in some corners of the world, in line with "geology" and "pharmacology." Politologists who focus on institutions can be said to concentrate on the limiting frames of political games. In his book on *Democracies* (1984), Arend Lijphart tackled these limiting frames on a broad front, inspiring others and setting up an inherent agenda for more detailed inquiry.

Arend Lijphart's work came to my attention soon after I switched from physics to political science in 1970, and he has influenced my own endeavors probably more than any other political scientist has. When I visited the Netherlands in 1976 I tried to visit him, but somehow the encounter did not materialize. Soon thereafter, however, he moved to California, and we did meet.

This comment on Arend Lijphart's work begins with some personal examples of how he has influenced my scholarly and political work. The focus will be on *Democracies* (1984), which is a major landmark in political science. This is the reason for having "Dimensions of Democracy" in my title. I'll also touch on Lijphart's more recent *Electoral Systems and Party Systems* (1994) that raises some dilemmas in visualization and operationalization of quantities such as effective threshold of representation and deviation from proportionality.

Lijphart's Democracies: Personal Impact

Arend sent me a copy of his freshly published *Democracies* in 1984, and it arrived as Mare and I were packing for Hawaii. I never take work with me on vacation, but this was the one exception, because the book looked so enticing. What's more, I actually did read it in between luaus and lonely hikes in the arid volcano terrain. Lacking graph paper, on the book's mainly empty page 149 I sketched a graph of effective number of parties versus the number of issue dimensions, on the basis of Lijphart's data. Then I wrote underneath:

> Res. Note. "Issue Dimensions Plus One Equals the Number of Parties"
>
> If this were a research note in physics, the title and Figure would suffice, along with a couple of footnotes. This being a worthier and wordier discipline, however, some paragraphs on definition of terms and implications of results are in order.

The next morning I got cold feet and scribbled in a hastier handwriting in the last available space on the page:

> "Artifact due to determination of issues as inter-party issues only."

Later on, I settled on middle ground between basic law and artifact. This Lijphart-inspired work was published as part of a collaborative article with Bernie Grofman (Taagepera and Grofman 1985)—see figure 4.1. As for wordiness, it had one of the longest titles in political science literature: "Rethinking Duverger's Law: Predicting the Effective Number of Parties in Plurality and PR Systems—Parties Minus Issues Equals One."

Another finding that resulted directly from Lijphart's *Democracies* was the "inverse square law of coalition durability" (see Taagepera and Shugart 1989: 99–103). It says that cabinet durability tends to be 400 months divided by the square of the effective number of parties in the parliament (see figure 4.2). Empirically, this flows directly from Lijphart's data (1984: 83 and 122). The theoretical explanation was longer in coming.[1] The findings became a conference paper (Taagepera 1987).

Given that the entire process began with data and comments in Arend's book I invited him to be coauthor on a more elaborate article. He graciously agreed and gave me further data and a list of sticky issues. It's my fault that the article still remains on the drawing board. Two factors intervened: the

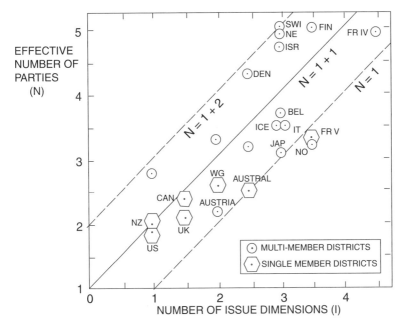

Fig. 4.1   **The relationship between the number of parliamentary parties and issue dimensions, based on data in Lijphart (1984: 122 and 130).**

From Rein Taagepera and Bernard Grofman (1985), "Rethinking Duverger's law: Predicting the effective number of parties in plurality and PR systems—parties minus issues equals one," *European Journal of Political Research* 13:341-52, fig. 1, © 1985 by Elsevier Science Publishers, with kind permission from Kluwer Academic Publishers.

onset of the so-called "singing revolution" in my native Estonia, and my collaboration with Matt Shugart on *Seats and Votes* (1989). This book included a short overview of the inverse square model. Thus, once *Seats and Votes* was published, the main result was in print, reducing the psychological urge to finalize the back-up article listed in the book's bibliography as unpublished "Taagepera and Lijphart." At the same time the Soviet occupation in Estonia began to crumble. For the first time in 43 years I was allowed to visit my homeland, and soon little time was left for theoretical work.

At my second visit to Estonia I had one political science book with me, and it was Lijphart's *Democracies*. I found it ideally concise for people who had to design makeshift democratic institutions without any previous political science background and little time to catch up on it during nighttime, after a harrowing day of practical politics, in which they also had little experience. Some backgrounds were more congenial than others for understanding Lijphart. People trained in physical sciences resonated with his use of data on

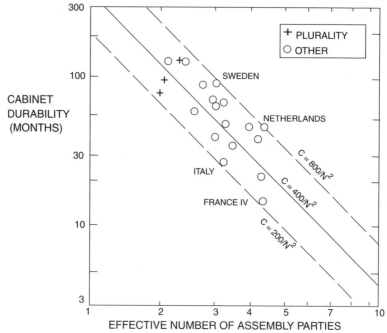

Fig. 4.2.   Inverse square law of cabinet durability, based on data in Lijphart (1984: 83 and 122).

From Rein Taagepera and Matthew S. Shugart (1989), *Seats and Votes*, Yale University Press, fig. 9.3, © 1989 by Yale University, with kind permission from Yale University Press.

what actual democracies do—and the physicists tended to know enough English to read the book. Soviet-trained law specialists tended to have the hardest time: they argued what democracy should be about on philosophical grounds, without having lived in democratic surroundings—and they tended to know less English. The atmosphere is described in a piece in *PS*:

> The [Legislative] Committee members locked horns on whether the Prime Minister should be able to call for new parliamentary elections in case of a vote of no confidence. The Committee vice-chair, physicist Peet Kask, referred to Arend Lijphart's *Democracies* (1984) to document the fact that almost all stable parliamentary regimes (with the exception of Norway) do give government such power. However, most of the Committee members still felt such power was "undemocratic" and the experience of stable democracies was irrelevant to Estonia's special condition. (Taagepera 1991)

On the opening day of Estonia's Constitutional Assembly (Taagepera 1994) I gave a scholarly overview of the differences between majoritarian and consensual democracies, based, of course, on Lijphart (1984). A draft of Shugart and Carey's *Presidents and Assemblies* (1992) served to review the strengths and weaknesses of parliamentary, premier-presidential, and presidential systems. The text of the talk was distributed to all Assembly members. Peet Kask became one of the most active members of the Constitutional Assembly, and he often had his copy of Lijphart's *Democracies* with him.[2]

Two Dimensions for Democratic Institutions

This concludes the specific examples of the scholarly and political impacts of Lijphart's *Democracies*, as observed directly. More generally, why is it a great book? The answer will be given first from the scholar's and then the teacher's viewpoint.

The main scholarly achievement of Lijphart's *Democracies* lies first in establishing two conceptual dimensions along which democracies organize their institutions, and then mapping the locations of various countries on these dimensional axes. These locations reflect the dilemma and uneasy compromise between desirable, yet mutually exclusive features. One axis ranges from majoritarianism to consensualism. The other goes from unitarism to federalism. Figure 4.3 graphs the factor scores tabulated by Lijphart (1984: 216).

The remarkable aspect of figure 4.3 is that the field is filled pretty evenly. Those who see the political world in terms of gradualism and compromise might expect more countries in the center, with those at the margins palpably less stable—but this is not the case. The failure of France IV cannot be blamed on an excess of consensualism, because Finland and the Netherlands have quite similar characteristics, yet have been stable. Those, on the other hand, who see the political world in terms of contrary and mutually exclusive principles might expect some of the corners of the graph to be heavily populated, reflecting healthy clear-cut choices. In their view, the center-field regimes that try to bridge the unbridgeable should be less stable—but this is not the case either. Italy's problems cannot be ascribed to its sitting on the fence between majoritarianism and consensualism, given that Japan and France V have similar characteristics.

Lijphart (1984: 43) classified the societies involved as nonplural, semiplural, and plural. The locations of semiplural and plural societies in figure 4.3 are intermixed. These societies tend to be consensual and federal, whereas nonplural societies tend to be majoritarian and unitary, as Lijphart expected. However, the separation line, also shown in figure 4.3, is far from clear-cut.

How novel was the delineation of these dimensions of democracy? After all, the notion of federalism as opposed to unitarism is pretty old. Moreover, it is evident that democracy has more dimensions than the institutional. The institutional aspect itself may well have further dimensions, in addition to the

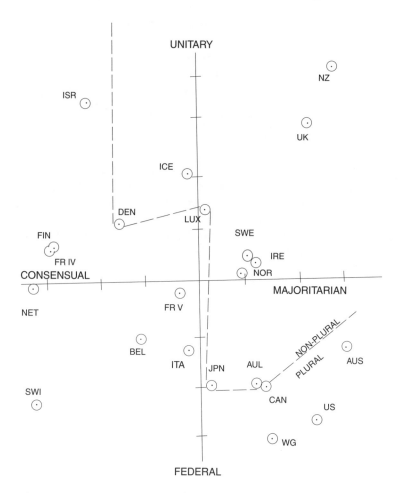

Fig. 4.3   Majority-consensus and unitary-federal scores, based on data in Lijphart (1984: 216).

two elucidated by Lijphart. By dimensions I mean bunches of properties that tend to come together, independent from other such bunches. Lijphart's factorial analysis showed, for instance, that referenda did not load significantly either on the unitary-federal or on the majoritarian-consensual dimension.

Though the unitary-federal dimension was fairly obvious a long time ago, this was not so for the consensus end of the other dimension. Modern political science largely developed in North America and took majoritarianism as a positive model, counterpoised only by a fuzzy, nameless dearth of majoritarianism. Lijphart's earlier work was important in giving this fuzzy end of the scale a name and some legitimacy.

In *The Politics of Accommodation* (1968) he showed that the majoritarian approach is risky in highly plural societies, and that consociation of elites actually has worked in some deeply divided countries. In *Democracy in Plural Societies* (1977) he coined the term "consociational democracy" to denote a style different from adversarial. In *Conflict and Coexistence in Belgium* (1981) the pure extremes are denoted as majoritarian and consociational democracies, respectively, and much of the framework of the 1984 book is already present. The later shift from "consociation" to "consensus" reflects a broadening, to include regimes that avoid the adversarial majoritarian spirit, yet also lack an explicitly consociational framework.

We can always find antecedents, but the emergence of consensus democracy as a notion and a respectable alternative in political science discourse owes much to Lijphart. And this was a precondition for even visualizing a majoritarian-consensual axis. However, in the beginning the unitary-federal features seemed to fit into the same package, so that institutions looked one-dimensional: purely majoritarian states would be unitary, and purely consensual states would be federal.

The evolution toward a two-dimensional field is in evidence from the first to the last chapters within Lijphart's *Democracies* (1984). In the light of the two-dimensional field in figure 4.3 the discussion could have begun with the presentation of four separate extreme or almost pure cases: New Zealand, the United States, Switzerland, and Israel. Instead, the book begins with a single axis ranging from consensual-federal Switzerland (and Belgium) to majoritarian-unitary New Zealand (and UK). The third corner, the majoritarian yet federal United States, is then presented (Lijphart 1984: 32–36) as a somewhat awkward mixed case. The starkly contrasting mixed case of Israel—consensual, yet unitary—is not noted.[3]

As the chapters in *Democracies* unfold, the aspects that in retrospect belong to the federal-unitary dimension (chapters 6, 10, 11) are randomly interspersed with the rest. Only in the concluding chapter does the two-dimensional nature of the field emerge from factorial analysis. This less-than-straightforward path is typical of scientific advances. In retrospect, we could proceed much more directly. To observe how the discovery actually meandered is fascinating—and also instructive for further basic inquiry.

How stable are these characterizations of institutions against errors of measurement and choice of specific variables? Nine years later Lijphart *et al.* (1993) reanalyzed the same countries in light of new evidence. These shifts are graphed in figure 4.4. The tip of the arrow indicates the reevaluated position, and the length of the arrow shows the extent of change. For individual countries these changes are appreciable. Instead of moderately majoritarian, Canada now looks like the most majoritarian country in the democratic world. The overall picture, however, is remarkably robust against reevaluation. In particular, only 4 out of the 22 regimes change quadrants (Belgium, France V,

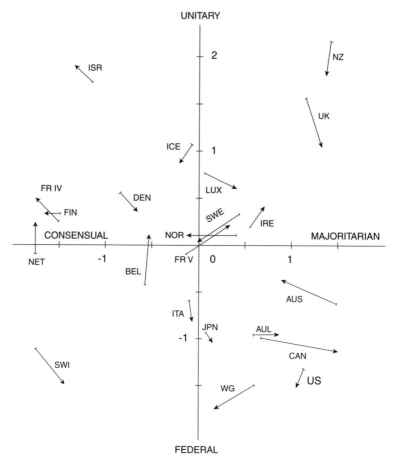

Fig. 4.4   Reevaluation of majority-consensus and unitary-federal scores, based on data in Lijphart (1984: 216) and Lijphart *et al.* (1993).

the Netherlands, and Norway), and all of them were and remain very much in the center of the field.

Teaching Democracy

It is time to address the teaching aspect of Lijphart's *Democracies*. Most books I try in class go through the following cycle: They look promising; during the first year of use in class a given book becomes familiar in the detail required for teaching. The second year is the most comfortable, but some flaws or gaps appear. During the third year flaws prove deep and begin to overweigh the advantages, as far as teaching goes, so I start looking for alternative textbooks.

In contrast to this habitual cycle, I have used *Democracies* ever since its publication. Sometimes it has been a slow presentation in an introductory course of which Lijphart's book was the centerpiece. The pace and style have been different in graduate courses. It has worked out in California and in newly democratizing Estonia. The book is clear and short. It finds simple ways to measure what stable democracies actually do, in terms of institutions, rather than what they should do on some abstract grounds.

We may feel that Lijphart's work can be appreciated but not readily extended to measurements on our own country of specialization. It may seem that for this purpose we must 1) be a generalist of a scope equal to Lijphart's, 2) be familiar with factorial analysis, and 3) enter the additional country data into factorial analysis along with the existing data. Yet, it can be simplified.

Table 4.1 reproduces an overview I prepared for freshmen, to be used in open-book exams. Armed with this table the top half of the students were reasonably able to place an unknown or hypothetical country among those in figure 4.3, when given information that any country specialist has in his or her head or closest bookshelf. By "reasonably close" to the known location (or my estimate of it) I mean the longest of the arrows in figure 4.4. For many purposes this is close enough, as long as we do not forget about the possible range of error.

Research Agenda

Given that widely divergent combinations in figures 4.3 and 4.4 lead to reasonably stable politics, we are led to the question that formed the title of the collection in which Lijphart's reanalysis was published: *Do Institutions Matter?* (Weaver and Rockman 1993). If all degrees of consensus and federalism can lead to stable politics, then why care about such details? The answer is that Lijphart's pioneering work begs for massive continuation. In addition to the democratic regimes he analyzed, various other democracies have achieved a degree of stability that makes them part of the club, and it should be checked whether they fall within the bounds found by Lijphart.

Equally important, the institutions of unstable and incomplete democracies must be evaluated. Some may fall in the usual ballpark. In this case the flaws in their democracy may be ascribed to features other than those included in the two dimensions, or else negatively synergistic combinations within the existing parameters may be located. Some newly stable regimes may have institutional characteristics outside the field observed earlier, and in this case the extreme limits of workable consensus, majority, centralization, and federation may be extended.

TABLE 4.1   Student Guidelines for Estimation of Country Scores along the Consensus-Majority and Federal-Unitary Dimensions

Factor loadings and country scores from Lijphart, *Democracies* (1984: 214 and 216).

	Consensus-Majoritarian Contrasts		
Factor loading [and page of major table in Lijphart 1984]	IDEAL CONSENSUS Approached by Israel Switzerland, Finland, Netherlands	Sample mixed case: Iceland (-.06)	IDEAL MAJORITARIAN Approached by U.S., New Zealand, Austria
.99 [122]	$N_s = 5$	$N_s = 3.5$ intermediary: 0	$N_s = 2$
.85 [61]	Close to 0% Minimum Winning Coalitions	86% MWC majoritarian: +1	Close to 100% MWC
.75 [130]	3 to 4 issue dimensions	3 issue dimensions consensus: −1	Only 1 issue dimension
.72 [83]	Cabinet duration about 20 months	37 months intermediary: 0	Cabinet duration about 80 months
.42 [160]	Deviation from PR = 1% (2 largest parties)	D = 3% intermediary: 0	D = 6 to 8%

Approximate average score for Iceland: (0+1−1+0+0)/4=0, compared to actual −.06

	Federal-Unitary Contrasts		
Factor loading [and page of major table in Lijphart 1984]	IDEAL FEDERAL Approached by U.S., Switzerland, Germany	Sample mixed case: Netherlands (−.06)	IDEAL MAJORITARIAN Approached by New Zealand, Israel
.76 [193]	Constitutional rigidity: written constitution, minority veto on changes, judicial review	WC, MV: yes JR: no Semi-federal: −.5	Constitutional flexibility: up to existing parliament
.65 [92, 99]	Strong bicameralism	Weak bicameralism semi-fed.: −.5	Unicameralism
.51 [178]	Central government tax share around 50%	Central share 98% unitary: +1	Central tax share close to 100%

Approximate average score for the Netherlands: (−.5 −.5 + 1)/4 = 0, compared to actual −.06

The properties measured by Lijphart must themselves be reviewed and possibly improved upon. After all, part of his genius in producing this deceptively simple book was to perceive the need to measure, say, the actual relative power of central and local governments, rather than what it should be according to formal arrangements. So he picked the central government's share of total tax receipts as something for which data were reasonably readily available. There are some surprises: Although Australia is formally federal, the central government still commands a whopping 80 percent of the tax money, whereas in formally unitary Sweden the figure is only 62 percent (Lijphart 1984: 178).

What is brilliant in a pioneering work can, however, amount to sloppiness in the follow-up. Are constitutional rigidity, strong bicameralism, and low central tax share the best indicators of federalism? Are they the only ones? Are they of equal importance? To what extent did they change over time, in individual countries? Lijphart was right in not getting stuck with such questions in 1984, for if he had, he would not have seen the forest but only trees. But now that the forest as a whole has been mapped it is time to consider the trees. At the same time, pioneering work must go on, in particular in extending Lijphart's approaches to less-than-democratic regimes. He himself has continued to investigate larger and smaller pockets within the general framework of democratic institutions. Among these, only some aspects of electoral systems will be touched on here.

Effective Threshold and Disproportionality

Lijphart's more recent *Electoral Systems and Party Systems* (1994) deals with an important subset of issues, which occupied about 2 chapters out of 13 in *Democracies* and in which Lijphart has a long-standing interest (cf. Lijphart and Grofman 1984, and Grofman and Lijphart 1986). Compared to *Democracies*, the later book is more technical in style. I have used it as textbook in California, both with undergraduates and graduates. I have recombined and graphed its data on the porch of the century-old granary at Estonia's Sacred Lake that has replaced Hawaii as our summer destination. Some methodological issues the book discusses may have broad implications for the future course of quantitative political science.

Whenever possible, politological inquiry must struggle to become more quantitative, but not in the sense of mindless number crunching. Qualitative thought must precede crunching. Lijphart's *Democracies* is a prime example. The final output is quantitative; it can be tabulated and graphed. But this output has meaning only because appreciable qualitative thought went into locating what needed to be measured. This qualitative background emerges throughout Lijphart's books on consociation (1977) and Belgium (1981)— books which themselves are relatively devoid of numbers.

When what to measure is clear on qualitative grounds, then the question remains of how to measure. On the basis of Lijphart's *Electoral Systems* (1994) two issues of measurement will be pointed out here: effective threshold of representation, and disproportionality. Each is quite central to analysis of electoral systems.

An electoral system's openness to small parties can be expressed in terms of an effective threshold or an effective magnitude. The two are essentially the inverses of each other (Taagepera and Shugart 1989: 117) or, as Lijphart (1994: 12) puts it: "Legal thresholds and district magnitudes can be seen as two sides of the same coin."

Is it then like resistance and conductance in electricity—where either is used in practice, depending on the specific problem? Or is it more like length and its inverse, which could be termed "shortness"? Length is used much more than shortness (although the unit "1/cm" also occurs in physics: e.g., in the so-called wave number). Which visualization will be more fruitful in devising theoretical rational models, and which will be more useful in practical construction of electoral laws? The specific example refers to electoral systems, but it reminds us of a more general issue in measuring politics: When trying to measure the analogue of length, how often are we inadvertently picking the less informative analogue of "shortness"?

Disproportionality presents a different problem. Fair proportionality between vote shares and seat shares is one of the desiderata in electoral design (balanced by desire to achieve workable majorities). But how should we measure deviation from proportionality? Two major competitors have emerged. Long-standing approaches (Rae 1968, Loosemore and Hanby 1971) sum the absolute values of the difference between vote and seat shares for each party. A more recent approach (Gallagher 1991) squares these differences.

The resulting rankings of electoral systems differ appreciably, and Lijphart (1994: 60-61) sees advantages in both. Special cases can be devised where one or the other measure leads to counterintuitive results. A more relevant criterion might be which measure correlates better empirically with other properties of the system (such as the effective threshold or magnitude). Lijphart (1994) takes this into account. I would add another consideration, namely, which measure is more conducive to construction of rational models to explain the correlations observed? Again, the particular issue refers to electoral studies, but the type of problem is more general.

The Limiting Frames of Political Games

To conclude, Arend Lijphart's work has been extraordinarily fruitful in expanding our notions of democratic institutions, both in terms of qualitative concepts and quantitative measurement to back them up. He has had impact on development of institutions in newly democratizing countries, from South Africa to Estonia. His work still presents the profession of political science with new challenges in mapping and explaining quantitatively the limiting frames of political games.

Notes

[1] The path that led to theoretical justification illustrates the importance of teaching in conjunction with research. Having found the empirical relationship, I got used to it, without thinking further about its possible causes. However, in a course on electoral systems I tried hard to point out which relationships were theoretical "laws" (in the sense of being backed by a rational quantitative model) and which were merely empirical observations. As I matter-of-factly told the students that the inverse square relation was of the empirical type, without theoretical explanation, a small voice piped up in the back of my mind: "But there's got to be a reason, and you better find it!" I told this to the students, and voicing it made something click in me. As I walked from the laboratory building to the office building, it occurred to me underneath the second-floor walkway, that cabinet duration must have something to do with the number of communication channels between parties, because communication channels are also possible dispute channels that break up coalitions. The rest was technicalities.

[2] In 1992 I was nominated presidential candidate in Estonia, and Peet Kask became my campaign manager (Taagepera 1993). In a four-candidate field we netted 23 percent of the vote and missed the run-off by 6 percentage points. Since then I have tried to build up social science education in Estonia, with mixed results. Peet Kask has returned to applied physics.

[3] Actually, if anything, it's Switzerland and New Zealand/UK that look like deviant cases in figure 4.3, because most countries are closer to the Israel-U.S. diagonal. This pattern becomes even more pronounced in figure 4.4—and New Zealand's recent shift to proportional representation further depopulates the unitary-majoritarian corner.

References

Gallagher, Michael. 1991. "Proportionality, disproportionality, and electoral systems." *Electoral Studies,* 10:33–51.

Grofman, Bernard, and Arend Lijphart, eds. 1986. *Electoral Laws and Their Political Consequences.* New York: Agathon.

Lijphart, Arend. 1977. *Democracy in Plural Societies: A Comparative Exploration.* New Haven: Yale University Press.

Lijphart, Arend. 1981. "Introduction: The Belgian example of cultural coexistence in comparative perspective." In A. Lijphart, ed., *Conflict and Coexistence in Belgium: The Dynamics of a Culturally Divided Society,* 1–12. Berkley: Institute of International Studies.

Lijphart, Arend. 1984. *Democracies: Patterns of Majoritarian and Consensus Government in Twenty-One Countries.* New Haven: Yale University Press.

Lijphart, Arend. 1994. *Electoral Systems and Party Systems: A Study of Twenty-Seven Democracies, 1945-1990.* Oxford: University Press.

Lijphart, Arend and Bernard Grofman, eds. 1984. *Choosing an Electoral System: Issues and Alternatives.* New York: Praeger.

Lijphart, Arend, Ronald Rogowski, and R. Kent Weaver. 1993. "Separation of powers and cleavage management." In R. Kent Weaver and Bert A. Rockman, eds., *Do Institutions Matter?* 302–344. Washington, DC: Brookings.

Loosemore, John, and Victor J. Hanby. 1971. "The theoretical limits of maximum distortion." *British Journal of Political Science,* 1:467–477.

Douglas W. Rae. 1968. *The Political Consequences of Electoral Laws.* New Haven: Yale University Press. Second edition in 1971.

Shugart, Matthew S. and John M. Carey. 1992. *Presidents and Assemblies: Constitutional Design and Electoral Dynamics.* Cambridge: University Press.

Taagepera, Rein. 1987. "The inverse square law of coalition durability." *International Conference on Coalition Theory and Public Choice.* Fiesole (Italy), 25–29 May.

Taagepera, Rein. 1991. "Building democracy in Estonia." *PS: Political Science and Politics,* 24:478–481.

Taagepera, Rein. 1993. "Running for president of Estonia: A political scientist in politics." *PS: Political Science and Politics,* 26:302–304.

Taagepera, Rein. 1994. "Estonia's Constitutional Assembly, 1991–1992." *Journal of Baltic Studies,* 25:211–232.

Taagepera, Rein, and Bernard Grofman. 1985. "Rethinking Duverger's law: Predicting the effective number of parties in plurality and PR systems—parties minus issues equals one." *European Journal of Political Research,* 13:341–352.

Taagepera, Rein, and Matthew S. Shugart. 1989. *Seats and Votes: The Effects and Determinants of Electoral Systems.* New Haven: Yale University Press.

Weaver, R. Kent, and Bert A. Rockman, eds. 1993. *Do Institutions Matter?* Washington, DC: Brookings.

CHAPTER 5

Power Sharing and the Constructionist Fallacy

Milton J. Esman

Ethnic Solidarities as Self-Standing Entities

Much of contemporary politics involves the competitive claims and counter-claims of ethnically or culturally defined communities. Some control the state apparatus, some struggle for inclusion, others demand autonomy, independence, or simply recognition and respect. Whether the struggles are peaceful and civil as in Belgium, Canada, Malaysia, and Kenya; violent as in Bosnia, Chechnya, Turkey, and Ruanda; or repressed as in Tibet, Nigeria, Peru, and Syria; the parties at conflict represent themselves as ethnic communities or distinct nationalities and are so regarded by attentive outsiders. Mainline political science, however, has experienced difficulty coming to terms with the ethnic phenomenon. Its recognition of the legitimacy of this global reality has been hesitant and reluctant, accompanied frequently by neglect and denial.

Until the late 1980s the prevailing expectation was that ethnic minorities would inevitably, though at different rates, integrate or assimilate into the dominant culture within their nation-state and that this was a desirable development. Ethnic solidarities were believed to be vestiges of premodern societies, bound to disappear in the process of political development, to be succeeded by more "rational" associations and cleavages, mainly economic or ideological. Ethnic politics was not considered an interesting phenomenon, except for students of some third-world systems; even there political development could be expected over time to diminish their importance.

With the termination of the Cold War, the disintegration of the multi-ethnic Soviet and Yugoslav polities, and the violent conflicts that ensued, it was no longer possible to neglect the ethnic dimension of politics. But instead of recognizing ethnic solidarities as authentic and objective realities, the tendency has been to evaluate and explain away what appears to the naked eye to be ethnically based political actors as:

1. Platonic shadow or surrogates for deeper, more fundamental reality, often economic (Banton 1983); the basic problem is believed to be economic disparities and only economic measures can mitigate ethnic conflicts

2. Expedient, rationally calculated associations, often manipulated by self-serving leaders, lacking intrinsic value, but instrumental to the competitive pursuit of individual or collective power, incomes, or prestige (Hechter 1986, Brown 1994)

3. Social constructs or imagined communities shaped by the imagination of intellectuals or culture brokers that enable individuals and groups to define and redefine their collective identities in response to changing threats and opportunities (Anderson 1983). The latter, especially, stresses the fluid, transitory, and contingent properties of ethnic solidarity.[1]

These various explanations have one thing in common: they construe collective ethnic identities and solidarities as epiphenomena or suspect categories, illusory, derivative of deeper forces, or instruments of extraneous purposes, casting doubt on their authenticity and longevity and disparaging them as causative forces in political competition and conflict. Those who propound these views are not prepared to take ethnic solidarities seriously or to accept them as legitimate, self-standing political actors comparable to class, regional, or ideological solidarities. One influential academic who addressed this phenomenon in the late 1980s was the historian Eric Hobsbawm. Although his main thesis is that nations are recent artifacts created by the ideology of nationalism, his references to ethnic solidarity are consistently derisory. He regards contemporary ethnic solidarity as "negative," "divisive," "defensive resistance against real or imaginary threats," irrational and reactive "protest against the status quo or, more precisely, against others who threaten the ethnically defined group," "no longer a major vector of historical development." Like fundamentalism, it is an expression of collective psychosis, of futile resistance to "the new supranational restructuring of the globe." In a global economy dominated by transnational corporations and informational-cultural networks, there is presumably no role for ethnically defined communities. This phenomenon should, as it must and as it will, join the dust heaps of history. This is an important historian's explanation of one of the most prominent and vital realities in contemporary public affairs. (Hobsbawm, 1990: 163–169).

Strangely, those who are so dismissive of the authenticity of ethnic communities that aspire to self-determination, nationhood, or recognition of their minority rights have no difficulty recognizing as legitimate ethnic communities that have already achieved the institutionalized status of nation-states in the current international order. The subdisciplines of International Relations and Comparative Politics assume their existence and their durability. They have no difficulty recognizing French, Russians, Thai, and Turks as collective identities, collectivities with distinctive cultures and interests, but have little patience with Quebecois, Ibo, Kurds, or Baluch attempting to validate their claims as distinct peoples with collective political rights. That such palpable and well established expressions of collective identity and solidarity should prompt such skeptical, even hostile and dismissive treatment by people who regard themselves as scientists calls for explanation.

The most convincing explanation of this culture lag stems from the intellectual hegemony during the past century of the competing liberal and Marxian paradigms. To Marxists, class is the principle objective societal cleavage; ethnic sentiments, which may have to be appeased for tactical reasons, represent a form of false consciousness that inhibits class solidarity, is destined to disappear with the movement toward proletarian internationalism, and should therefore be discouraged (Connor 1984). To liberals the individual is the basic unit of social value; ethnic allegiances are residues of earlier, less enlightened eras, associated often with primordial, irrational hatred of outsiders. Preferences or discrimination based on involuntary, ascriptive status— race, religion, or ethnic origin—should be eliminated, as individuals are freed to strive for their life goals according to objective rules based on merit and achievement. All rights inhere in individuals, none in collectivities (Van Dyke 1977).[2] American political scientists especially have been strongly influenced by the liberal paradigm.[3] The modernization version of liberalism predicts that with the global processes of industrialization, urbanization, secularization, and the information revolution, individuals will become more and more similar in their needs and aspirations, while ethnic distinctiveness loses its social function and gradually withers away (Deutsch 1953, Newman 1991).

The emergence and salience of ethnic solidarity as a modern political phenomenon represents an unwelcome challenge both to liberals and Marxists. The dominant reaction has been one of hostility and distaste, associating politicized ethnicity with cynical manipulation and irrational, atavistic collective behavior. During the decades following World War II the subject was virtually taboo in public discourse and in Western academic circles. The world remembered the Nazi holocaust against a people they defined as an ethnic community; it recalled the perverse success of the Nazis in exploiting the ethnic aspirations of Sudeten Germans, Flemings, Bretons, Croats, Slovaks, and Ukranians. Except for self-determination of peoples emerging from European colonialism, human rights were defined in international circles as individual, not collective entitlements.[4] What resulted was a pronounced normative rejection of ethnic solidarity as a legitimate social and political phenomenon. In the literature on social movements, for example, ethnic-based movements have

been conspicuously absent (Tarrow 1994). As an expression of these sentiments, a long-standing friend and collaborator on the political science faculty
of a major university advised me recently that he liked my book on *Ethnic
Politics*, but "detested the subject" (Esman 1994).[5]

Social construction is one of the reigning and dogmatic fashions in contemporary social science (Onuf 1989: 35–65; Said 1978). In this post-
modernist discourse, societal phenomena are "invented." Hence, ethnicity is
more an intellectual construct than the objective outcome of historical experience. Far from being deep-rooted and enduring solidarities, ethnic affinities
are likely to be fluid, opportunistic, contingent, arbitrary; most are recent cre-
ations prompted by social change and especially by political conflict and
struggles for power; much of their history is contrived, to fortify collective
self-esteem and distinguish the invented "us" from a hostile or threatening
"them." Community, so deconstructed, is the product of imagination and ideology, not the reverse. As circumstances and intellectual predispositions
change, ethnic affinities may dissolve or be reconstituted along different lines.
The constructionist perspective thus stands on its head the conventional
understanding that ideology is constructed to meet the needs and aspirations
of human collectivities that constitute objective reality. As a result of this
reversal of causality, ethnic communities emerge as precarious entities, neither robust nor resilient, vulnerable to contingencies and to ideological reconstruction along different and unpredictable lines of collective identity.

There are, of course, real world examples of the contingent character of
some ethnic solidarities, of new formations that emerge with changing circumstances including government policies, and of others that coalesce as
small communities facing similar pressures seek the benefits of larger scale.
With its emphasis on the shifting, tentative, and opportunistic character of collective ethnic identities, constructionism is a useful hypothesis for explaining
ethnogenesis, the origins of ethnic solidarity. Thus the examples often cited to
illustrate the constructionist hypothesis tend to be drawn from less developed,
relatively unmobilized societies—indigenous peoples in South Asia, aborigi-
nals in the Americas, tribal societies in Africa.

Dogmatic assertions to the contrary, social constructionist skepticism has
no explanation for the many ethnic solidarities that are demonstrably long-
lasting, whose roots are decades and centuries deep, and which have survived,
adapted, and maintained the loyalty of constituents over successive genera-
tions. Periods of activism may be succeeded by periods of quiescence, strategies may be contested and revised, but the community with its distinct
collective identity in relation to outsiders persists. Can any objective observer
dismiss Chinese/Malays, Serbs/Croats/Muslims/Albanians, Hausa/Yoruba,
Turks/Kurds/Arabs, English/Scottish as imagined or invented entities or
recent "constructions" manipulated by ideology and likely to be transformed

or disappear in the near future? Or is it more convincing to believe that ideology and strategy are created and reinterpreted to meet the needs of established ethnic communities, rather than the other way around?

In assessing the causes of violent ethnic conflict, constructionists often point out that individual members of warring parties only recently coexisted peacefully, transacted business, even found occasions to cooperate. But this hardly demonstrates that these communities have been recently invented or that their boundaries are fluid and permeable. Many have developed their distinctive cultures and sense of cohesion over centuries. Though this does not prevent them as individuals from living on peaceful or even friendly terms with others, it does not erode their separate collective identities and collective historical memories.[6] That the very opposite is more likely to be the case is the reluctant conclusion of the journalist, Neal Ascherson, from his extended study of peoples who live near the Black Sea:

> People who live in communion with other people for a hundred or a
> thousand years do not always like them—may, in fact, have always
> disliked them. As individuals the "others" are not strangers, but
> neighbors, often friends. But my sense of Black Sea life, a sad one,
> is that latent mistrust between different cultures is immortal (p. 9).
> All multi-ethnic landscapes...are fragile. (Ascherson 1995: 244)

Instrumentalists and social constructionists are inclined to dismiss those who confront them with the historically based reality of ethnic solidarity as "primordialists," often intended as a pejorative category, similar to the Marxist dismissal of "bourgeois social scientists." Among contemporary social scientists "primordialism" has become a straw man. The notion that ethnic groups embody ineffable and unchanging cultural essences that have survived unaltered since the onset of time is a caricature that has no support in responsible academic circles. Those who are mislabeled primordialists do, however, believe that 1) ethnic communities are real and objective, not imagined or invented entities; 2) they serve intrinsic as well as instrumental needs of their members, which accounts for their cohesiveness and longevity; and 3) they are political structures that adapt continuously to threats and opportunities in their external environment.[7] These solidarities may be exploited and manipulated by cynical priests and politicians, but unless the underlying sense of community is present in the first place combined with a latent distrust of the "other," there would be no audience, no sentiment for unscrupulous entrepreneurs to exploit.

> Assertions that many modern ethnies are artificially created, fabri-
> cated, instrumentally formed or imagined are mostly irrelevant for
> the conclusions to be drawn from ethnic revivals and upsurges. The
> intense passions...make pointless the constructionist skepticism; the
> solidarities clearly do exist and are accompanied by strong senti-
> ments and collective actions. (Williams 1994)

Rejection of constructionism does not imply that collective ethnic identity is a static phenomena or that it can claim monopoly status. It is one of several collective identities by which individuals define themselves. Occupation, economic status, religion, political affiliation, gender, age cohorts may represent collective identities that, along with ethnic identity, coexist within an individual; together and in combinations they situate individuals in their social milieu and impart meaning to their lives. Under different circumstances any one of them may take precedence in determining an individual's behavior. As a determinant of collective action, ethnic identity may be passive and ill-defined over extended periods. Even when it has been activated, the boundaries of an ethnic community may change in response to changing circumstances; new individuals or groups may be accepted and incorporated, and others pass out of its ranks. Cultures may evolve as customs, and practices from outside are adopted and others abandoned. Individuals may transact business, establish and maintain friendships, even intermarry across ethnic boundaries. The content of culture—beliefs, social markers, and practices— may be reinterpreted, as French-Canadians after World War II defined the French language rather than the Catholic faith as the principal marker of their collective identity and as Americans of African origin chose to shift their designation successively from Colored to Negro to Black to African-American. Yet, these communities maintained their integrity and continuity. They were not formed by ideology, but by historical experience.

Notwithstanding these processes of continuous adaptation and reinterpretation, the shifting content of strategies, and internal divisions, most ethnic communities and their collective identities persist as real and objective social entities that command the allegiance of their members and the attention of outsiders. It is for these reasons, not because they are unchanging essences, that mobilized ethnic solidarities can claim to be treated as "givens" for policy analysis.

Like other collective identities, ethnic allegiances can be mobilized and politicized by apparent threats to their security, survival, collective dignity, or common interests, or by opportunities to promote their collective welfare. Mobilization is promoted by ethnic entrepreneurs who, for a variety of motives ranging from political ambition to social obligation, organize and arouse the community to action. For these leadership and mobilizing roles there may be competitors who interpret the community's interests differently and articulate internal divisions; there are intellectuals who help to shape and popularize a common ideology or belief system suitable to the times; and activists who carry out the organizing tasks and implement the strategies of action selected by the leadership. The activities of the modern state have stimulated the process of competitive ethnic mobilization as the state, during the twentieth century, became the principal allocator of values that affect the status of ethnic communities and the life chances of their members. This is why politics and political parties in so many countries tend to express and reflect, in fact if not in name, the interests of particular ethnic communities; and why the proliferation of new states resulting from European decolonization and from the recent disintegration of the Soviet empire prompted so many instances of ethnic mobilization and of interethnic and ethnic-state conflict.

Once mobilization occurs, ethnic identities tend to become dominant, eclipsing and superseding all others. This distinguishes ethnic solidarities from other collective identities. Although class, occupational, regional, and ideological identities remain active within mobilized ethnic communities, cross-cutting memberships have difficulty surviving. Cross-cutting affiliations, a standard prescription of many analysts who hope to break down ethnic solidarities in favor of other collective identities that they consider to be more rational or less amenable to violence, become nearly impossible to maintain or establish.[8.] Constructionists have no explanation for the primacy of ethnic solidarities over others. This can, however, be traced to the socialization process that inducts individuals into these communities at an early age, that facilitates internal communication, and that binds individuals emotionally and often materially to their ethnic community. As the latter may also function as vehicles through which individuals promote and defend emotional as well as political and economic interests, they serve both affective and instrumental needs (Bell 1974).

Competitive, even hostile ethnic communities may become amalgamated into a more inclusive collective identity, but only over extended periods of time measured in centuries and under a common political authority. Thus, Normans, Saxons, and Danes eventually merged into English; Parisians, Gascons, Burgundians, and Alsaciens into French; but Catalans and Basques never became Spaniards, nor did Irish Catholics identify as British. Efforts to promote the process of amalgamation over short time spans by social engineering, to create an overarching Yugoslav, Soviet, or Indian identity at the cost of abandoning or subordinating the original identities of constituent communities uniformly fail. Social constructionists to the contrary, ethnic identities, once mobilized, tend to be durable, for combinations of emotional and material reasons sufficiently valuable to their constituents that they are not readily surrendered. Ideologies and strategies are constructed and changeable, but ethnic communities, once they are consolidated, tend to persist. Smith concludes, correctly, that "whatever and however national identity is forged, once established it becomes immensely difficult, if not impossible (short of genocide) to eradicate" (Smith 1993 cited in Kymlicka 1995). Prior to the "forging" of ethnic communities, constructionism is a plausible description of the limited and transitory loyalties they command. Once they have been forged (mobilized) and launched on their careers, constructionism fails as an explanation.

In the realm of action rather than of speculation, of policy rather than explanation, political scientists are confronted with a critical choice. Whether the conflict they encounter is conducted by civil means or by violence, have they any practical alternative but to treat the contesting parties and the solidarities they represent as "givens"? And to proceed from that point, if they can, to search for practical formulas to moderate the conflicts, mitigate human suffering, and work out consensual patterns of coexistence within a single polity if possible, or in separate states if necessary? Once lines of conflict have been drawn, how futile it is to remind Hutu and Tutsi, Sinhalese and Tamils, Bosnian Serbs and Muslims, that not long ago they or their ancestors lived side by side in peace, that they share many common traits, that the lines between them were often vague and uncertain, but that they have become hapless victims of manipulation by self-serving politicians? To them the existential reality is the ongoing conflict between communities that are clearly demarcated in the minds of their members and of relevant outsiders, the congealing of solidarities that cannot be unscrambled, and the yearning for belonging and protection that are available only among their own kind. For beneath that reality are an established sense of community and a latent distrust of the other, in the absence of which the mobilizing appeals of politicians would have fallen on deaf ears.

It is as arrogant as it is futile for outsiders, academics included, to inform people who identify as members of an ethnic community under great stress that they have been the victims of manipulation, that there is little historical validity or objective justification for their distinctive identity or for the claims asserted in their name, like the Israeli Prime Minister who presumed to inform Palestinians that there was, in fact, no such category of people, or the Turkish Government's long-standing practice of referring to their large Kurdish minority as "Mountain Turks."

Both the "primordialist" and the "instrumentalist" insights contribute to an appreciation of contemporary ethnic politics. The former, that these are enduring, real-world collectivities that serve important needs of their members; the latter, that they are adaptive structures through which individuals and groups strive and compete for security, power, prestige, and economic resources. The fusion of these insights produces a synthesis that is useful for understanding, explanation, and policy. Constructionism, on the contrary, denies the existence of collective ethnic identity as the objective product of historical experience, ascribing it instead to the creative imagination of intellectuals, in effect a fabricated product. Having misconstrued the essential qualities and functions of ethnic solidarity, constructionism is barren of insights on how to manage the conflicts it generates.

If, as the constructionist perspective would have it, collective ethnic identities are imagined or invented entities rather than objective realities, then they must be as fragile as the ideas that contrived them and as vulnerable and pre-

carious as intellectual fashions—including the one that spawned constructionism itself. Such insubstantial images are not consistent with the observed
structure and behavior of most ethnic communities. This error involves more
than mere hairsplitting. It feeds the propensity of many social scientists to
denigrate the authenticity of ethnic solidarities, dismiss them as derivative of
other forces, as myths or inventions; in short, to find explanations for their
activity in extraneous forces and not in their internal dynamics. A correct
appreciation of the ethnic phenomenon in public affairs requires their accep-
tance and recognition as existential, self-standing realities.

Ethnic communities are not static entities. They evolve in response to material and intellectual challenges and changes. The content of their cultures, criteria for membership, and strategies toward the external world may be interpreted,
reinterpreted, and contested. But interpretation is not the same as construction.
Interpretation implies that the collectivity exists as an objective phenomenon,
construction that it is created by cerebration. The latter construes it as contingent
and transitory, the former as robust and resilient. Constructionism is useful in
explaining the origins of ethnic communities, but this is the limit of its utility. It
fails entirely to appreciate the dynamics of ethnic solidarities as they evolve over
time. For such reasons the constructionist claims leave too much of collective
ethnic behavior unexplained, including its most obvious and manifest features.
By confusing rather than clarifying the subject it seeks to explain, constructionism has impaired and set back the academic appreciation of ethnic politics.

In his influential scholarship, Arend Lijphart has never been tempted by
constructionism. He wisely chose to accept the contending parties in ethnic
conflicts as existential givens. And instead of deploring their existence, chal-
lenging their legitimacy, attempting to deconstruct them, ascribing their
claims or their very existence to manipulation, he accepted as genuine the participants' own definitions of what constituted their collective identities. He
was prepared to accept ethnic solidarities on their own terms as self-standing
phenomena that command the respectful attention of political scientists and
deserve to be analyzed and evaluated as objective phenomena. He was less
concerned that these solidarities might be frozen in place than with the more
creative search for processes by which conflicts between competitive, even
hostile ethnic communities might be controlled and regulated so that these
communities might learn to coexist, preferably within the same political
space, in peace. Lijphart neither celebrates nor denigrates ethnic solidarity, but
instead treats it as a reality and a challenge to public policy.

Power-sharing and Conflict Management

With the publication three decades ago of his book, *The Politics of
Accommodation: Pluralism and Democracy in the Netherlands* (1968), Lijphart

dropped a bombshell on the unsuspecting ranks of political scientists. In this and subsequent work, notably *Democracy in Plural Societies* (1977), he challenged the conventional wisdom of the time, which held that a normal and stable state was necessarily the homeland of a single nation, a nation-state. As it was believed that political community requires a set of common values and a common culture, ethnic pluralism posed a threat to the maintenance and development of a well-functioning and durable polity. Therefore, the prime responsibility of statesmanship was nation-building, to strengthen and homogenize the nation associated with the state; the duty of minorities was to accept integration as individuals into the mainstream culture.

In his consociational theory Lijphart argued that societal pluralism was no impediment to democratic stability. A common culture is not essential to a democratic state, nor is it necessary or even desirable that such a polity split into independent, culturally uniform entities. Contrary to constructionist logic, he accepted manifest ethnic solidarities as political givens and sought to discover rules and practices that would enable them to coexist within the same political space, to share consensually the responsibilities and the benefits of maintaining a common state that would provide all its members with the benefits of a common political, economic, and security community.

He identified a number of practices as methods for regulating a complete consociational system in which allegiance to the state and commitment to an ethnic community would be entirely compatible. Among them were the grand, inclusive coalition; proportionality in representation and in the allocation of benefits and costs; segmental autonomy—territorial or cultural; and the mutual veto. Favorable but not essential conditions for a consociational polity were a multiple balance of power, multiparty politics, small size, cross-cutting cleavages, overarching loyalties, segmental isolation, and traditions of elite accommodation. Conspicuously absent was the presence of a common enemy, a circumstance that in the opinion of many observers facilitates interethnic cooperation. In Lijphart's scheme, the presence of some but not all the components of the complete consociational package can contribute to peaceful coexistence, though such regimes are likely to be less stable.

This powerful insight soon became a lively topic of discussion among political scientists.[9] Graduate student in comparative politics learned the rules of consociationalism and debated their applicability. Along with its distant cousin, democratic corporatism, which also recognized social collectivities as intermediaries between state and citizen, it began to undermine the intellectual hegemony of the monolithic Jacobin state.

Many scholars attempted to apply consociational logic to a variety of ethnically plural societies and in doing so to refine the concept. Others attacked it, in some cases harshly. Some objected on normative grounds that it would employ state sanctions to freeze existing, often arbitrary ethnic definitions into rigid boundaries that would limit freedom of individual choice and inhibit the normal and desirable evolution of fresh collective identities. Others feared that it was profoundly undemocratic, since it implied elite domination and deferential publics that acquiesce in the compromises negotiated by their elites. This would subject individuals to unwanted exploitation by power-holders within their ethnic community; it would undermine democratic accountability by inflating the power of elites who would govern the state within interethnic cartels, arriving at decisions in smoke-filled rooms in the interest of their own transethnic class. Not only was it attacked as antidemocratic, but as blocking the inevitable and desirable evolution of class struggle or of the process of individual integration into a common cultural and political community. The integrationist alternative to the management of ethnic conflict, along with a set of instruments and incentives for reducing the political salience of ethnic solidarities, was vigorously promoted.[10]

The most sophisticated attack was launched by Rabushka and Shepsle (1972). They begin with the observation that there are necessarily competing factions within ethnic communities and aspirants to leadership and power who are committed to displacing existing elites. Based on the dynamics of "outbidding," they identified incentives for competitive aspirants to leadership to accentuate the extreme demands of their constituents. As unfulfilled demands are converted into grievances by the arguments of counter elites, constituents begin to distrust their leaders; accommodationist elites are compelled by their survival needs in competitive elections to espouse more extreme positions. This blocks interethnic compromises that are essential to the maintenance of a consociational polity; as the support of established elites melts away, the regime loses its consociational character or collapses. Thus, consociationalism and democracy are incompatible. This critique assumes that the rank and file are likely to be more extreme than elites in their definition of their community's interests and vulnerable to competitive manipulation.

A generation of debate, empirical testing, and reflection have tended to devalue the specific rules and practices identified with the consociational strategy for conflict management, while confirming its fundamental insight: that ethnic communities are long-lasting structures in many societies, that integrating and homogenizing strategies are likely to fail, that the successful structuring and operation of political systems must take explicit account of these realities, and that power sharing among them is the only alternative to partition, disorder, or coercive domination by a single community. The logic of his insight, as Lijphart later discovered, was less the specific rules of consociationalism than a rationale for power sharing in divided societies:

> Power sharing can be defined in terms of four characteristics: the
> two primary characteristics are the participation of the representa-
> tives of all significant groups in the government of the country and a

high degree of autonomy for these groups. The secondary characteristics are proportionality and the minority veto. (Lijphart 1990)

While asserting that all four of these characteristics are required for a
"complete" power-sharing system, he also argues that it is the principle of
power sharing that matters, more than specific rules, and that the principle can
be applied to a variety of circumstances.[11] A sympathetic reader might resolve
this ambiguity by concluding that power sharing need not conform to specific
practices and need not be an all or nothing proposition. In reviewing the examples he cites—Belgium, Malaysia, India, Nigeria, Zimbabwe, Canada—none
practice the minority veto and few adhere to formal proportionality. Symbolic
recognition and some measure of participation seem essential. Underlying
these principles is the recognition of ethnic solidarities as self-defined political actors and of their right to protect their security and promote their collective interests by participation in the processes of government. This is the
essence of power sharing; it can be implemented by a wide variety of methods including, but not limited to, those identified by Lijphart. These arrangements may have to be adjusted with changing circumstances. Power sharing
may be realized imperfectly, not to the full satisfaction of all parties but sufficiently to achieve peaceful and consensual coexistence.[12]

An example of imperfect and incomplete power sharing is Malaysia, one
of the cases cited by Lijphart. In this semiauthoritarian polity, Chinese and
Indians, as well as Malays are recognized as ethnic communities and incorporated into the political system through participation in the governing
National Front. But it is an asymmetrical arrangement in which Malays are
politically and culturally dominant; non-Malays participate as junior partners,
but there is neither autonomy, proportionality, nor minority veto. Indeed, the
majority of Chinese often vote for an opposition party that is not represented
in the government coalition. There are elements of power sharing in that
Chinese as a community have a voice and some influence over minority language elementary education, but it is far from conforming to the properties
that Lijphart posits as complete. Yet it qualifies as power sharing, though
incomplete and imperfect, because it recognizes and accords to the non-Malay
communities the rights to recognition and representation, to a minority voice
but not a veto, and to significant economic opportunity, a dimension of power
sharing that Lijphart has overlooked. Despite continuing grievances, these
arrangements have for four decades provided non-Malay minorities with sufficient security and satisfactions to maintain a tolerable pattern of coexistence
in a dynamic economy (Esman 1994, 1987).

Economic opportunity may be implied in Lijphart's concept of proportionality, but the Malaysian case suggests that it requires separate treatment. It
applies especially to countries where ethnic relationships have been stratified
or segmented and some ethnic communities have been economically disad-

vantaged. Individual competition, even on a nondiscriminatory basis, for employment or university admissions, is likely to benefit those from better educated backgrounds; market competition for control and management of economic resources always privileges those with capital, business experience, and contacts. Where economic differences are pronounced, the rules governing access to education, employment, and economic resources become contested issues. Thus, economic opportunity is likely to become a necessary dimension of power sharing. This may require not only substantial government investment and expanded services in areas where disadvantaged ethnic communities are located, but also measures calculated to insure their access on favorable terms to education, employment, business licenses, and credit (Esman 1987). Absent economic opportunity, power sharing could be perceived by economically disadvantaged ethnic communities as tokenism or deception.

Ethnic power sharing need not be fully equitable to be effective, to enable peaceful and consensual coexistence among ethnic communities in the same political system. On the other hand, it must encompass more than a minimal set of minority rights, such as management of their own cultural and educational institutions. Though the threshold between minority rights and power sharing is indistinct, combinations of extensive autonomy, participation in government, and substantial economic opportunity are required before a relationship can qualify as genuinely inclusive power sharing. Some who are skeptical of power sharing on normative grounds continue to argue that collectivities are no proper basis for political structures and that rights should properly be exercised only by individuals. Others who are skeptical on more expedient grounds believe that power sharing is inherently unstable and likely to lead to demands for separation or to domination by a single community (Miller 1989). But short of separation, which in many situations is impossible, how can we visualize the future of Northern Ireland, of Sri Lanka, India, or Bosnia, or of Belgium, Spain, Ethiopia, Bolivia, or the Russian Federation except through some variation on the theme and process of power sharing? Once ethnic communities have been mobilized, what are the alternatives to domination or separation other than power sharing? This was Lijphart's seminal insight.

Democratic and Authoritarian Systems

The literature on consociationalism and power sharing, including Lijphart's contributions, has heretofore focused on democratic polities. The underlying premise has been that effective and consensual power sharing is possible only in a democratic political system that enables and legitimates political activity by ethnic communities and whose authority is grounded in popular consent. But unless we believe that liberal democracy and capitalist economics represent the universal wave of the future, that the end of history is imminent, many peoples seem destined to be governed by authoritarian regimes of one kind or another for many years to come. China, Indonesia, Vietnam, and Burma; Iran, Iraq, Syria, and Saudi Arabia; Sudan, Congo, Zimbabwe, and Uganda are examples of large societies under authoritarian rule, several of which enforce the domination over others of a single ethnic community. Many of the states that now qualify as "democratic," in that they permit some freedom of expression and practice the formalities of electoral politics, are fragile and unstable systems with very shallow roots. In some that combine mixed democratic and authoritarian features, the democratic elements are conceded more to impress international audiences than in response to domestic pressures. Unable to insure order, control official corruption, or meet the minimal economic expectations of their population, they are vulnerable to displacement by coups, as happened in Algeria and Sudan, to manipulation by strongmen as in Croatia and Peru, or to repudiation by angry and frustrated electorates, as occurred in the December 1995 elections in Russia. Except for the Baltic republics, it is uncertain whether democracy will survive in any of the successor states of the Soviet Union.

What this indicates is that a number of states, several with large populations and including diverse ethnic communities, are likely to be governed by regimes that do not conform to democratic principles or processes. Is ethnic power sharing possible in such systems?

There are strong incentives for authoritarian rulers to accommodate ethnic communities other than their own. Some authoritarian rulers allocate the fruits of their control of the state to their fellow ethnic constituents whom alone they can trust, and rely on intimidation and repression to pacify others. They may divide minorities by co-opting selected members of their elite stratum into the regime. Such policies have been followed by the ruling Alowite minority in Syria, the Burman, Hausa, and Mestizo-dominated military in Burma (Myanmar), Nigeria, and Guatemala, respectively. They may ignore or suppress the claims of ethnic communities other than their own; they may attempt to promote an overarching national identity that seldom conceals the reality of ethnic domination. But the cost of sustaining such repression and of alienating large sections of the population can be high— high enough to produce incentives for some rulers to try a more inclusive policy. That policy would provide other ethnic communities with some of the elements of power sharing—symbolic recognition, a measure of representation and participation (voice) in decision-making, cultural or territorial autonomy, and economic opportunity—sufficient to persuade a substantial number of their more influential members that their basic needs are being respectfully considered and attended to.

This more inclusive and responsive style of accommodative politics requires a higher level of political sophistication than the practice of exclusion and repression, but it is likely to yield a higher level of stability. In their "theory of democratic instability" Rabushka and Shepsle argued that consociational arrangements destabilize democratic societies because they are unable to cope with the politics of outbidding. Authoritarian systems, by contrast, can limit outbidding, while providing ethnic communities with sufficient security and satisfactions to enable peaceful coexistence.

The purpose of this discussion is not to endorse authoritarian rule—though a standard justification for such systems is precisely that they are necessary to preempt or prevent violent conflict in ethnically divided societies—but to indicate the possibility that some measure of ethnic power sharing is possible in authoritarian systems.[13] A number of empirical examples come to mind. There are several such cases in post-colonial Africa, including the Ivory Coast during the long reign of Houphuey-Boigny, Uganda under the one-party government of Yoweri Musaveni, Zambia during the presidency of Kenneth Kuanda, and more recently the Ethiopian experiment with ethnic federalism (Rothchild 1991, Cohen 1995). In Latin America, Paraguay, which has been governed for most of this century by dictators, accords official status to Guarani, the language of the principal indigenous community. In Bolivia the current convention requires that a high office, at present the vice presidency, be held by an Indian, that substantial public expenditures and services be allocated to indigenous communities, and that their distinctive cultural needs be recognized and accommodated.

There are numerous historical examples. The Ottoman millet system for half a millennium provided substantial autonomy, economic opportunity, and ready access to decision-making circles for its Christian and Jewish communities under an authoritarian Islamic regime (Karpat 1988). The complex arrangements and concessions by which the authoritarian Austro-Hungarian dual monarchy attempted, after the events of 1848, to manage its ethnic pluralism with minimal repression was undermined less by internal dissension than by defeat in the first World War. Prominent socialist opponents of that government proposed a regime of political-cultural autonomy for the nationalities and ethnic minorities that would enable them to continue to enjoy the benefits of an economic and security community within a reformed Hapsburg empire (Bauer 1907–1975).

What I have attempted to demonstrate is that the logic of power sharing can be extended beyond genuinely democratic polities to encompass authoritarian systems as well, and to stipulate some of the practices that may be conducive to its success. Power sharing need not be complete or symmetrical to qualify as an effective formula for conflict regulation. Not all the properties or elements cited earlier need to be present in every case; nor must any of them meet the test of proportional equity or minority veto. A viable power-sharing formula cannot fulfill all the aspirations of participating ethnic communities, resolve all their grievances, or prevent the emergence of ethnic-based disputes. It need only satisfy attentive publics that their status is recognized, their security protected, opportunities for economic advancement provided, and their access to governmental decision-making insured, sufficiently to maintain their acquiescence to the polity. Such arrangements require adjustments as circumstances change, but given the conflict potential of ethnic-based grievances, expedient power-sharing practices represent no mean achievement.

Success with such initiatives cannot be guaranteed. Militant factions may reject the terms or even the desirability of power sharing, agitate against them, and, like Basque separatists and Chechen militants, resort to violence. The Mexican revolutionary championing of Indian rights (indigenismo) with its message of liberation was never translated into power sharing; it soon atrophied, leading to alienation of the Indian peoples and eventually to the Chiapas rebellion. Soviet practice depended excessively on symbolic recognition and economic opportunity. It provided too little genuine autonomy and no effective participation, while relying excessively on ill-concealed repression of nationalist sentiments among the non-Russian peoples (Connor 1984).

Examples of power sharing such as those previously cited require respectful recognition of ethnic communities as legitimate political actors and claimants on the state. Once they are mobilized, once people define their identity as members of these communities, whether they have persisted and evolved over centuries or whether they have emerged in recent years, makes scant difference to the participants. What matters is whether their current conflicting claims can be somehow accommodated and destructive violence averted. Mobilized ethnic communities evolve over time in response to changing aspirations and changing circumstances; but short of genocide they cannot be deconstructed by political engineering as integrationists propose, or dismissed as artificial, contingent, or expedient intellectual inventions as social constructionists argue. In authoritarian, as in democratic systems, they must be recognized as self-standing political actors with legitimate claims on the state.

Lijphart's insight on power sharing, originally intended to apply only to democratic systems, can and should be universalized. The alternatives to power sharing among mobilized communities in ethnically divided systems, whether they be democratic or authoritarian, are separation, domination cum repression, or violence. In many cases separation (partition) is unfeasible and not desired by any of the parties. Thus, international efforts to mediate violent conflicts in such ethnic hot spots as Angola, Tadjikistan, Indonesia, and Bosnia where prospects for democratic politics range from uncertain to poor usually propose some version of power sharing. Successful formulas for the politics of accommodation, in authoritarian as in democratic polities, must be worked out case by case by structural arrangements or by conventions that respect the collective interests of ethnic communities.[14] They must incorporate in varying combinations some of the main elements of power sharing, notably symbolic recognition, participation in decision making, proportionality, cultural or territorial autonomy, and economic opportunity.

Notes

[1]See Crawford Young's elaboration of the social constructionist paradigm as it applies to ethnic politics in Young (1993) 21–5. See also Leigh Mullings, (1994), and Sheila L. Croucher (1999).

[2]The liberal tradition from Hobbes, Locke, Rousseau, and Mill to contemporary scholars such as John Rawls regard the individual as the only unit of social value. Even such pluralists as Gierke, the early Laski, and G. D. H. Cole failed to recognize ethnic or cultural communities as intermediaries between the individual and the state.

[3]A survey of five selected texts in comparative politics, all published during the 1980s, found that none contained a chapter on ethnic or nationality tensions or cleavages (Almond and Powell 1988; Bishop and Meszaros 1980; Deutsch *et al.* 1981; Mahler 1989; McLennan 1980). There were descriptive references to ethnic conflict in individual countries. One text implied the inevitability of assimilation, but at varying rates (Deutsch *et al.*). During the 1980s panels on ethnic politics at the annual meetings of the American Political Science Association were rare; in recent years their number has multiplied. A handful of political scientists did focus their research and writing on ethnic politics, but this was considered outside the mainstream of the discipline. Among them were Crawford Young, Walker Connor, Donald Horowitz, Daniel Patrick Moynihan, this author, and, of course, Arend Lijphart.

[4]The 1948 Universal Declaration of Human Rights and the 1966 International Human Rights Covenants focus on human rights for individuals (Hannum 1992).

[5]It should be noted that, unlike political scientists, sociologists during most of the twentieth century have studied and written about ethnic solidarity, often under the rubric of "intergroup relations." Prominent among them are Robin Williams, Nathan Glazer, E. J. Francis, and Leo Kuper. Perhaps the most sophisticated treatment is that of R. A. Schermerhorn (1970).

[6]Collective memories are important contributors to ethnic solidarity. Thus, many Serbs refer to Bosnian Muslims as "Turks," recalling the Serbs' humiliating 14th century defeat and long domination by the Ottoman Empire.

Northern Ireland Protestants ritually recall the exploits of the apprentice boys and King Billy's (William III) victory over the Catholic James II in 1689. Although such symbols are exploited by political activists, they could not be effective unless they resonated with deep-seated collective memories.

[7]Exceptions can be found in immigrant societies with a strong individualistic and inclusive ethos where ethnic communities have not coalesced in territorial enclaves such as the United States and Australia. English-speaking Canada has witnessed a rapid integrative process, but in Quebec, French-speakers vigorously assert their ethnic distinctiveness, and Indian tribes resolutely refuse to assimilate into either of the White communities.

[8]The literature contains a number of examples of the erosion of cross-cutting affiliations as ethnic mobilization intensifies: the collapse of a multi-ethnic labor union in Nigeria (Melson 1971); the disintegration of the Muslim-Christian trade unions in Lebanon (Hanf 1988); and the withdrawal from the Canadian Labor Congress in 1970 of their Quebec affiliates and the formation of a separate Quebec Federation of Labor (FTQ).

[9]Lijphart became one of the most frequently cited political scientists (Klingmann *et al.* 1989). The Buthelezi Commission searching for a way out of the South African impasse was inspired by the consociational model (Buthelezi 1982); see also Slabbert and Welsh (1979). In a 1977 book on ethnic conflict edited by this author, Lijphart's model of consociational politics was the dominant paradigm among the contributors (Esman 1977).

[10]For example, by Donald Horowitz (1985, 1990).

[11]In a recent article, "The Puzzle of Indian Democracy: a Consociational Interpretation," *American Political Science Review,* 90/2 June 1996, 258–268, Lijphart seems to revert to his earlier view that an effective consociational regime requires all four of its basic principles. As India has relaxed the principles of cultural autonomy and the minority veto, the polity has become more unstable and violence prone. The question, of course, is the direction of causality: did the instability provoke the relaxation of consociational practices, or vice versa?

[12]For a well-documented review and critique of the literature on power sharing, see Sisk (1996).

[13]In the early 1960s I asked a member of President Tito's ruling elite whether, in view of the more relaxed posture of the Titoist regime and their successful resistance against Soviet pressure, the time had come to open Yugoslavia to competitive politics. His immediate reply was that unconstrained competitive politics would immediately crystallize along ethnic lines with potentials for

extremism and violence that would put at risk the Yugoslav experiment with ethnic cooperation in a multinational polity.

[14]Post-apartheid South Africa has opted for an integrative system to govern its plural society, in which the rights of individuals of all racial and ethnic backgrounds are protected by a constitutionally entrenched bill of rights. The languages of all the major ethnic communities are accorded official status, though English is the lingua franca and the language of government. These arrangements may prove unstable unless they are accompanied by power-sharing conventions that protect the collective interests of its white, especially its Afrikaner minority, as well as those of its principal African communities, for example, the Zulu.

References

Almond, Gabriel, and G. Bingham Powell. 1988. *Comparative Politics Today: A World View*. Glenview, IL: Scott-Forsman, 4th edition.

Anderson, Benedict. 1983. *Imagined Communities: Reflections on the Origins and Spread of Nationalism*. London: New Left Books.

Ascherson, Neal. 1995. *Black Sea*. New York: Hill and Wang

Banton, Michael. 1983. *Racial and Ethnic Competition*. Cambridge University Press.

Bauer, Otto. c.1975. *Die Nationalitaten Frage und die Sozialdemocratie*. Wien: Europaverlag. (First published in 1907).

Bell, Daniel. 1974. "Ethnicity and Social Change" in Nathan Glaser and Daniel Patrick Moynihan, eds., *Ethnicity: Theory and Experience*. Cambridge Harvard University Press, 141–75.

Bishop, V. F. and J. W. Meszaros. 1980. *Comparing Nations: the Developed and the Developing World*. Boston, MA: D. C. Heath.

Brown, Michael E. 1994. "The Causes and Regional Dimensions of Internal Conflict." In Brown (ed.) *The International Dimensions of Internal Conflict*. Cambridge, MA: MIT Press.

Buthelezi, M. Gatsha. 1982. *Report of the Buthelezi Commission: the Requirements for Stability and Development in Kwa Zulu and Natal*, 2 vols. Durban, South Africa: H and H Publications.

Cohen, John M. 1995. "Ethnic Federalism in Ethiopia." Development Discussion Paper 519. Cambridge, MA: Harvard Institute for International Development.

Connor, Walker. 1984. *The National Question in Marxist-Leninist Theory and Strategy*. Princeton University Press.

Croucher, Sheila L. 1999. "Constructing the Ethnic Spectacle: Identity Politics in a Postmodern World." In Stack and Hebron.

Deutsch, Karl. 1953. *Nationalism and Social Communication*. Cambridge, MA: MIT Press.

Deutsch, Karl, Jorge C. Dominguez, and Hugh Heclo. 1981. *Comparative Government: Politics of Developing and Industrialized Nations*. Boston, MA: Houghton-Mifflin.

Esman, Milton J. 1994. *Ethnic Politics*. Ithaca, NY: Cornell University Press.

Esman, Milton J. 1987. "Ethnic Politics and Economic Power." *Comparative Politics*. 19/4 July 395–418.

Esman, Milton J., ed. 1977. *Ethnic Conflict in the Western World*. Ithaca, NY: Cornell University Press.

Hanf, Theodor. 1988. "Homo Economicus—Homo Communitaris Cross-Cutting Loyalties in a Deeply Divided Society: the Case of Trade Unions in Lebanon." In Esman, Milton J. and Itamar Rabinovich, eds., *Ethnicity, Pluralism and the State in the Middle-East*. 173–84. Ithaca, NY: Cornell University Press.

Hannum, Hurst, ed. 1992. *Guide to International Human Rights Practice.* 2nd edition. Philadelphia: University of Pennsylvania Press.

Hechter, Michael. 1986. "Rational Choice Theory and the Study of Race and Ethnic Relations." In John Rex and David Mason, eds., *Theories of Racial and Ethnic Relations.* Cambridge University Press.

Hobsbawm, Eric J. 1990. *Nations and Nationalism Since 1780: Programme, Myth, and Reality.* Cambridge University Press.

Horowitz, Donald. 1985. *Ethnic Groups in Conflict.* Berkeley: University of California Press.

Horowitz, Donald. 1990. "Making Moderation Pay: The Comparative Politics of Ethnic Conflict Management." In Montville, Joseph.

Karpat, Kemal. 1988. "The Ottoman Ethnic and Confessional Legacy in the Middle-East." In Esman, Milton J. and Itamar Rabinovich, eds., *Ethnicity, Pluralism and the State in the Middle East.* Ithaca, NY: Cornell University Press.

Klingmann, Hans-Dieter, Bernard Grofman, and Janet Compagna. 1989. "The *PS* 400: Citations by Ph.D. Cohort and by Granting Institutions." *PS: Political Science and Politics* 21/1, 158–65.

Kymlicka, Will. 1995. *Multicultural Citizenship: A Liberal Theory of Minority Rights.* Oxford University Press.

Lijphart, Arend. 1968. *The Politics of Accommodation: Pluralism and Democracy in the Netherlands.* Berkeley: University of California Press.

Lijphart, Arend. 1977. *Democracy in Plural Societies: a Comparative Exploration.* New Haven: Yale University Press.

Lijphart, Arend. 1990. "The Power-Sharing Approach." In Montville, Joseph.

Mahler, Gregory S. 1992. *Comparative Politics: an Institutional and Cross-National Approach.* Englewood Cliffs, NJ: Prentice-Hall.

McLennan, Barbara. 1980. *Comparative Politics and Public Policy.* Belmont, CA: Wadsworth Inc.

McKay, James. 1982. "An Exploratory Synthesis of Primordial and Mobilizational Approaches to Ethnic Phenomena." In *Ethnic and Racial Studies,* 5/4: 395–413.

Melson, Robert. 1971. "Ideology and Inconsistency: the 'Cross-Pressured' Nigerian Worker." In Melson and Harold Wolpe, eds., *Nigeria: Modernization and the Politics of Communalism.* 581–605. East Lansing: Michigan State University Press.

Miller, David. 1989. *Market, State, and Community: the Foundations of Market Socialism.* Oxford University Press.

Montville, Joseph, ed. 1990. *Conflict and Peacemaking in Multiethnic Societies.* Lexington, MA: D. C. Heath.

Mullings, Leigh. 1994. "Ethnicity as Representation." In George C. Bond and Angela Gilliam, eds., *Social Construction of the Past: Representation as Power.* London: Routledge.

Newman, Saul. 1991. "Does Modernization Breed Ethnic Political Conflict?" *World Politics* 43/3.

Onuf, Nicholas. 1989. *World of Our Making: Rules and Rule in Social Theory and International Relations.* University of South Carolina Press.

Patterson, Orville. 1977. *Ethnic Chauvinism: the Reactionary Impulse.* New York: Stein and Day.

Rabushka, Alvin and Kenneth E Shepsle. 1972. *Politics in Plural Societies: A Theory of Democratic Instability.* Columbus, Ohio: Charles E. Merrill Publishing Co.

Rothchild, Donald. 1991. "An Interactive Model for State-Ethnic Relations." In Francis Deng and William Zartmen, eds., *Conflict Resolution in Africa.* Washington, DC: The Brookings Institution.

Said, Edward. 1978. *Orientalism.* New York: Pantheon Books 1–28.

Schermerhorn, R A. 1970. *Comparative Ethnic Relations: A Framework for Theory and Research.* New York: Random House.

Sisk, Timothy D. 1996. *Power-Sharing and International Mediation in Ethnic Conflicts.* Washington DC: US Institute of Peace Press.

Slabbert, F. Van Zyl and David Welsh. 1979. *South Africa: Options and Strategies for Sharing Power.* Cape Town: David Philip; London: Rex Collings.

Smith, Anthony. 1993. "A Europe of Nations—or the Nations of Europe." *Journal of Peace Research* 30/2, 129–35.

Stack, John F., Jr., and Lui Hebron, eds. 1999. *The Ethnic Entanglement: Conflict and Intervention in World Politics.* Westport, CT: Praeger.

Tarrow, Sidney. 1994. *Power in Movement: Social Movements, Collective Action, and Politics.* Cambridge University Press.

Van Dyke, Vernon. 1977. "The Individual, the State, and Ethnic Communities in Political Theory." *World Politics* 29: 343–69.

Williams, Robin. 1994. "The Sociology of Ethnic Conflict." *Annual Review of Sociology* 20: 58.

Young, Crawford, ed. 1993. *The Rising Tide of Cultural Pluralism.* Madison: University of Wisconsin Press.

CHAPTER 6

Expanding the Spectrum of *Democracies:* Reflections on Proportional Representation in New Zealand

Jack H. Nagel

In 1984, Arend Lijphart put New Zealand on the radar screen of international political science when his book *Democracies* singled it out as "a virtually perfect example" of majoritarian or Westminster democracy, even better suited to illustrate the type than Britain, where that model originated (Lijphart 1984: 16–19). Condemned to obscurity during most of the twentieth century by small numbers, remote location, and relative tranquillity, New Zealanders are pleased to receive attention from overseas, and they normally delight in claiming to be first, best, or highest in any global ranking. Uncharacteristically, however, they quickly sought to shed the mantle of distinction Lijphart had bestowed on their country.

Just two years later, the government-appointed Royal Commission on the Electoral System (1986) proposed that New Zealand abandon one of the key components of its majoritarian democracy—the method of single-member-district plurality elections, better known in Britain and New Zealand as first-past-the-post (FPP). In its place, they recommended a central feature of Lijphart's consensus model of democracy—list-based proportional representation, specifically the German system, which the Commission dubbed "mixed-member proportional" (MMP). The Commissioners understood that electoral reform would set in motion a sequence of changes away from the majoritarian pattern in as many as four other elements of Lijphart's model: The two major parties (National and Labour) would lose their parliamentary duopoly, and a multiparty system would develop. The party system would no longer be organized by one dimension of conflict (socio-economic class), but instead would probably express and represent other social divisions (such as race and post-materialism). One-party majority governments would give way to multiparty coalitions. Consequently, cabinets would be less able to dominate Parliament.

By accepting the Royal Commission's plan without collateral reforms (some of which were also discussed at the time), New Zealand retained other features of majoritarian democracy—an unwritten constitution and parliamentary sovereignty, fusion of legislative and executive power, unicameralism, and centralized unitary government.[1] Nevertheless, the electoral reform and its predictable effects entailed a major shift from the majoritarian end of Lijphart's spectrum toward "consensus." The word had special appeal to New Zealanders because so many of them were dismayed with the adversarial style of their politicians, which former Prime Minister Sir Geoffrey Palmer (1987: 254–255) depicted in the following unflattering terms:

> Much effort is wasted in perpetual party conflict and constant electioneering....The confrontational style of New Zealand politics produces a lot of hot air and not much enlightenment. Much of the political debate in Parliament and outside is both sterile and acrimonious....[W]e tend to descend to personalities quickly and offensively. Political debate in New Zealand proceeds by way of slogan and cliché. It is both mindless and meretricious. In such circumstances rational argument is frequently the first casualty. Half truths, distortions and sensational allegations make better headlines.

To Palmer, who had appointed the Royal Commission, electoral reform "would change substantially the adversary nature of our current political process. It would move towards a co-operative style."

In the protracted national debate over electoral reform, which culminated in 1992 and 1993 with successive referendums, Lijphart's ideas were prominently featured. Political scientists played important roles as advocates and public educators, and most of them drew implicitly or explicitly on his concepts of majoritarian and consensus democracy. A best-selling booklet by a professional writer (Temple 1993) prominently reproduced Lijphart's (1991) diagram showing New Zealand's extreme position among 23 democracies and featured his data on the superior performance of moderate PR systems. After the 1993 referendum, the major political-science analysis of the vote was entitled *Towards Consensus?* because, as the authors noted, "Much of the debate about MMP focused on whether or not it might promote greater consensus in New Zealand politics." They went on to describe the themes of "less conflict and more consensus" as the "siren songs" of the electoral reform movement (Vowles *et al.* 1995: xiii, 8).

In the aftermath of the decisive 1993 referendum, politicians at first appeared to have heeded the consensus message. On the night of the referendum, Prime Minister Jim Bolger of the National Party won praise for his conciliatory and temperate remarks: "The country has spoken in a way that, I believe, says 'We want you collectively, ninety-nine Members of Parliament, to work more constructively and co-operatively together.'" In a similar vein,

Jim Anderton, leader of the Alliance Party, proclaimed, "We are going to have a co-operative, consultative and more consensus style of government." (Vowles *et al.* 1995: 1–2) The only discordant note was struck by Mike Moore of the Labour Party; but his combative, power-oriented speech became a major reason why his party's caucus subsequently replaced him as leader.

As they jockeyed for position in the first MMP election, which was to be held three years after the referendum, party leaders attempted to keep open lines of consultation to potential coalition partners, but the divisive effect of competition soon became dominant. By 1995, a leading journalist could write, "On election night in 1993..., many false promises were made of a new style of consensus-driven government. It was to be a new era of full consultation between parties so that legislation could be drafted and passed into law by mutual consent. Instead, the parliamentary trench warfare has continued unabated—the same cynical games, the same arrogant disdain of public opinion." (Ralston 1995: 38)

In the October 1996 election, one major promise of MMP was fulfilled, as five parties surpassed the 5 percent threshold to win significant representation (and a sixth, United, won a single constituency as a result of a deal with National). The traditional major parties, National and Labour, held the largest blocks of seats, but neither had won a majority. Occupying the pivotal position was the New Zealand First (NZF) Party, led by Winston Peters, a former National Minister of Maori Affairs. Peters and his NZF colleagues engaged in protracted bargaining with both Labour and National, meeting in the mornings with one and in the afternoons with the other. After two months of negotiations, they decided to join forces with National (Boston and McLeay 1997).

The resulting two-party coalition held the smallest possible majority of seats—61 of 120. Hopes of widespread cooperation were disappointed as the partners excluded National's erstwhile ideological allies, United and the free-market Association of Consumers and Taxpayers (ACT). Labour, spurned in its courtship of NZF, reacted bitterly, as did members of the other opposition parties. Acrimonious attacks and personal accusations again filled the newspapers. Tensions also persisted within the governing coalition. In one sensational incident, Winston Peters (at the time, Deputy Prime Minister) and a National MP engaged in a physical altercation inside the Parliament building. In August 1998, the Coalition fell apart and the New Zealand First Party disintegrated. National clung precariously to power as a minority government. Polls reported widespread disillusionment with MMP, in part because it seemed to offer no quick fix for the combative style of New Zealand politics (Vowles, Banducci, and Karp 1998).

If "the idea of government by 'consensus' proves to be a dream too far" for New Zealand (Boston *et al.* 1996: 10), three explanations might be offered for the resulting disillusionment. Two are obvious and already widely recognized in New Zealand. The third involves a criticism of Lijphart's framework and leads to the major points I want to make in this essay.

First is the problem of cultural lag. As National Party President Geoff Thompson (1994) put it in a speech, "The real problem we have is whether in New Zealand's traditionally adversarial system we can adapt to a more cooperative and consensual approach." That tradition, after all, had developed during 140 years before the adoption of MMP, and it remains an open question whether politicians socialized within it can change with sufficient alacrity to make the new system a success in the eyes of the public.

Second, in opting for proportional representation, multiparty politics, and coalition governments, New Zealand instituted only some of the features Lijphart identifies with the full consensus model of democracy. With its unitary system, unicameral legislature, and absence of a formal constitution, New Zealand continues to lack the elements his empirical analysis associates with federalism. In addition, of the core consensual institutions, New Zealand does not have separation of powers, and there is neither a requirement nor an expectation that grand coalitions will form. As the authors of a preview of New Zealand under MMP summed up, "[D]espite the rhetoric, New Zealand's experience of 'consensus' government will be somewhat limited. There may be some disappointment, therefore, with some of the fruits of MMP..." (Boston *et al.*: 1996 181–82).

Strictly speaking, therefore, New Zealand's post-reform polity is not an example of consensus democracy. In Lijphart's two-dimensional classificatory scheme, it has only moved to an "intermediate" position on Dimension I and remains strictly majoritarian on Dimension II (Lijphart 1984: 219). In this position, it would probably be grouped with Iceland and Luxembourg, still far from Switzerland, the exemplar of the consensus type, and not even as far along toward that pole as Norway, Sweden, and Denmark, which New Zealanders often take as models for their post-Westminster politics (Boston 1998).

New Zealand political scientists, who have done an outstanding job of educating their fellow citizens about MMP and its likely consequences, have clearly conveyed this more modest truth about the reform:

> Some people argued for MMP on the grounds that it would encourage consensus politics. Few people knew what that meant. The notion of consensus coupled with proportional representation (PR) and majoritarianism coupled with FPP comes from political scientist Arend Lijphart. The proposition that PR can foster consensus more successfully than FPP is easy to argue. The assumption that it can always be successful in so doing does not follow. Consensus building is unavoidable for minority governments (Harris & McLeay 1993). Coalitions, however, can be more decisive. After all, they usually have the numbers....[Under MMP] decisions will have to be made on

a somewhat broader base with a greater need for bargaining and compromise. Such a process will tend to foster more consensus than has existed in recent New Zealand politics. It will not bring about universal harmony and good will among politicians and people...
(Vowles et al., 1995: 206–7)

In part it is a hazard of the very popularity of Lijphart's concepts that enthusiasts in the general public would lose their nuances and take "consensus" too literally as harmonious unanimity. After all, "a new era of consensus politics" makes far better rhetoric than "a new system intermediate between majoritarian and consensus democracy" or "decisions will be made on a somewhat broader base with a greater need for bargaining and compromise."

Nevertheless, part of the problem lies with Lijphart's analysis itself. It is not so much that he has labels only for the "majoritarian" and "consensus" endpoints of his continuum, nor that he devotes most of his exposition to the pure types rather than the intermediate mixtures. These were doubtless necessary aspects of the intellectual process of producing an innovation that has proven extraordinarily fruitful for democratic theory and practice. Nevertheless, I contend that if we are to realize the full benefit of his discovery—and also lessen New Zealanders' disappointment with the imperfect "consensus" MMP has given them—then we need to reorganize our understanding of democracies by recognizing two crucial modifications: (a) Lijphart's typology spans only half the continuum of possibilities, and (b) "majoritarian" democracy properly understood is near the middle, not at an endpoint, of the extended democratic spectrum.

Lijphart's distinction between majoritarian and consensus democracy fundamentally derives from two different answers to a basic question: How many people have their preferences taken into account in the policy decisions of government? Majoritarian democracy answers "more than half the people," but with no requirement of a supermajority. Consensus democracy, according to Lijphart (1984: 4), answers "as many people as possible"—a rather ambiguous number! A literal, dictionary definition would answer "everyone," and unanimity is indeed Lijphart's aspiration: "An ideal democratic government would be one whose actions were *always* in *perfect* correspondence with the preferences of *all* its citizens" (p. 1). His subsequent analysis obscures this standard by positing the existence of conflict: "Who will do the governing and to whose interests should the government be responsive when the people are in disagreement and have divergent preferences?" (p. 4).

In categorizing political systems according to the number who rule, Lijphart follows a classical tradition. Aristotle distinguished rule by one, a few, or many; but Lijphart, considering only democracies, singles out instead just two versions of "many"—a majority and (as close as possible to) everyone. He apparently assumes that governments in which the preferences of less than a majority prevail are not democratic. In actuality, however, Westminster systems typically function to produce rule by a plurality, not a majority. To be sure, the political theory by which they are justified is stated in terms of majority rule, and the distinction is further obscured by the British fondness for using "relative majority" in place of "plurality."

The pure Westminster model produces rule by pluralities in two respects: First, at the electoral level, the first-past-the-post decision rule is plurality, not majority. When there are only two contenders, of course, the distinction remains academic; and, in the opinion of its advocates, the great virtue of FPP is its supposed ability to produce two-party politics. Through Duverger's mechanical effect, FPP systems do tend toward two-partyism, especially at the legislative level; but the psychological effect of FPP on politicians and voters has proven less inexorable, so elections are frequently contested by more than two significant contestants. As a result, victorious parties typically are supported by less than a majority of voters. In New Zealand from 1954 through the last FPP election in 1993, not one of fourteen governments was elected with an absolute majority of the popular vote. From 1972 on, the average vote for the winning party was 43.6 percent. Similarly, in Canada and Britain during the 1970s, 1980s, and 1990s, governing parties won average popular vote shares of only 42.4 percent and 42.3 percent, respectively.

Second, at the legislative level, pluralitarian processes also prevail in Westminster parliaments. Although the two-party bias of the electoral system usually manufactures an absolute majority of seats for one party, party discipline enables a plurality of MPs to control legislation, because the ruling majority within the governing party's caucus is likely to comprise only a plurality of the legislature as a whole. Shrinking the ruling fraction even further, the doctrine of collective responsibility in the cabinet may enable a bare majority of the executive to impose its will on the entire caucus.

Because pluralities typically rule both electorally and legislatively, I have suggested that Westminster systems like Britain and prereform New Zealand should be described as *pluralitarian*, rather than majoritarian (Nagel 1994a, 1994b, 1998). Even this label can be too generous when plurality votes in elections are compounded by party discipline in the legislature and cabinet solidarity within the caucus. The interaction of the three processes may produce a government that enacts policies supported by only a small minority of voters. Moreover, it is easily possible that influences other than voting— expertise, money, personal domination—can produce outcomes that respond to the preferences of very small numbers indeed; at the limit, democracy can mask rule by a small elite or even an elected dictator.

Thus, even when analyzing ostensibly democratic systems, we ought to think in terms of a full neo-Aristotelian continuum, from rule by one (dictatorship) to rule by all (unanimity or perfect consensus).[2] Along this extended spectrum (depicted in fig. 6.1), majoritarianism strictly defined occupies the region just above the halfway point. Below that mark occur the regions of pluralitarian democracy and what might be called factional rule.[3] Above it, we can distinguish supermajoritarian decision rules (such as the 60% cloture requirement in the U.S. Senate) and a region approaching unanimity that may be properly described as consensus democracy.

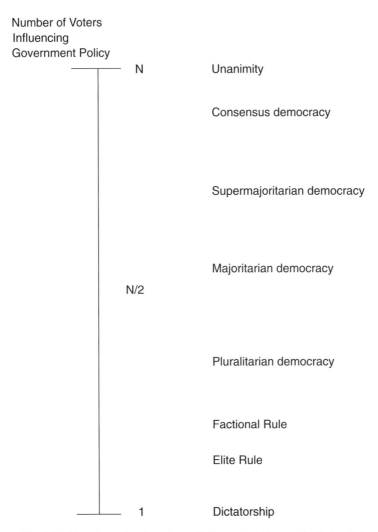

Number of Voters
Influencing
Government Policy

N — Unanimity

Consensus democracy

Supermajoritarian democracy

Majoritarian democracy

N/2

Pluralitarian democracy

Factional Rule

Elite Rule

1 — Dictatorship

**Fig. 6.1   The Expanded Spectrum: Patterns of Influence in Ostensibly
Democratic Systems**

For many New Zealanders, the decision to reject FPP and embrace MMP was motivated by the belief that pluralitarian processes had run amok in their country, enabling a small elite to enact drastic policy changes against the wishes of, or at least without the consent of, a majority of voters. Elsewhere (Nagel 1998), I have recounted how a combination of party discipline, cabinet dominance within the ruling caucus, implicit logrolls, a monopoly of expertise, and skillful tactics enabled a handful of determined ministers to impose radical free-market reforms that revolutionized New Zealand's economy in the period from 1984 to 1991. This sweeping liberalization delighted the international financial community, but left many New Zealanders dismayed that their pluralitarian institutions had proved so vulnerable to capture by an "elective dictatorship." Their disillusionment and its relation to electoral reform have been eloquently expressed by the political theorist Richard Mulgan (1995b: 88): "In essence," he writes, the economic liberalizers adhered to "an ideology of philosophical dictatorship, familiar in its assumptions to readers of Plato's *Republic* and Lenin's *What is to be done?* and profoundly anti-democratic."

> [T]he policy-making elite... had usurped the power offered by the Westminster system, and abused the democratic trust implicit in that power. The only way to reestablish such trust seemed to be by creating a new electoral system which would replace unwritten political conventions of accountability and impose a more formal constitutional requirement on governments to listen and negotiate. The constitutional change involved may be radical and revolutionary but the inspiration and support behind it is conservative and counter-revolutionary. (Mulgan 1995a: 279)

Although Mulgan may be justified in his portrayal of the philosophy and tactics of the liberalizing elite, the suggestion in his language that governments were utterly unresponsive to voters may be overdrawn. There was an electoral base for the economic reforms, but at key stages that support (and the incentive it provided) came from only a narrow (but pivotal) minority of voters (Nagel 1998). Democracy in New Zealand had thus deteriorated beyond the pluralitarian level to factional dominance, if not literally to elite rule or dictatorship. "The essential flaw in our present arrangements," wrote political scientist Jack Vowles (1991) during the reform debate, "is a simple one: power is given to minorities who think they have a majority."[4]

How would politics differ under proportional representation? In the relation between electors and the legislature, PR increases the popular support base for governments and makes it more likely that a parliamentary majority will have been elected by a majority of voters. In a perfectly proportional system, with no wasted votes, the correspondence between shares of votes and seats would be one-to-one, so any parliamentary majority would represent a majority of voters. In actual PR systems, including New Zealand's with its five percent threshold, there remains some tendency toward manufactured majorities, but it is much less than under FPP. In the first New Zealand Parliament elected under MMP, the two parties in the bare-majority governing coalition (National and New Zealand First) won a combined 47.2 percent of the party vote. In contrast, in the last election under FPP in 1993, the National Party was able to form a single-party government with a similarly narrow majority of seats after winning only 35.1 percent of the vote (Electoral Commission 1997: 18, 126). Thus what Crepaz (1996) calls the *popular cabinet support* (the sum of popular votes for parties that make up a government) increased by more than a third and was much closer to (though still short of) an absolute majority.[5]

Does PR also move politics within parliament away from the pluralitarian pattern? The answer at the legislative level is more debatable. Within a multiparty coalition, party discipline inside the separate caucuses might enable an overall plurality (the sum of intraparty majorities) to prevail; the arithmetic is not much different than for a one-party governing caucus. Similarly, through informal processes, we can imagine a handful of leaders in cabinet bullying their respective caucuses. The possibility of factional power through interparty bargains is certainly present in multiparty PR systems, as the influence of religious parties in Israel conspicuously demonstrates.

Nevertheless, proponents of electoral reform in New Zealand argued that an MMP parliament would be less susceptible to domination by dictatorial prime ministers, cabinet elites, special-interest factions, or legislative pluralities. Under PR as compared with FPP, disenchanted members of a caucus arc more able to survive electorally as a new party, so caucus majorities and party leaders have a greater incentive to consult and satisfy backbenchers. The availability of alternative partners in a multiparty environment limits the concessions a party can be compelled to make by coalition partners. The fact that key bargains are made through public, interparty agreements rather than in the secrecy of caucus raises MPs' consciousness of policy tradeoffs and discourages deals likely to provoke an electoral backlash.

Just as the clear-cut upward shift in popular cabinet support only produces an electoral base for governments near the majority level, so also the less certain parliamentary changes produced by PR are likely to fall far short of an encompassing consensus. As long as majority rule remains the formal requirement for enacting bills, inevitable policy conflicts combined with desires to limit claimants for distributive goods (notably ministerial portfolios) will produce a powerful pressure toward minimal winning coalitions. In short, by adopting MMP, New Zealand did not move towards consensus from majoritarianism, but instead shifted from pluralitarian towards majoritarian democracy.

The foregoing argument applies to PR generally, not just to MMP in New Zealand. Proportional representation and the effects that follow most closely from it—multiparty legislatures and coalition (and/or minority) govern-ments—are institutions of majoritarian, not consensus democracy. Only when coupled with other elements in Lijphart's consensus model—separation of powers, bicameralism, supermajority decision rules or consociational norms—will PR be associated with the more encompassing agreement that the term "consensus" normally implies. Within a unicameral parliamentary system, PR as compared with FPP represents a wider "range of parties and interests...in the policy process [and a] greater need to negotiate public poli-cies rather than merely imposing them." (Boston *et al.* 1996: 155) But the range of parties and interests included within the negotiated agreement is not likely to be much more than a majority. Recognizing this argument, Vowles *et al.* (1995: 206–207) write: "The notion linking majoritarianism and FPP is actually misleading. FPP decisions require a plurality (most over any other), not a majority (50 percent plus one)....PR makes it more likely that decision will be based on the preferences of 50 percent plus one."

Richard Katz (1997: 304–307) has independently reached a similar con-clusion. After a close reading of the *Report* of New Zealand's Royal Commission on the Electoral System, he takes issue with Lijphart's (1987) interpretation of it as "based on a general philosophical dislike of the under-lying Westminster principle of concentrating power in the hands of the major-ity and great sympathy for the contrasting consensus principle of sharing, dispersing, and limiting power." Instead, Katz contends the Commission

> ...was proposing an alternative institutionalization of popular sover-
> eignty, which is to say majoritarianism....[M]ost of the problems of
> Westminster democracy are attributed to governments that have less
> than majority support, not to those with bare majorities....The virtue
> of mixed-member proportional from [the Commission's] perspective
> is not that it makes coalitions more likely, but that it makes more
> likely that whatever government forms, whether single-party or
> coalition, will have received the votes of a majority of the electorate.

In light of this argument, we can better understand the contention of Richard Mulgan, who was himself a member of the Royal Commission, that the inspiration behind MMP was "counter-revolutionary." The Westminster system in New Zealand had traditionally been justified by a majoritarian, pop-ulist ideology (Vowles 1987), but when the experience of the 1970s and 1980s revealed how susceptible that system was to capture by groups much less than a majority (whether we see them as a plurality, a faction, or a ruling elite), Mulgan and his colleagues sought to restore majority rule through propor-tional representation.

The shift from plurality to majority may seem modest compared with New Zealand's supposed decision to move towards consensus democracy. Terminological accuracy nevertheless has the great virtue of avoiding the collapse of inflated hopes that a thorny reality will inevitably puncture. Majoritarianism is, after all, inherently adversarial, so it is not surprising that politics in New Zealand remain contentious.

Nevertheless, it is crucial to recognize the impact on policy of broadening a government's electoral base, even if only from 35 percent (in 1993) to 47 percent (in 1996). If New Zealand had used FPP for its 1996 election, survey data indicate the National Party would have been able to form a single-party government with an overwhelming 58.6 percent of seats based on a mere 38.1 percent of the popular vote (Vowles 1997). It then presumably could have continued its own policies without any electoral or parliamentary need to attend to the concerns of the remaining 61.9% of the electorate.

The policy concessions required by a broader popular cabinet support base are illustrated by the compromises the National Party was compelled to make in its Coalition Agreement with New Zealand First, notwithstanding the short life of that pact. Two social groups heavily represented among NZF voters were the elderly and Maori (Ganley 1997). To form a government, National had to make substantial concessions toward NZF policy with respect to both groups. For the elderly, the Coalition Agreement promised abolition of the superannuation surcharge, removal of means testing for long-stay geriatric services, and protections for the home equity of pensioners and nursing home residents. For Maori, the agreement promised to discontinue the hotly disputed "fiscal envelope" under which National had limited (to NZ$1 billion) the total payments it would accept as reparations for settlements ordered by the Waitangi Tribunal (which judges claims arising from violations of the 1840 treaty between Maori chiefs and the British). The agreement also included numerous other pro-Maori initiatives, and the coalition cabinet included three Maori members, including Winston Peters as Deputy Prime Minister and Treasurer. Beyond its appeal to those two groups, NZF had sought to stake out a general position as a center party, somewhat to the left of National. Accordingly, the agreement moderated economic and social policies at NZF's behest. The two parties pledged to reduce long-term unemployment, provide job-seekers with community work and training, increase funding for early-childhood education, restore the health system to a public service rather than commercial profit objective, increase health funding, freeze public-housing rents, raise welfare benefits, and address underlying causes of crime. These initiatives required a significant relaxation of National's previously stringent fiscal policy, with a delay in a planned tax reduction and additional expenditures totaling NZ$5 billion over three years.[6] In short, the substantive significance of a shift from pluralitarian to majoritarian democracy should not be slighted.

The relation between theory and practice must always be reciprocal. As in so many other places around the world, Arend Lijphart's contributions to democratic theory greatly influenced political reform in New Zealand. The fact that New Zealanders were not only inspired but also, to a degree, confused and disappointed by the concept of consensus democracy, together with the account offered here about what electoral reform actually meant in that country, suggests the value of modifying Lijphart's pioneering analysis of patterns of democratic government. Specifically, I suggest the following refinements:

- The conceptual spectrum should be extended to make explicit the possibility of submajoritarian patterns of rule within ostensibly democratic systems.

- In particular, it should be recognized that pure Westminster systems, although justified by majoritarian ideology and sometimes majoritarian in practice, are in their basic workings, pluralitarian.

- Closer attention should be paid to the character of intermediate systems, which in the extended spectrum include majoritarian democracies properly understood.

- Proportional representation per se, and its immediate effects, should no longer be seen as necessarily conducive to consensus democracy. Instead, as compared with first-past-the-post, PR fosters true majoritarianism.

Notes

I wish to thank Richard Chou for research assistance and Jonathan Boston, Paul Harris, André Kaiser, Richard Mulgan, and Jack Vowles for comments on an earlier draft.

[1]See Jackson (1993) for a discussion of other ways in which New Zealand has been evolving away from majoritarianism. He contends that electoral reform "will constitute the culminating point in emancipating the country from the Westminster-majoritarian model."

[2]Such a continuum is hardly a new idea in democratic theory. Compare Buchanan and Tullock (1962) and Mansbridge (1980).

[3]I suggest "factional" rather than "minority" (or Dahl's "minorities") rule because pluralities are also minorities.

[4]This widespread sentiment was probably the single strongest factor influencing voters to support electoral reform. Stephen Mills, a pollster and strategist for the pro-FPP Campaign for Better Government, commented after the referendum: "[The reformers'] best argument was that FPP allowed a small group in cabinet to do whatever they want. That was just a nuclear argument. If they'd used that with the level of ferocity we used our arguments, we'd

never have got within 25 or 30 points of them." (Interview with the author, Wellington, November 9, 1993.)

[5]If a minority government formed in a multiparty PR system, the popular cabinet support could be a smaller plurality, but to enact bills the governing party would require votes from another party or parties. In such cases, the relevant measure would be the sum of popular votes for parties in the legislating coalition, which might be called the *popular legislative support*.

[6]The Coalition Agreement is available at (http://www.knowledge.basket. co.nz/gpprint/coalition.html). See also Boston 1997.

References

Boston, Jonathan. 1997. "Coalition Formation." In Raymond Miller, ed., *New Zealand Politics in Transition*. Auckland: Oxford University Press.

Boston, Jonathan. 1998. *Governing under Proportional Representation: Lessons from Europe*. Wellington: Victoria University of Wellington, Institute of Policy Studies.

Boston, Jonathan, Stephen Levine, Elizabeth McLeay, and Nigel S. Roberts. 1996. *New Zealand Under MMP: A New Politics?* Auckland: Auckland University Press.

Boston, Jonathan, and Elizabeth McLeay. 1997. "Forming the First MMP Government: Theory, Practice and Prospects." In Jonathan Boston, Stephen Levine, Elizabeth McLeay, and Nigel S. Roberts, eds., *From Campaign to Coalition: New Zealand's First General Election under Proportional Representation*. Palmerston North, N.Z.: The Dunmore Press.

Buchanan, James, and Gordon Tullock. 1962. *The Calculus of Consent*. Ann Arbor: University of Michigan Press.

Crepaz, Markus M. L. 1996. "Consensus versus Majoritarian Democracy: Political Institutions and Their Impact on Macroeconomic Performance and Industrial Disputes." *Comparative Political Studies*. 29:1 (February), 4–26.

Electoral Commission. 1997. *The New Zealand Electoral Compendium*. Wellington.

Ganley, Marcus. 1997. "Who Voted for NZ First?" Paper presented to the New Zealand Political Studies Association Conference, Waikato University, Hamilton (June 6–8).

Harris, Paul, and Elizabeth McLeay. 1993. "The Legislature." In G. R. Hawke, ed., *Changing Politics: The Electoral Referendum 1993*. Wellington: Institute of Policy Studies.

Jackson, Keith. 1993. "Problems of Democracy in a Majoritarian System: New Zealand and Emancipation from the Westminster Model?" *The Round Table* 328 (October), 401–17.

Katz, Richard S. 1997. *Democracy and Elections*. New York: Oxford University Press.

Lijphart, Arend. 1984. *Democracies: Patterns of Majoritarian and Consensus Government in Twenty-One Countries*. New Haven: Yale University Press.

Lijphart, Arend. 1987. "The Demise of the Last Westminster System? Comments on the Report of New Zealand's Royal Commission on the Electoral System." *Electoral Studies* 6:2 (August), 97–104.

Lijphart, Arend. 1991. "Majority Rule in Theory and Practice: The Tenacity of a Flawed Paradigm." *International Political Science Review* 29, 483–93.

Mansbridge, Jane J. 1980. *Beyond Adversary Democracy*. New York: Basic Books.

Mulgan, Richard. 1995a. "The Westminster System and the Erosion of Democratic Legitimacy." In B. D. Gray and R. B. McClintock, eds., *Courts and Policy: Checking the Balance*. Wellington: Brooker's.

Mulgan, Richard. 1995b. "The Democratic Failure of Single Party Government: The New Zealand Experience." *Australian Journal of Political Science* 30 (Special Issue), 82–96.

Nagel, Jack H. 1994a. "Market Liberalization in New Zealand: The Interaction of Economic Reform and Political Institutions in a Pluralitarian Democracy." Paper presented at the 1994 Annual Meeting of the American Political Science Assn., New York.

Nagel, Jack H. 1994b. "What Political Scientists Can Learn from the 1993 Electoral Reform in New Zealand." *PS: Political Science & Politics* 27:3 (September), 525–29.

Nagel, Jack H. 1998. "Social Choice in a Pluralitarian Democracy: The Politics of Market Liberalization in New Zealand." *British Journal of Political Science* 28 (April), 223–67.

Palmer, Geoffrey. 1987. *Unbridled Power: An Interpretation of New Zealand's Constitution and Government*, second edition. Auckland: Oxford University Press.

Ralston, Bill. 1995. "Politics." *North & South*. 38–9.

Royal Commission on the Electoral System. 1986. *Report of the Royal Commission on the Electoral System: Towards a Better Democracy*. Wellington: V. R. Ward, Government Printer.

Temple, Philip. 1993. *Making Your Vote Count Twice*. Dunedin, NZ: McIndoe Publishers.

Thompson, G.W.F. 1994. "Coping with MMP." Speech to the Rotary Club of Auckland (14 November).

Vowles, Jack. 1987. "Liberal Democracy: Pakeha Political Ideology." *New Zealand Journal of History* 21, 215–27.

Vowles, Jack. 1991. "A Case for Electoral Reform." *The New Zealand Herald* (29 May 1991). Reprinted in Alan McRobie, ed., *Taking it to the People: The New Zealand Electoral Referendum Debate*. Christchurch: Hazard Press, 1993, 178–80.

Vowles, Jack. 1995. "The Politics of Electoral Reform in New Zealand." *International Political Science Review* 16:1 (January) 95–115.

Vowles, Jack. 1997. Communication to the author.

Vowles, Jack, Peter Aimer, Helena Catt, Jim Lamare, and Raymond Miller. 1995. *Towards Consensus? The 1993 Election in New Zealand and the Transition to Proportional Representation*. Auckland: Auckland University Press.

Vowles, Jack, Susan Banducci, and Jeffrey Karp. 1998. "Electoral System Opinion in New Zealand." New Zealand Election Study Mid-Term Survey, University of Waikato, August 5.

CHAPTER 7

The New South African Constitution:
A Case of Consensus Democracy?

Thomas A. Koelble

In his book *Democracies: Patterns of Majoritarian and Consensus Government in Twenty-One Countries*, as well as numerous other contributions, Arend Lijphart outlines the essential institutional features of two ideal-type democracies.[1] On the one hand, the conception of democracy, which holds that a true democracy is one in which a majority should rule, leads to the establishment of institutions that concentrate political decision-making powers with the political party representing this majority. On the other hand, the conception of democracy that holds that democracy is a governmental system in which as many people as possible should be included in the decision-making process leads to the establishment of institutions that diffuse political power and encourage coalition government. Majoritarianism is the guiding principle of governments such as those of Britain or, until very recently, New Zealand. Consensus democracy is the guiding principle of governmental institutions such as those found in Belgium and Switzerland.[2]

Lijphart argues that although majoritarian systems are suitable for homogeneous societies, they are likely to exacerbate divisions in heterogeneous or plural societies. Lijphart prescribes consensus democracy for such divided societies as a system better able to deal with conflict resulting from ethnic, language-based, religious, or socio-economic division than majoritarian rule.[3] Although there are some relatively homogeneous nation-states for which a majoritarian democracy may be advantageous, there are few societies that are not to some extent plural. Particularly newer, less established democratic systems in Asia, Africa, Eastern Europe, and Latin America have to contend with such plural societies and should therefore adopt consensus democracy. Majoritarianism could well lead to increased conflict since certain groups may find themselves disadvantaged in the struggles for scarce resources or have policies, particularly on cultural and educational issues, imposed on them against their will. The advantage of consensus systems is that their institutions provide multiple access points for minorities by instituting federalism or mechanisms such as power sharing at the executive and legislative levels of governance. Some consensus systems even provide minorities with veto rights over certain kinds of policies deemed to be crucial to the existence of the group. Segmental or cultural autonomy provide mechanisms for participation in decision-making and may avert conflict, confrontation, and unrest. In the worst case scenarios, majoritarian impositions of policy can lead to civil war and calls for secession by minority groups.[4]

To Lijphart, South Africa has been a case of great interest since it is a prototypical divided society, not only in terms of race, ethnicity, and language, but also of crass socio-economic disparity. Lijphart devoted *Powersharing in South Africa* and numerous articles to the proposition that South Africa ought to adopt a consensus-oriented system of government.[5] Lijphart's personal involvement in the South African debate provides a good example of how academic work can influence constitutional developments as well as how high the personal costs of such involvement can be. The political left in Europe interpreted Lijphart's involvement in the Buthelezi Commission of the early 1980s as a legitimization of the apartheid regime. The political right in South Africa misused the concepts and terms of Lijphart's suggestions to justify the continuation of apartheid after the constitutional reforms of 1983. This reform called into existence a tri-chamber parliamentary system that was portrayed as consociational by the apartheid government when it, in fact, was nothing of the sort.[6] Lijphart endured attacks on his work and character as a result of his involvement in the South African debate. This chapter assesses to what extent the new South African constitution of 1996 establishes a consensus democracy.

Institutions of a Consensus Democracy

A consensus democracy is, according to Lijphart, one in which eight majority-restraining elements can be found.[7] Not every one of these features is necessary to identify a system as consensus oriented, since various combinations between these features and majoritarian features are possible. However, the principle guiding a consensus democracy is that it aims to include as many diverse groups in the decision-making process as possible and that political power is shared among the contending groups. The eight institutional features are as follows: executive power sharing, the separation of powers, balanced bicameralism and minority representation, multiparty systems, a multidimensional party system, proportional representation, territorial and nonterritorial decentralization and federalism, and a written constitution and minority veto rights.

Executive Power Sharing

The first criterion, executive power sharing and a commitment to grand coalition government, was a subject of much acrimony and debate in South Africa. The nature of South Africa's transition, a negotiated settlement rather than the collapse of an authoritarian regime, necessitated a grand coalition government. The African National Congress (ANC) was not in a position to take over government forcefully from the National Party (NP), but the NP government was not in a position to deny the representatives of the black majority input into government decision-making.[8] The Government of National Unity (GNU), formed after the first general elections in April of 1994, was supposed to preside over the entire process of transformation until the year 1999 when the second full elections took place.[9] The GNU included the three major political parties—the ANC, the NP, and the Inkatha Freedom Party (IFP). Each party was given a number of cabinet portfolios and the coalition government survived until shortly after the first draft of the Constitution was completed in May of 1996. The NP withdrew from government arguing that it would be better served by opposing ANC policies than having to defend the ANC's actions.[10]

The new constitution does not expressly require coalition governments. The National Party was the only party that demanded such a constitutional ruling, arguing that parties representing various ethnic or racial groups should be given a constitutional right to representation in the cabinet. The ANC opposed any such mechanism, arguing instead that should the election produce a result where there is no clear parliamentary majority, only then should a coalition government come into existence. Further, some ANC negotiators suggested that a voluntary coalition government could be created if the majority party so desired.[11] The ANC took the position that a power-sharing clause in the constitution was not a negotiable item and the NP soon dropped its insistence on such a provision.

The ANC's position that power sharing at the executive level was not an option got support from academic circles. Defenders of majoritarian principles, such as Shapiro and Jung, argued that such an arrangement might only freeze the current political constellation and provide apartheid's supporters with a security blanket they did not deserve.[12] Such arguments echoed the sentiments of the Pan Africanist Congress, which also suggested that power sharing between ANC and the NP would be an unacceptable situation for its members and voters since it provided the perpetrators of apartheid government power. Clarence Makwetu, then leader of the PAC, expressed his delight with the constitution precisely because it did not afford the NP with a mandated slice of governmental power.[13]

There are few consensus democracies that actually require coalition governments in their constitutions. Belgium and Switzerland represent the closest approximations to the ideal-type consensus democracy, but even in the Swiss case coalition government is an informal rule in the composition of the Federal Council rather than a formal requirement.[14] The Belgian constitution requires that equal numbers of Dutch- and French-speaking ministers comprise the government, but Belgium provides an exceptional case. Most consensus democracies rely on the electoral mechanism and proportional representation to produce parliaments in which a governing coalition must be forged to support cabinet decisions in the legislature.

Given that the ANC is likely to be a majority party for a number of years, it is unlikely that it is going to be forced to coalesce with other, smaller parties because of electoral reasons. There are simply no sizable parties with constituencies that could possibly hope to challenge the ANC's electoral base at this point. The ANC leadership may choose to seek coalition partners to form oversized coalitions, as it has done throughout 1996 to 1999 and, again, after the 1999 elections. However, such a consensus-seeking gesture is a discretionary power. Only if the party should disintegrate into a number of competing political parties, will it be possible to imagine a situation of coalition governments due to electoral pressures.

Separation of Powers

The new constitution provides for a parliamentary form of government in which the cabinet is dependent upon the confidence of its legislative branch of government. Chapter 5 of the constitution stipulates that Parliament, in its first session after a general election, must elect a President. The President then selects a cabinet. Cabinet members are accountable to both the President and Parliament. There is no formal separation of powers between legislature and executive, and in this sense the institutional arrangement is much more akin to the Westminster system than to the Swiss system, for instance, where the Federal Council is protected from the legislature.

Lijphart distinguishes between formal and informal mechanisms by which a separation of power is achieved.[15] A formal separation of powers defines the U.S. system of governance in which the constitution clearly sets up the legislative and executive branches as independent units. A presidential system separates legislative and executive powers rather than fusing power as cabinet governments do. Presidents are elected for a fixed term and by either a popular election or through an Electoral College as in the U.S. case. Despite the fact that South Africa has a president, he or she is elected by Parliament, as a Prime Minister would be. South Africa is therefore a parliamentary and not a presidential system.

An informal way of achieving such separation of powers is to have a parliament consisting of many different political parties and large and/or non-cohesive coalitions. Such an informal separation of powers is again unlikely to occur in South Africa as long as competitive political parties do not fundamentally challenge the ANC's electoral dominance. In other words, on both the issue of power sharing and separation of powers the new South African constitution tends towards majoritarianism rather than consensus democracy. However, a movement towards consensus democracy is conceivable if and when more political parties become viable electoral entities and the parliamentary distribution of power shifts away from the dominant position the ANC currently holds.

Balanced Bicameralism

The third criterion for consensus democracy is balanced bicameralism and minority representation as opposed to unicameralism. On this dimension the South African constitution is clearly more in the consensus rather than in the majoritarian camp. Parliament is divided into a National Assembly and a National Council of Provinces. Clearly the National Assembly is the most important chamber in the sense that all national legislation will be passed in this forum. However, the Council of Provinces has veto powers over legislation directly affecting the provinces, although it is again a question of praxis to determine precisely how much autonomy the provinces will have in decision-making. The section governing the relationship between provincial and national government set out in Chapter 3 of the constitution is quite vague and general. The first constitutional draft was rejected by the Constitutional Court in September of 1996 largely because the judges felt that the provinces were not given sufficient powers and that the jurisdiction of these nine provinces was so unclear as to require further definition.[16] Although the new constitution passed the judges' muster in November, provincial rights will undoubtedly be a subject of some contentiousness and litigation in the future.

The reason why provincial powers were so limited and undefined in the first constitutional draft was that the ANC leadership was quite opposed to the possibility of strong provincial government. However, the champion of federal decentralization, the Inkatha Freedom Party, isolated itself from the negotiations around the constitution and therefore had no impact on the federalism sections of the document.[17]

The National Council of Provinces consists of 10 delegates selected by the legislatures of the provinces. Four of these are "special delegates" including, if and when available, the premier of the province. Six delegates are permanently appointed. The selection of these delegates raises some questions as to their legitimacy since the provincial parliament and not the electorate selects them. Further, every province will have only one vote, so unanimity is expected of the provincial delegation even if it should consist of members from rival political parties. As Humphries and Meierhenrich argue, it is, at this point, unclear exactly what role the Council of Provinces is likely to play and it remains to be seen whether the second chamber will be truly coequal in stature to the National Assembly.[19]

Multiparty System

The 1994 elections resulted in seven political parties being represented in the National Assembly. The ANC was by far the largest party with 252 of the 400 seats and 62.65 percent of the vote. The IFP occupied 43 seats based on 10.5 percent of the vote and formed part of the governing coalition. The National Party (NP) with 82 seats (and 20.3 percent of the vote) left the GNU in 1996 and became the largest opposition party. It was followed by the Afrikaner-based Freedom Front (FF) with 9 seats, the Democratic Party (DP) with 7 seats, the Pan African Congress (PAC) with 5 seats and the African Christian Democratic Party (ACDP) with 2 seats.

The 1999 elections saw a disintegration of the NP's constituency, the mete-oric rise of the DP, and a net gain in the vote for the ANC. Both the parties to

TABLE 7.1   Results of the South African National Assembly Elections, 2 June 1999

Party	National Percentage of Vote		Seats in National Assembly	
	1994	1999	1994	1999
ANC	62.6	65.6	252	266
NP	20.3	6.8	82	28
IFP	10.5	8.5	43	34
FF	2.1	0.8	9	3
DP	1.7	9.5	7	38
PAC	1.2	0.7	5	3
ACDP	0.4	1.4	3	6
AEB		0.2		1
APO		0.1		1
FA		0.5		2
MF	0.07	0.3		1
UCDP		0.7		3
UDM		3.4		14

(AEB — Afrikaner Eenheids Beweging (Afrikaner Unity Movement); APO — Azanian Peoples' Organization; FA — Federal Alliance; MF — Minority Front; UCDP — United Christian Democratic Party; UDM — United Democratic Movement.)

Source: Adapted from Electoral Institute of South Africa (EISA), *Election Update 99*, No. 14, 12. June 1999, p. 17–18.

the right of the NP and to the left of the ANC were decimated. While the rightist FF and the leftist PAC each lost votes, they retained some representation in the National Assembly with 3 seats each. The ANC carried the elections with an overwhelming 66.35 percent of the vote. It received 266 seats in the 400 strong National Assembly. The DP was able to overtake the NP as the main opposition party with 9.5 percent of the vote and received 38 seats. The NP slipped to 6.8 percent of the vote, thereby retaining only 28 seats. The IFP slipped to 8.5 percent and 34 seats. The party, however, remained part of the governing coalition. Numerous smaller parties achieved representation. One of these parties, the Minority Front, ceded its seat to the ANC after the elections giving the governing party a two-thirds majority in the Assembly. The ACDP was able to increase its share of the vote from 0.45 to 1.4 percent of the vote and increased its parliamentary delegation to six. The UDM with 14 seats and 3.4 percent of the vote achieved the most spectacular result amongst the newcomers.

Although South Africa's party system is definitely a multiparty one, one large party also dominates it. The ANC's electoral weight vis-à-vis the other parties is overwhelming. Unlike most European consensus democracies where many parties of relatively equal electoral strength compete with each other for votes and governmental power, South Africa's party system is essentially a one-party dominance system. Pempel and others have investigated one-party systems in Israel, Sweden, Italy, and Japan but unlike these political systems where other parties did eventually wrest political power from the dominant party, the electoral swing necessary to do so in South Africa is enormous.[20] We might be encouraged by speculation that the ANC's dominance is temporary and due to the overriding electoral factor in 1994—the ANC stood for liberation and a break with the apartheid regime. Although this electoral bonus still applied in the 1999 elections, it is doubtful whether this advantage will last much beyond the next election. Various opposition parties might well emerge from within the ANC's wide antiapartheid mantle should the government fail to deliver its electoral promises.

Multidimensional Party System

The South African party system is a multidimensional one. Lijphart lists seven possible issue dimensions along which political parties might form: socioeconomic, religious, cultural-ethnic, rural-urban, regime support, foreign policy, and post-materialism. Although the last three dimensions do not play much of a role in South African politics—there is neither a significant Green Party nor one that opposes South Africa's new regime or foreign policy—Lipset and Rokkan's four fundamental cleavages exist and have played a role in producing political parties.[21] The overriding cleavage in South Africa, however, is the racial division that plays into the other dimensions of partisan conflict.

The religious cleavage is perhaps the least important in terms of party formation. The small ACDP, despite its small parliamentary representation, does, however, draw on a rather large potential constituency. The growth of various evangelical churches in South Africa, particularly among Black South Africans, has been remarkable over the last decade. Though most of these religious groups and their followers voted for the ANC, the religious groups oppose the ANC's abortion policy. Although abortion was virtually illegal under apartheid, the ANC adopted a very liberal policy that allows abortion on demand within the first trimester. Religious affiliations also play a role in the predominantly white political parties. The NP, for instance, has been inextricably linked to the Dutch Reformed Church and the smaller Reformed Churches active within the Afrikaner community. These churches played a major role in the promulgation of the apartheid doctrine. They provided biblical justifications for the system of racial separation. They were also instrumental in bringing about a reconsideration of the morality of apartheid during the 1980s when the Dutch Reformed Church admitted that apartheid was, after all, a sin.[22] However, some of the more conservative clergy adopted the position that ethnic and racial separation is natural and sanctioned by God, and formed the Afrikaanse Protestantse Kerk.[23]

The rural-urban dimension of partisan conflict is also prevalent in South Africa, but especially so in KwaZulu/Natal. The IFP's electoral strongholds are in the most rural areas of KwaZulu where traditional leaders still hold sway over their communities. The ANC has taken an ambivalent position on the issue of traditional leadership. On the one hand, it has accepted that most rural communities (not just those in KwaZulu/Natal) are structured in such a way that the chiefs and headmen have a great deal of power over the rural population. In order to bind the chiefs and headmen to the government and state, the ANC introduced a controversial parliamentary act in which headmen and chiefs are to be paid by the central government.[24] Opponents of this plan argue that it is designed to establish a patronage relationship between nonelected local community leaders and the central state. Others, such as the IFP, suggest that the plan represents a strategy to undermine the IFP's electoral stronghold in KwaZulu/Natal's rural regions. On the other hand, there are many voices inside the ANC who argue that traditional leadership is patriarchal, out-dated, and that it represents a backward aspect of African traditions that ought to be overcome in a modern state and economy.[25] The ANC is essentially a modernist party. It views such traditional structures with suspicion, especially since they are tainted by the fact that traditional leadership was based upon the homelands concept that provided the foundation for the apartheid regime.

The conditions in KwaZulu/Natal, where ANC, IFP and United Democratic Movement (UDM) sympathizers are still engaged in a low level civil war, have led some observers to believe that ethnic conflict is at the heart

of the confrontation. The ANC is often seen as a political movement dominated by Xhosas, whereas the IFP was a Zulu cultural movement and now represents Zulus in KwaZulu/Natal as well as Zulu migrants in the urban areas.[26]
However, the ANC-IFP confrontations in the province involve mainly Zulu
activists on different sides of the political fence. Ethnicity plays a defining
role in the FF and IFP's political self-understanding, but again is not the only
factor at work in party formation or allegiance.

Ethnicity plays a much more important role in township politics, divisions within the labor forces of various firms and mining operations where
frequently new migrants of one particular ethnicity live together in com-
pounds. Such newly arrived migrants often find themselves in competition
with township dwellers or squatters over various scarce resources, and in these
situations ethnicity then plays an important role in mobilization.[27] There are
also indications that frequently, confrontations in the townships between long-
term residents and squatters involve ethnicity since the long-term residents
tend to be of one ethnic group, whereas the newcomers are often from another
area of the country.[28]

The socio-economic division between the races, but also among the various ethnic and linguistic groups, is highly salient in party allegiances. The
ANC is clearly the political party representing the urban poor, workers, and
others disadvantaged by the colonial and apartheid regimes, even though these
groups are often in conflict at the local level. Resentments by established,
working class township residents against squatters and the unemployed pau-
pers frequently lead to confrontations. Yet, the very nature of the party as an
alliance between the trade unions, the South African Communist Party
(SACP), and the various social movements (United Democratic Front (UDF),
South African National Civics Organization (SANCO), South African
Students Organization (SASO) to name a few) suggests that it has succeeded,
so far, to plaster over this fragmented class base.[29] The party united those
opposed to apartheid and that, not surprisingly, constituted an overwhelming
majority of black South Africans. Its electoral appeal is based on promises of
socio-economic betterment for the vast majority of South Africa's citizenry.[30]
In the 1994 elections the party obtained some 94 percent of its support from
black South African voters, 4 percent from Colored voters in the Western
Cape (some 0.5 million votes), 1.5 percent from the Indian community
(150,000 votes), and another 0.5 percent from white South Africans (50,000
voters).[31] The 1999 elections yielded similar results.

In contrast to the black electorate, white South Africans, colored, and
Indian voters are quite fragmented in their voting behavior. Although the FF
could rely on an exclusively ethnic base amongst Afrikaners, the National
Party finds itself straddling a rather interesting divide.[32] Erstwhile the party of
apartheid, Afrikaner nationalism, and racial segregation, now finds itself

being supported by a large number of colored voters in the Western Cape on whom the party depends if it wants to hold onto the only provincial government it is still part of. There is a fierce debate among electoral behavioralists as to the motives of the colored population. Some argue that Cape Coloreds, who speak Afrikaans, associated with their linguistic group despite the long years of oppression at the hands of Afrikaner nationalists. Others argue that Cape Coloreds, who hold better jobs than black South Africans in the Cape Province, voted for the NP for socioeconomic reasons rather than linguistic ones. Others again suggest that Cape Coloreds voted against the ANC because they feared an ANC government in the province that would steer patronage opportunities and other benefits to the African rather than the Colored communities. Robert Mattes argues that class, ideology, and expectations of future government performance explain voting behavior among Cape Coloreds much better than essentially ethnic or racial explanations.[33]

The NP suffered a humiliating defeat in the 1999 elections. While the colored community in the Western Cape remained largely loyal to the party (although there were significant defections to both the DP and ANC), much of its white Afrikaner constituency deserted it. These Afrikaners voted for the DP. The DP ran a confrontational campaign against the ANC stressing the government's failures in terms of crime prevention and corruption. The NP's campaign was a lackluster affair reflecting the internal confusion of the party. The DP was successful in moving away from its rather narrow electoral base among white, affluent, and English-speaking voters. The party was able to win numerous white and Afrikaans-speaking voters and scored impressive electoral victories in some of the most ardently conservative, NP strongholds. Even in the Western Cape, the DP was able to woo votes away from the NP. While the good news, so to speak, was that the political right suffered tremendous electoral losses, the bad news is that the electorate appears to still be racially divided.

The 1994 elections may not afford us a true picture of the ethnic and other divisions in South African society since the election was really about one issue—the end of the apartheid regime.[34] This circumstance tended to unite the black South African electorate and split the white South African electorate into competing parties—one supportive of the change (DP), one defending its change of heart and mind (NP), and one opposing the transformation (FF). Although the classic Lipset and Rokkan model does help to describe the formation of South Africa's party system, each party has ethnic, cultural, racial, religious, urban-rural, and socio-economic dimensions to its electoral appeal. South Africa's political party system is therefore one that does not easily collapse into the categories outlined.

The 1999 election result only reaffirmed the huge electoral advantage of the ANC in relation to all other parties. The party was able to extend its constituency and held off all challengers to its left such as the PAC and

APO. Both of these parties campaigned on a perceived weakness of the ANC—that the delivery of houses, jobs, social and other services had not been met as promised. While the ANC consolidated its electorate, no strong opposition to the party emerged from the contending parties. Although the DP was able to increase its share of the vote in spectacular style, none of the opposing parties reached the 10 percent mark. In other words, the electoral hegemony of the ANC remains unchallenged and is likely to remain that way for a number of elections raising the specter of a one-party dominant system as predicted by Giliomee and Simkins.[35]

It remains to be seen whether other competitive parties will emerge, particularly from within the ANC. Not only has the ANC been able to cobble together diverse interest groups, political movements, and distinct political parties under its wide antiapartheid umbrella, it has also been able to downplay socio-economic, linguistic, cultural, and ethnic divisions under its "nonracialism" policy. How far the ANC is able to continue to do so is a question of some importance for the future trajectory of South Africa's party system and democracy.

Proportional Representation

A consensus-oriented feature of the new constitution is the adoption of proportional representation. Proportional representation was used in the 1994 and 1999 general elections. South Africa is a single constituency with between 350 and 400 representatives. The electorate then casts its votes and parties are provided seats on a proportional basis, much like the Dutch system. Although the issue was raised on several occasions during the constitutional debates whether South Africa should not adopt a mixed system of proportional party and direct constituency representation such as the German system, lawmakers retained the proportional-representation-only system.[36] The constitution stipulates that the choice of electoral systems is to be taken by an Act of Parliament.

Although proportional representation is, according to Lijphart, a central mechanism of any consensus democracy, the way in which the central party controls the placement of potential representatives on the party lists should also be an important aspect of democratic and participatory politics. In this case the ANC's central leadership exercises a great deal of influence over the positioning of various preferred candidates on the provincial lists. The ANC also insisted that a representative who "crosses the floor" from one party to another loses his or her seat. The party has the right to fill the vacant position with another representative from within its ranks and the defector loses the seat. This ensures that defections from one party to another are kept at a minimum. A politician risks his or her political career when contemplating such a move unless the other party assures the defector of a high list placement in the next election. In other words, the list system provides the central party leadership with a great deal of power over candidates and their political careers.[37]

Territorial and Nonterritorial Federalism and Decentralization

South Africa is a federal republic, but the issue of provincial powers and the relationship between federal and provincial government was perhaps the most difficult and contentious issue of the constitutional writing process. The debate over federalism took a back seat because the IFP decided to withdraw from the constitutional deliberations, but that did not diminish the importance of the decisions taken. The ANC's attempt to greatly reduce and limit provincial powers when compared to those of the central government were dealt a blow by the rejection of the draft constitution by the Constitutional Court in September of 1996.[38] The court insisted that provincial powers would not only have to be extended to approximate the original intention of the interim constitution, but they needed to be clearly defined.

The powers of the provinces are, nevertheless, rather limited. Although the final constitution grants the provinces more powers over the local police forces, the provinces have exclusive power only over such issues as abattoirs, roads and traffic, ambulances, recreation and amenities, and sports; hardly policy areas of great controversy. When the Constitutional Court finally accepted the constitution as compatible with the interim constitution in December of 1996, the court found that the powers of the provinces had, in fact, been reduced when compared to those granted by the interim constitution.[39] However, the court decided that although provincial rights were less than before, they had not been fundamentally weakened and the reductions were such that the spirit of the interim constitution had not been violated.

Written Constitution and Minority Veto

South Africa now has, of course, a written constitution. Although it does not provide minority groups with veto powers, the constitution contains an unusually long Bill of Rights. Unlike the U.S. Bill of Rights, the South African version is part of the constitution and constitutes the entire second chapter of the document. This Bill of Rights guarantees South African citizens a myriad of rights ranging from the freedom of speech, movement, association, and equality, to a slew of socio-economic rights such as housing, health, education, food and water, sewer, electricity, and social security. However, these rights are "ideal" rights rather than actual ones since the preamble to the list of rights states that the courts and the state can limit these rights. Constitutional lawyers distinguish between first, second, and third generation rights, which introduces the notion of a "rights hierarchy." The government is, for instance, not obliged to house every citizen. Nor is it under an obligation to provide water, sewer, or electricity to everyone. Rather, the Bill of Rights portrays an ideal situation in which the state commits itself to attempting to provide such services. Other rights, such as those to free speech, association, and so forth are considered first generation rights and inviolable by the state.

To safeguard that these rights are also respected, particularly by the state, the constitution calls into existence several watchdog agencies, which are there, along with the courts, to monitor the actions of the state and government. The Commission for the Promotion and Protection of the Rights of Cultural, Religious, and Linguistic Communities is a rather unique institution that was called into being as an attempt to mollify the Afrikaner Freedom Front. The FF threatened to use the schooling issue to mobilize Afrikaner opposition to the constitution and demanded a constitutional right to educate pupils in Afrikaans. This commission provides a platform from which to defend the rights of such communities to their culture and language. The Human Rights Commission, the Commission for Gender Equality, the Electoral Commission, the Public Protector (formerly known as the Ombudsman), the Auditor General, and the Independent Broadcasting Authority are all agencies designed to assist individuals and groups in bringing cases of alleged discrimination before the courts. They also mediate disputes as the Human Rights Commission has already done on numerous occasions concerning schooling policies.

Contextualizing the Constitution

Lijphart uses Dahl's concept of polyarchy to define conditions that have to be present before it can be argued that a democracy exists. If the following eight conditions are not met, democracy cannot be said to exist:

- Freedom to form associations and organizations
- Free speech
- The secret ballot and voting rights for all citizens
- Eligibility for public office
- The right of political leaders to compete for support and votes
- Alternative sources of information
- Fair and free elections
- Popularly elected institutions for policy-making[40]

Undoubtedly, the new South African constitution guarantees these institutional foundations of polyarchy, and much more. However, it should also not be forgotten that South Africa emerged from a long period of authoritarian government, of political turmoil, even civil war only in the last few years, and some of these rights and concepts are still very much in question. The country finds itself in a process in which these rights are given substance in both theory and political praxis.

The concept of fair and free elections is an appropriate test case of such "democratic substance." Johnson and Schlemmer's edited volume *Launching Democracy in South Africa* presents a well-balanced assessment of the question whether the April 1994 general elections were indeed fair and free.[41] Although all of the participant observers agree that the elections held have been partially fair and free, the context within which the elections were held are somewhat more troubling. Most, if not all voters, were able to participate and cast their vote in secrecy. However, it is not so certain if one can speak of an unfettered right to form and join associations, of free speech, of various sources of information in some of the townships across the country.

Goetz and Shaw present an analysis of township electioneering that complicates the assessment of the concept of polyarchy in South Africa.[42] The authors suggest that although township residents were able to rely on a broad range of organizations for information, campaigning for political parties, which did not control a certain territorial space, was quite difficult. In some areas, election posters did not signal a normal political campaign but indicated territorial boundaries. Political information was not freely available for all residents from all the political parties since it proved to be difficult for rival parties to distribute their materials in hostile environments. In areas controlled by the IFP, ANC campaigners were not tolerated, and vice versa. NP and DP candidates had an even harder time campaigning in the townships and frequently took to distributing their campaign materials from the air, which only reinforced the impression that the "white parties" did not care to know about conditions on the ground in the townships. Township politics is far removed from the ideal of democratic politics in the sense that open and participatory debates take place and that rival points of view can be openly discussed without candidates being intimidated.

The issue of township politics and electioneering raises wider questions about the nature of the regime change in South Africa. In a perceptive article, Richard Joseph suggests that the current wave of democratization in Africa is a highly precarious one.[43] Since many of the preconditions for democracy such as a certain level of economic development, certain sets of cultural values and support from broad social groups are not present or only marginally so, many third-world democracies are "virtual democracies" rather than actual ones. Joseph suggests that such virtual democratic systems display some institutional forms akin to democracy, but the balance of economic and social power is such that the representative institutions do not determine issues such as fundamental economic policy. Joseph suggests that given time and favorable conditions, such virtual democracies may develop into real democracies, but that they are just as likely to revert to some form of autocratic, even dictatorial system.[44] Such a development is likely if the new democracy fails to bring about socio-economic betterment for the vast majority of the citizenry. Although South Africa certainly possesses the economic basis for a democratic system, the ANC does face many obstacles in bringing about fundamental socio-economic change. Though we can imagine a situation in which South African democracy takes root and produces social policies designed to address the injustices of the past, it is also imaginable that failures to produce such socio-economic betterment will lead to disenchantment, demobilization, nonparticipation, and corruption. Such a vicious cycle has taken hold in numerous other would-be democracies.

The 1999 elections took place in a far calmer atmosphere than the 1994 elections. They would indicate that South Africa had embarked on a virtuous rather than the vicious cycle outlined by Joseph. Although the townships were still difficult terrain for some parties to campaign in, and there were some political assassinations in the Western Cape and in KwaZulu/Natal prior to the election, the elections were held to be fair and free by all observers and participants. In fact, the election was as routine as elections in established democracies, with few procedural or organizational hiccups. If they are a portend of development to come, South African democracy can be held to be securely founded in both principle and action. But one election does not a democracy make! Several other developments have to coincide with the institutionalization of fair and free elections.

Polyarchy and the Internal Politics of the ANC

Questions concerning free speech, the powers of provincial government and the ANC's provincial substructures, the right to join associations, and concepts of intraparty debate are currently at the core of some of the most severe problems facing the ANC political leadership. In four of the seven ANC-controlled provinces, the ANC's national leadership intervened either to remove problematic ANC local leaders (even premiers of provinces) or to back its chosen leaders against a grassroots revolt among the membership.[45] In the Free State, the former antiapartheid and UDF leader Patrick "Terror" Lekota was removed from his position of State Premier and made a Senator. The ANC leadership imposed Dr. Ivy Matepe-Casaburri as Premier on a rather unwilling provincial party. The preceding story is a tortuous one involving charges and counter-charges of corruption in the state party involving both Lekota and his rivals for the leadership of the provincial party. After the 1999 elections, Matepe-Casaburri was also replaced by the relatively unknown Winkie Direko. In the Eastern Cape the party leadership persuaded the

Premier, Raymond Mhlaba, to step down in favor of the leadership's chosen candidate, Alfred Stofile.

In June 1997 an attempt was made to remove the ANC's Northern Province premier, Ngoako Ramathlodi, from office. At first, the ANC's national leadership persuaded all of Ramathlodi's rivals to stand down but then changed its mind to support another rival, George Mashamba, to replace Ramathlodi as chair of the provincial party.[46] Although Ramathlodi held onto his position as premier he was forced to purge his cabinet of a number of office holders who were alleged to have squandered public funds.[47] There are also reports that Ramathlodi's removal from his position as chair of the provincial party has an ethnic dimension to it since he was backed by the Pedi, whereas his rival was backed by an alliance of Shangaan and Venda chiefs. These chiefs have, in some cases, signed up entire villages to the ANC. The provincial ANC depends on their continued support if it is to retain political power in the region.[48]

In Gauteng, by far the most prosperous and important of provinces, the popular premier, Tokyo Sexwale, was persuaded not to stand against Thabo Mbeki in his bid to become President Mandela's successor. Sexwale, widely believed to be a future presidential candidate, has since declared his intention to withdraw from politics and, like the ANC's chief constitutional negotiator and former trade union leader Cyril Ramaphosa, join the world of business.[49] Mathole Motshekga, who won the support of the provincial party and defeated the candidate favored by Thabo Mbeki, the Reverend Frank Chicane, replaced Sexwale. Yet, Moshekga never gained the confidence of the party leadership and, in turn, was replaced after the 1999 elections by Sam Shilowa as premier of South Africa's richest and most important province. Shilowa was the leader of the trade union movement, COSATU, after Ramaphosa's departure and is considered a close ally of Mbeki's.[50]

Although none of these personnel-related issues are a direct challenge to the constitution or democracy as such, they point to some rather interesting tensions between democratic theory and its praxis within the ANC itself. One of the dimensions of the power struggles within the party is the relationship between central party and the provincial organizations. The ANC struggles with the issue of how much power to decentralize to the various organizations. The tendency so far has been to centralize rather than decentralize policy and personnel decision-making. Although many party organizations insist on central decision-making, the ANC is not a conventional party with central, hierarchical structures, but an alliance of organizations ranging from the trade unions to the South African Communist Party. This organizational structure and history does not bode well for a top-down decision-making style.

What is clearly the case is that the ANC is itself having troubles adjusting from being a liberation movement to a democratically organized political party.

As a liberation movement the ANC was essentially an umbrella organization containing numerous organizations and groups. Tensions between these rather diverse groups and between exiles who returned to South Africa and those who were active in the United Democratic Front are commonplace within the ANC. The events surrounding Patrick Lekota is just one example of frictions between former UDF members such as Lekota and his "exile" adversaries. The economic and social policy reversals of the ANC, particularly in terms of the scaling down of the Reconstruction and Development Program (RDP), since coming into office exacerbated these conflicts. Some populists argue that it is time to reverse 300 years of colonial and apartheid rule. In contrast, most members of the governing elite caution against large-scale social and economic experiments. Faced with mounting internal criticisms, the ANC leadership has adopted a fairly heavy-handed approach to its internal critics. Even its external critics have not been spared. At various press conferences, newspaper editors were also asked to "cut the government some slack." After all, the media had gotten what it wanted, as one government official put it—democracy. They should now stop criticizing the government's actions at every turn![51]

The new constitution finds itself in a still rather precarious environment. South Africa's economic situation and its domestic political stability are still in a process of adjustment and far from settled. To deal with unemployment, grave social needs in housing, education, health services, and the provision of basic infrastructure to large parts of the country, the ANC needs resources. However, it finds itself in an international environment that does not favor redistributive action in the domestic sphere. Further, to address domestic socio-economic inequalities is part and parcel of the set of expectations that the ANC's voters have of the new government, the new political system and the new leadership. Democracy is, to many people, an effort to redistribute resources. This places the ANC in an unenviable position of having to please a number of pipers whose interests are diametrically opposed, yet whose support the ANC desperately needs to keep its electoral majority together and to ensure economic growth to generate the resources for distributive programs.

The Role of the ANC as Agent of Democratization

Lijphart argues that consensus democracies are designed to restrain the majority by requiring or encouraging the sharing of power, the dispersal of power, a fair distribution of power, a delegation of power, and a formal limit on power.[52] These criteria are as much institutional rules and organizational structures as they are a question of political praxis and a definition of what democratic rule is all about. Given the overwhelming electoral position the ANC currently occupies in South African politics, it is up to this party and its underlying mass movement to institute democratic praxis. Not only does the

ANC represent the majority of voters, but also it is up to the party to ensure that South Africa remains on the path to a consensus democracy.

Lijphart himself has argued that he views the South African interim constitution as essentially a consensus-oriented one.[53] Since, except for the power-sharing provision, this interim constitution has guided the constitutional process towards the new document, it would be quite obvious to argue that South Africa has a consensus-oriented democratic regime. The point I would like to make is that political practice should be given a higher value-ranking in the assessment and categorization of the South African situation, or indeed any so-called democratic regime, than the institutional shell within which politics is conducted. Although institutions undoubtedly shape, sometimes even determine, the actions and preferences of politicians, as I have argued in earlier work on social democracy, institutions also reflect the interests of the dominant political actors and can be shaped to meet the perceived needs of these actors.[54]

As should have already become clear in the previous sections, on a number of issues the actions of the ANC become important markers of future development. Perhaps the most important issue is how the ANC defines and carries out its role as chief agent of the democratization process. The commitment to a constitutional process, open political debate concerning certain policy issues, heightened access to government information, the extension of the electoral process to all citizens, and the constitution itself indicate that the ANC is seriously committed to democratization. However, the ANC's rather heavy-handed approach to intraparty dissenters cast some doubt over this commitment to openness and participation.

South Africa's path towards a consensus democracy is very much linked to the future trajectory of the ANC as a political party from its origins as a liberation movement. Should the ANC's political fortunes produce a number of rival political parties, a movement towards coalition government and a greater separation of powers at the national level might occur. Similarly, we could then, with good conscience, talk of a truly multidimensional and multiparty party system. However, the ANC is obviously attempting to overcome internal division. It remains to be seen whether the sometimes rather heavy-handed actions against internal dissenters will produce the desired effect—party unity—or whether it will encourage the unintended consequence—internal fragmentation and breakaway parties. There are already signs that the disgruntled factions around popular but expelled leaders such as Bantu Holomisa or out-of-favor leaders such as Winnie Madikizela-Mandela might be able to mobilize significant sections of the electorate.

There is certainly room for a populist movement, which might appeal to the poorest sections of the townships, and squatter camps on the grounds that the ANC has not delivered the "promised goods" fast enough. Should such a fragmentation occur, the path towards a consensus democracy is only safeguarded if conditions at the local level improve in terms of the freedom of electioneering, campaigning, and the dissemination of information. It is, however, just as likely that the emergence of such a party will lead to increased confrontations and conflict along ethnic and class lines. A replication of the violent clashes between the ANC, IFP, and various other groups such as the PAC or the Azanian People's Organization are then quite likely.

South Africa: A Case of Consensus Democracy?

There is certainly some potential for South Africa to develop a consensus democracy. The constitution and the political institutions it calls into existence allow for the development of consensus-oriented political praxis. This essay has focused only on the major political party in South Africa, the ANC, to highlight some of the quite formidable obstacles still in the path of such a democratic system. I have done so because the ANC is, by far, the most important agent of the democratization process since the other political parties are either tainted by their past or are simply too small to determine which path the country is likely to take. I have also avoided a debate on external factors although South Africa's political development is related to its economic trajectory which, in turn, is connected to external markets, the perceptions of the international business, banking, and trading communities.

The point the article intends to make is that the substance of consensus-oriented politics is still very much at stake in this case. The actions of the ANC leadership in terms of filling the concepts of democracy with meaning and substance is, in my mind, as important a process in determining the shape of democratic interaction and politics as is the institutional arrangement. The constitution writers of South Africa have achieved something rather remarkable. They have been at the center of a process of transformation as well as reconciliation in a country in which conditions for either appeared to be rather limited. Now the question is how this constitution and its principles are to be implemented and transformed from a text into a reality. It is too early to tell at this point whether this process will produce a consensus democracy, even if the institutions and political structures called into existence by the constitution point in that direction.

Notes

[1]Arend Lijphart. 1984. *Democracies: Patterns of Majoritarian and Consensus Government in Twenty-One Countries*. New Haven: Yale University Press. See also A. Lijphart, "Democratic Political Systems: Types, Cases, Causes and Consequences. *Journal of Theoretical Politics*, Vol. 1, No. 1, January 1989.

[2]Lijphart, 1984: 3–4.

[3]See also A. Lijphart. 1977. *Democracy in Plural Societies*. New Haven: Yale University Press, pp. 177–222.

[4]See Lijphart, 1977: 41–52.

[5]Arend Lijphart. 1985. *Powersharing in South Africa*. Berkeley: Institute for International Studies.

[6]Laurence Boulle. 1983. *Constitutional Reform and the Apartheid State*. New York: St. Martin's Press, presents an in-depth analysis of consociationalism and the South African constitution of 1983 to dispel the notion that consociationalism was or could be the intellectual and theoretical foundation for that regime.

[7]Lijphart, 1984: 23.

[8]There are several excellent accounts of the South African transition in the late 1980s and early 1990s. See, for instance, Timothy Sisk, *Democratization in South Africa*, Princeton: Princeton University Press, 1995; and Martin Murray, *The Revolution Deferred*, London: Verso, 1994.

[9]Initially, the new constitution was to take effect in 1999 as well but President Mandela suggested that the constitution should be signed, ratified, and adopted as soon as possible. The Constitutional Assembly agreed, and on December 10, 1996 Mandela signed the document in Sharpeville, site of the 1960 massacre. "Signing of the constitution closes circle." *The Star*, December 5, 1997.

[10]"Drama of the Nat Caucus revealed." *The Star*, May 10, 1996, where speculations are voiced that the party leaders were split on the issue of leaving the GNU. However, since the party is fast losing electoral support from its Afrikaner base, the leadership decided that it would lose even more support if it stayed in government.

[11]Thomas Koelble and Andrew Reynolds. "Powersharing in the New South Africa." *Politics and Society*, Vol. 23, No. 3, September 1996.

[12]Ian Shapiro. "South African Democracy Revisited." *Politics and Society*, Vol. 24, No. 3, September 1996.

[13]"Hand in hand to a brighter Future." *Mail and Guardian*, May 10, 1996.

[14]Lijphart, 1984: 23–4.

[15]Lijphart, 1984: 24–5.

[16]"It's broke, so they'll fix it." *Sunday Times*, September 8, 1996.

[17]The IFP leadership argued that the interim constitution demanded international mediation in the actual constitutional process. Since the ANC stead-

fastly refused to bring international mediators into the constitutional deliberations, the IFP deemed the constitutional assembly as an illegitimate forum. It did not participate in the constitutional writing process, nor did it vote on the final constitution. The party rejected the constitution as illegitimate as well.

[19]Richard Humphries and Jens Meierhenrich. "South Africa's New Upper House: The National Council of Provinces." *Indicator South Africa*, Vol. 13, No. 4, Spring 1996.

[20]T. J. Pempel, ed. 1990. *Uncommon Democracies: The One-Party Dominant Regimes*. Ithaca: Cornell University Press.

[21]Seymour Martin Lipset and Stein Rokkan. 1967. "Cleavage Structures, Party Systems, and Voter Alignments: An Introduction." In Seymour M. Lipset and Stein Rokkan, *Party Systems and Voter Alignments: Cross-National Perspectives*, New York: Free Press.

[22]For a sensitive description of these issues see the interviews with various members of the clergy and church groups in June Goodwin and Ben Schiff, *The Heart of Whiteness*, New York: Scribner, 1995.

[23]For an excellent analysis of the role of the Nederduitse Gereformeerde Kerk (Dutch Reformed Church) see Donald H. Akenson, *God's Peoples: Covenant and Land Use in South Africa, Israel, and Ulster*, Ithaca: Cornell University Press, 1992.

[24]"Bruising battle looms between ANC, Controlesa." *Southern Africa Report*, December 1, 1995.

[25]Nozizwe Madlala-Routledge. "Do we really need traditional leaders?" *Sunday Times*, April 27, 1997.

[26]Donald Horowitz, 1991, *A Democratic South Africa?*, Berkeley: University of Califormia Press. pp. 54–60 points out that the ANC contains a disproportionally high number of Xhosas in its leadership cadres as does the PAC.

[27]See for instance Carol Paton, "Rumours of War," *Sunday Times*, December 15, 1996, where the author describes a confrontation between Sothos and Xhosas over the alleged killing and castration of a Sotho for stealing milk. Sotho hostel dwellers went on a rampage, killing the shop owner. The ensuing melee took the lives of 32 people in Rustenburg's Freedom Park squatter camp. Part of the confrontation took place on a soccer field where Sothos wore shirts and Xhosas took theirs off to identify allegiances.

[28]See the excellent chapter "The Roots of Political Violence" in Martin Murray, *The Revolution Deferred*, London: Verso, 1994: 93–116.

[29]There is considerable controversy over whether the election result is merely an ethnic census as R.W. Johnson claims in "The 1994 Election: Outcome and Analysis," in R.W. Johnson and L. Schlemmer, eds., *Launching Democracy in South Africa*, New Haven: Yale University Press, 1996: 319, or whether the results should be interpreted in a much more nuanced manner as Robert Mattes claims in *The Election Book*, Cape Town: IDASA, 1995.

[30]Tom Lodge, "The African National Congress and its Allies." in Andrew Reynolds, ed., *Elections 1994: South Africa*, New York: St. Martin's Press, 1994: 23–42.

[31]Andrew Reynolds. "The Results." 1994: 191.

[32]Herman Gilliomee. "The National Party's Campaign for a Liberation Election." In Reynolds, 1994: 43–72.

[33]Robert Mattes, "Dispelling the myth of racism in coloured vote." *Opinion Poll*, Vol. 1, No. 1, October 1995: 1.

[34]Robert Mattes. 1996. *The Election Book*. Cape Town: Idasa Publications. Also, R.W. Johnson and L. Schlemmer, eds. *Launching Democracy in South Africa: The First Open Elections*, New Haven: Yale University Press, 1999.

[35]Herman Giliomee and Charles Simkins; (eds.) *Awkward Embrace; One Party Domination and Democracy*. Cape Town, Tafelberg.

[36]Andrew Reynolds. "The Case for Proportionality." *The Journal of Democracy*, Vol. 6, No. 4, 1995; and "Constitutional Design in South Africa." *Journal of Democracy*, Vol. 6, No. 2, 1995.

[37]For a discussion of such organizational issues see Thomas A. Koelble, *The Left Unraveled*, Durham; Duke University Press, 1991.

[38]"Constitutional Court rejects vital clauses of the new constitution." *The Star*, September 6, 1996.

[39]*The Star*, December 5, 1996: 1.

[40]Lijphart, 1984: 2.

[41]Johnson and Schlemmer, 1995.

[42]Graeme Goetz and Mark Shaw. "The Election on the Reef: Choice and First-time Voters in Gauteng." In Johnson and Schlemmer, eds. 1996: 212–46.

[43]Richard Joseph. "Democratization in Africa: Comparative and Theoretical Perspectives." *Comparative Politics*, 29, 3, April 1997, pp. 363–82.

[44]Joseph, 1997: 378.

[45]Ray Louw, "ANC's National Executive Committee forces four wayward provinces to toe the party line." *Southern Africa Report*, Vol. 14, No. 50, December 13, 1996, pp. 1–2.

[46]"Another ANC bombshell as fourth premier plans to quit." *The Star*, June 17, 1997.

[47]Carol Paton. "Reshuffle pushes Ramatlhodi out of the firing line." *Sunday Times*, July 6, 1997.

[48]Ray Hartley, "Tribalism steps out of the closet." *Sunday Times*, December 22, 1996, p. 26.

[49]"Why Tokyo wants to quit the tracksuit brigade." *Mail and Guardian*, May 30–June 5, 1997.

[50]"Gauteng boss Shilowa puts reds in power," *Southern Africa Report*, June 25, 1999.

[51]Personal interview with Ray Louw, former chief editor of the *Rand Daily Mail* and the editor of *Southern Africa Report*, November, 1995.

[52]Lijphart, 1984: 30.

[53]A. Lijphart. "Prospects for Power-sharing in South Africa." In Andrew Reynolds, ed. 1994: 221–31.

[54]Thomas A. Koelble. "The New Institutionalism in Political Science and Sociology." *Comparative Politics*, Vol. 27, No. 2, January 1995.

References

Akenson, Donald. 1992. God's Peoples: *Covenant and Land Use in South Africa, Israel and Ulster*. Ithaca: Cornell University Press.

Boulle, Laurence. 1983. *Constitutional Reform and the Apartheid State*. New York: St. Martin's Press.

Gilliomee, Herman. 1994. "The National Party's Campaign for a Liberation Election." in Andrew Reynolds, ed., *Elections 1994: South Africa*. New York: St. Martin's Press.

Gilliomee, Herman and Charles Simkins, eds. 1999. *The Awkward Embrace: One Party Domination and Democracy*. Cape Town: Tafelberg.

Goetz, Graeme and Mark Shaw. 1996. "The Election on the Reef." In R. W. Johnson and L. Schlemmer, eds., *Launching Democracy in South Africa*. New Haven: Yale University Press.

Goodwin, June and Ben Schiff. 1995. *The Heart of Whiteness*. New York: Scribner.

Humphries, Richard and Jens Meierhenrich. 1994. "South Africa's New Upper House." *Indicator South Africa*, vol. 13, no. 4, spring 1994.

Horowitz, Donald. 1991. *A Democratic South Africa? Constitutional Engineering in a Divided Society*. Berkeley: University of California Press.

Johnson, R. W. and L. Schlemmer, eds. 1996. *Launching Democracy in South Africa: the First Open Elections*. New Haven: Yale University Press.

Joseph, Richard. 1997. "Democratization in Africa." *Comparative Politics*, vol. 29, no. 3, April 1997.

Koelble, Thomas and Andrew Reynolds. 1996. "Powersharing in the New South Africa." *Politics and Society*, vol. 23, no. 3, September 1996.

Koelble, T. 1995. "The New Institutionalism in Political Science and Sociology." *Comparative Politics*. vol. 27, no. 2, January 1995.

Koelble, T. 1991. *The Left Unraveled*. Durham: Duke University Press.

Koelble, T. 1998. *The Global Economy and Democracy in South Africa*. New Brunswick: Rutgers University Press.

Lijphart, Arend. 1977. *Democracy in Plural Societies*. New Haven: Yale University Press.

Lijphart, A. 1984. *Democracies: Patterns of Majoritarian and Consensus Government in Twenty-One Countries*. New Haven: Yale University Press.

Lijphart, A. 1985. *Powersharing in South Africa*. Berkeley: Institute for International Studies.

Lijphart, A. 1989. "Democratic Political Systems: Types, Cases, Causes and Consequences." *Journal of Theoretical Politics*, vol. 1, no. 1, January 1989.

Lijphart, A. 1994. "Prospects for Powersharing in South Africa." In A. Reynolds, ed., *Elections 1994: South Africa*. New York: St. Martin's Press.

Lipset, S. M. and S. Rokkan, eds. 1967. *Party Systems and Voter Alignments*. New York: Free Press.

Lodge, Tom. 1994. "The African National Congress and Its Allies." In A. Reynolds, ed., *Elections 1994: South Africa.* New York: St. Martin's Press.

Mattes, Robert. 1995. *The Election Book.* Cape Town: Idasa Publications.

Mattes, R. 1995. "Dispelling the Myth of Racism in the Coloured Vote." *Opinion Poll,* vol. 1, no. 1, October 1995.

Murray, Martin. 1994. *The Revolution Deferred.* London: Verso.

Pempel, T. J. 1990. *Uncommon Democracies: The One-Party Dominant Regimes.* Ithaca: Cornell University Press.

Reynolds, Andrew. 1995. "The Case for Proportionality." *The Journal of Democracy,* vol. 6, no. 4, 1995.

Reynolds, A. 1995. "Constitutional Design in South Africa." *The Journal of Democracy,* vol. 6, no. 2. 1995.

Reynolds, A., ed. 1994. *Elections 1994: South Africa.* New York: St. Martin's Press.

Shapiro, Ian. 1996. "South African Democracy Revisited." *Politics and Society,* vol. 24, no. 3, September 1996.

Sisk, Timothy. 1995. *Democratization in South Africa.* Princeton: Princeton University Press.

CHAPTER 8

Majoritarian or Power-Sharing Government

Andrew Reynolds

Electoral systems may be key to conflict resolution in a divided society, but even their power can be submerged by the bundle of other institutional structures and political practices that combine together to form a nation's democratic type. It is important to note here that the terms I use relate to formal political and institutional practices as opposed to informal economic relationships. A political system may consist of majoritarian institutions, but power sharing goes on in the economic sphere (as in Zimbabwe). For the purpose of assessing the conflict-mitigating potential of various democratic types, it is useful to go beyond the simple, majoritarian versus power-sharing dichotomy to a more nuanced typology, which recognizes that there are choices to be made within each family. To illustrate this new categorization I focus on the fledgling democracies of southern Africa, which represent a useful array of institutional arrangements and proposals for constitutional engineering.[1]

Table 8.1 outlines the ethos and defining institutional characteristics of five democratic types—three majoritarian, two power sharing—all of which at some stage have been advocated for use in the new democracies of southern Africa. The component parts of classic (or unadulterated) majoritarianism consist of the following: single-party parliamentary governments (or powerful single-person presidents), plurality SMD elections, unicameralism, and a unitary state. Ideally, pure majoritarianism will create two inclusive, broadly based, moderate political parties, effectively alternating between government and opposition. Qualified majoritarianism seeks to remedy some of the more exclusionary aspects of straight majoritarianism by including one, or all, of the following institutions: list PR elections, a degree of government decentralization and federalism, and reserved seats for territorially dispersed ethnic minorities. Lastly, Donald Horowitz recommends for South Africa a type of integrative majoritarianism, in which a number of accommodation-inducing institutions are incorporated into classic Westminster-style democracy to encourage the growth of moderate and multi-ethnic political parties.

TABLE 8.1.   The Characteristics of Majoritarian and Power-Sharing Democracy

	Majoritarian Democracy		Power-Sharing Democracy		
Type	*Unadulterated*	*Qualified*	*Integrative*	*Consociational*	*Consensual (Integrative)*
Ethos	Classic winner-take-all Westminster-style democracy. Two broadly based political parties alternating in government and opposition.	Winner-take-all democracy moderated by PR (making coalition governments more likely), rectifying minority exclusion through affirmative action remedies, and providing multi-access points to political power.	Majoritarian democracy with in-built incentives for interethnic party appeals. There is a centripetal spin to the system where elites are encouraged to gravitate to the moderate, and multi-ethnic center.	Government includes the representatives of all significant groups and revolves around interethnic cooperation and log rolling. Minority rights are protected through minority vetoes.	Inclusive power sharing between all significant political forces but no ethnically based minority vetoes or segmental autonomy. The electoral system encourages the growth of multi-ethnic political parties based on ideology rather than ascriptive communal traits.
Institutional Traits	Single party (or person) executives, unicameralism, plurality SMD, unitary state, and a flexible constitution.	Single party (or person) executives and other majoritarian institutions, qualified by PR, and/or federalism, and/or reserved positions for ethnic minorities.	Presidentialism (with a supermajority criterion), the alternative vote, and multi-ethnic federalism.	Parliamentarism, grand coalitions, proportionality in electoral system (list PR) and bureaucracy, mutual vetoes, segmental autonomy for ethnic groups.	Parliamentarism, grand coalitions, the single transferable vote (PR), decentralization of power alongside moderate federalism.

In contrast, it is unfortunate that much of the discussion about the potential importance of conflict resolving political arrangements assumes that power sharing is embodied in a single type. The great error that critics of the proposal that consociationalism would be best for South Africa continue to make is the presumption that, if ethnically based consociationalism is not appropriate, then the only alternative is majoritarian democracy, and likewise if the interim and permanent South African constitutions of 1994 and 1996 were not consociational then they had to be majoritarian constructs.[2] Regardless, of the relative values of consociationalism and majoritarianism the view that these are the only two choices, in theory and in practice, is erroneous and demonstrates a weak understanding of the diverse nature and consequences of institutional structures. In this chapter I argue that contrary to this received wisdom there are in fact two distinctive types of power sharing that rest on different assumptions and, in some areas, prescribe different institutions. In essence, consociationalism rests on the premises that society is deeply divided along ethnic lines and is segmented into a number of nonconversing and antagonistic cultural groups, and that voting affiliation is driven primarily by such ascriptive identities. Conversely, integrative consensus "systems" rest on the premise that society is conflictual, but those divisions are not necessarily determined by ethnic identities. Other cleavages along the lines of class, wealth, regionalism, and clan may be more salient. In such societies, there may be correlations between ethnic group and patterns of voting behavior, but there are enough exceptions to the "elections as an ethnic census" rule to render a casual link doubtful at best.

Before too much confusion about terminology sets into your mind let me outline what I take to be the distinction between the majoritarian-consensus dichotomy, the majoritarian versus power-sharing choice, and the difference between those categories and the consociational versus integrative consensual democratic types that I address in this chapter. First, "majoritarianism" is both an ideal type and a specific set of institutions. When I talk of majoritarianism versus power sharing I am referring to majoritarianism as a type and when I talk of the majoritarian-consensual continuum I am referring to specific institutional arrangements and party system characteristics. "Consensual" institutions facilitate power sharing between groups and they are found in both "consociational" and "integrative consensual" types. However, for a democracy to be truly consociational it must have segmental autonomy and minority vetoes for communal groups as well as grand coalitions. In contrast, an integrative consensual system also has grand coalitions, but it does not have cultural segmental autonomy or minority vetoes, and makes use of a STV electoral system instead of a list PR system.

Majoritarian Democracy

Unadulterated and Qualified Majoritarianism

The vast majority of cited benefits of majoritarian government for divided societies—for example, coherent single-party executives, a strong parliamentary opposition, and the close territorial link between MPs and their constituents—stems either from criticisms of power-sharing structures (some valid, others not), or from the belief that Anglo-American democracy will work in Cape Town and Lilongwe the way it works in Westminster and Washington DC. However, though there are indeed benefits to single-party cabinets and single-member districts, those benefits are subsumed by the all too often catastrophic zero-sum game that accompanies majoritarianism.[3] Horowitz notes that where Anglo-American democracy was practiced in the segmented societies of the developing world, "ethnic parties developed, majorities took power, and minorities took shelter. It was a fearful situation, in which the prospect of minority exclusion from government underpinned by ethnic voting, was potentially permanent... Civil violence, military coups, and the advent of single party regimes can all be traced to this problem of inclusion-exclusion."[4] In the 1990s, the cases of Angola, Algeria, and Bosnia all show how disastrous majoritarianism can be if imposed on a society where exclusion from political office is equated with the threat of social extinction.

Because such winner-take-all structures increasingly are recognized to be destabilizing forces in the fledgling democracies of Africa, majoritarian institutions have been adapted to incorporate some of the consensus elements. In Mozambique, Liberia, and Sierra Leone, PR was used instead of plurality SMD, which in Mozambique and Sierra Leone facilitated the entrenchment of strong opposition parties, and, in the cases of Liberia and Sierra Leone, informal governments of national unity. In Angola, if a settlement between Savimbi's UNITA rebels and the government of Dos Santos is ever to be achieved it will likely entail PR, executive power sharing, and a degree of federalism, which will mitigate some of the winner-take-all aspects of the system. Moreover, the Zimbabwe Lancaster House constitution was a classic case of qualified majoritarianism: there was no mandated power sharing in the executive, but one-fifth of the parliamentary seats were reserved for whites, and PR was used to ensure the proportional representation of the Shona and Ndebele.[5] Although these qualifications to straight majority rule make minority inclusion slightly more likely, they do not guarantee it, nor do they offer any hope of breaking down ethnic allegiances and replacing them with cross-cutting ideological cleavages. Thus in most cases, simply using PR is not enough if one group has more than 50 percent of the votes, and federalism will be ineffective if minorities are not geographically concentrated enough to win control of state legislatures.

Integrative Majoritarianism

The underpinning principle of Horowitz's integrative majoritarianism is that elites be given incentives to appeal outside of their primary and narrowly defined ethnic constituencies. The key to integrative majoritarianism is that in the long run, internal incentives are more powerful than external constraints. As noted by Sisk, "the aim is to engineer a centripetal spin to the political system by providing electoral incentives for broad-based moderation by political leaders and disincentives for extremist outbidding."[6]

For Horowitz, a combination of integrative institutions and accommodation-inducing policies will engender such centripetalism. On the institutional side, he recommends the following. Vote-pooling electoral systems should be used, specifically the alternative vote in multimember districts at the parliamentary level. This should be combined with a directly elected president, chosen either by a national election on the basis of the alternative vote, or through a super-majority requirement where the winning candidate must win, not merely a national majority, but surmount a threshold in all regions of the country.[7] Lastly, Horowitz advocates federalism, which will provide increased access points to power, thus mitigating the extremes of winner-take-all exclusion; promote intraethnic political fragmentation; and encourage the proliferation of parties. In conjunction to these institutional arrangements, Horowitz argues for socioeconomic policies that recognize and advantage nonethnic communities of interests and that reduce overall socioeconomic inequalities.

Departing from Sisk's framework, I categorize this bundle of centripetal institutional mechanisms as being part of the majoritarian family. This is not just because the alternative vote produces classically majoritarian results, and because presidencies (even with supermajority election rules) are essentially winner-take-all institutions, but because integrative majoritarianism seeks to include minorities by proxy rather than by full appearance.[8] In contrast to consociational and consensual democracy, nothing within Horowitz's proposals will inherently guarantee that political power is shared between majority and minority groups. That is not to say that accommodation cannot take place under such institutional provisions, but such accommodation is dependent on the social and demographic environment within which institutions operate. For the alternative vote to give parties incentives to behave in an ethnically conciliatory manner, constituencies must be heterogeneous, with no one group holding an absolute majority of the votes. Similarly, in order to elect a president beholden to inclusive nation-building, rather than ethnically divisive exclusion, no one group can be in the absolute majority if the voting rule is preferential. Horowitz's other suggestion, a supermajority distributional formula, might better ensure that the president has multi-ethnic support. However, as I will outline in greater detail at the end of this chapter, such arrangements have often proved unworkable in both theory and practice.

All three types of majoritarianism might give rise to power sharing, but their efficacy is ultimately contextual. Pure majoritarian structures are least likely to give rise to ethnic inclusion. Qualified majoritarian structures stand a better chance of engendering accommodation, whereas integrative majoritarian institutions give the most incentives for parties to make cross-cutting appeals. The appropriateness of each type for a divided society, however, ultimately depends on where people live in that society and the numerical balance between groups. This is what distinguishes majoritarian structures from power-sharing structures in both consociationalism and consensual government types. For under power-sharing systems, where people live and the size of the population have far less impact on the operation of the institutions because electoral institutions are less influenced by demographics and the geographical voting patterns. From the evidence outlined within this chapter, it becomes apparent that these five African case studies do not exhibit the correct demographic cleavages for the vote-pooling incentives of integrated majoritarianism to be given a chance to work. Political party supporters are too geographically concentrated for constituency-based legislative elections to be competitive. And, in each of the case studies, ethnic/regional/racial majorities make vote-pooling incentives in presidential elections unnecessary. Integrative majoritarianism will become an option in southern Africa only when neighborhoods are more ethnically and racially mixed and patterns of party support are more fluid. Of course, once this social integration has occurred, there will be far less need for politically coercive integrative mechanisms.

Power-Sharing Democracy

Consociationalism

The Theory

One of the most important prescriptions for plural (segmented) societies remains that of consociationalism, a term first used by Althusius, and rescued from obscurity by Lijphart in the late 1960s. Consociationalism entails a power-sharing agreement within government, brokered between clearly defined segments of society that may be joined by citizenship but divided by ethnicity, religion, and language. Examples of consociational societies have included Belgium, the Netherlands, Austria, and Switzerland. Cyprus and Lebanon are cited as countries which had, but no longer have, a consociational ethos. The mechanics of consociationalism can be distilled into four basic elements that must be present to make the constitution worthy of the consociational name. They are: 1) executive power sharing among the representatives of all significant groups (grand coalition); 2) a high degree of internal autonomy for groups that wish to have it (segmental autonomy); 3) proportional representation and proportional allocation of civil service positions and public funds (proportionality); and 4) a minority veto on the most vital issues (mutual veto).[9]

These four basic elements ensure that government becomes an inclusive multiethnic coalition, unlike the adversarial nature of a Westminster winner-take-all democracy. Lijphart cites Riker's minimum winning coalition theorem in support of his view of consociationalism or oversized government coalitions, in that they are not just desirable in plural societies but are the most rational product of bargaining among elites under such conditions. Riker's theory is based upon the zero-sum game of coalition bargaining. However, he concedes that when there are common advantages for coalition players the zero sum game disappears, and it is logical to see oversized coalition governments.[10]

As previously noted, in bitterly divided societies the stakes are too high for politics to be conducted as a zero-sum game. Also, the risks of governmental collapse and state instability are too great for parties to view the executive branch of government as a prize to be won or lost. As Rousseau observed, "the more grave and important questions discussed, the nearer the opinion that is to prevail approach unanimity."[11] The fact that grand coalitions exist in Westminster democracies at times of particular crisis further supports the consociational claim.[12] This is because it is reasonable to assume that they should always exist in the constant crisis management environment of a deeply divided plural society. During peacetime in these more established democracies, parties may accept a total loss in executive power at one election because they know that eventually the pendulum is likely to swing back in their favor and they will have another turn at governing. This is due to a significant floating vote, which determines whether Labour or the Conservatives take office in Britain and whether the Democrats or Republicans win the executive branch in America. In plural societies, the segments competing for power are more clearly delineated and the floating vote is negligible. Therefore, alternation of power is far less likely than one dominant segment seizing power and never being obliged to relinquish it. If majoritarianism (and one-party cabinets) were used in plural societies, it could lead to the dangerous permanent exclusion of one or a number of minority groups.

For Lijphart, the constitutional incentives or obligations to form a grand coalition need to be supplemented by three other mechanisms, the first of which amounts to negative minority rule represented by a mutual veto. Even within grand coalitions, the rights of minorities may be overridden if there is not an effective supermajority clause or absolute right of veto for all coalition partners. The mutual veto invokes Calhoun's "concurrent majority" principle, which stated that each segment should be invested with "the power of protecting itself, and places the rights and safety of each where only they can be securely placed, under its own guardianship."[13] In response to the cited danger of engendering legislative deadlock and minority tyranny, Lijphart argues this need not be the case as other bargaining considerations come into play in the grand coalition. First, as it is a mutual veto, minorities would not wish to use their veto unreasonably at every turn because they would know that another segment could retaliate against their proposals. It would thus create instability, which in the long run would upset the common advantages of the consociational pact. Second, the mere availability of a minority veto makes its threat, and not use, the most common employment. Partners in government will realize that any legislation will have to be designed with the interests of all groups in mind—otherwise, a veto will be used and all the preparation will have gone for nothing.[14]

In most consociational democracies it is a requirement of the segmental groups that the proportionality principle extends beyond the political arena and into such government controlled areas as the civil service and the distribution of resources. This seems not only desirable within normative criteria of equality, but also may have practical benefits for the smooth working of the consociational partnership. If only one segment in a society controls the bureaucracy and dominates resource allocation, then regardless of parity in the executive arena, this group will have an overwhelming advantage in society as a whole. However, the equality principle is not an absolute, and in some societies, where segments are of unequal size, the proportionality principle will mean that smaller groups have a correspondingly smaller influence on the policies of government. If this were not so, they would have power beyond their size, which could be a further recipe for alienation and instability in society.

The underlying ethos of consociationalism stresses that although there is joint decision making over common interests, regarding a cultural minority's area of exclusive domain the minority should be autonomous. This requires a clear definition of groups and group rights, which has led to the criticism that consociationalism may well perpetuate divisions rather than alleviate them. Indeed, Lijphart argues that "it is in the nature of consociational democracy, at least initially, to make plural societies more thoroughly plural. Its approach is not to abolish or weaken segmental cleavages but to recognize them explicitly and to turn the segments into constructive elements of a stable democracy."[15]

Favorable Conditions

The following nine variables make the establishment and maintenance of consociationalism in a country more or less likely.[16]

1. The most important factor is that there should be no one majority segment. If there is a dominant segment with over 50 percent support nationwide, it is much more likely that majoritarianism will take hold.
2. Negotiations among leaders will be facilitated if segments are of equal size.
3. Too many segments will require complicated and bilateral bargaining between elites, which will engender gridlock within legislation. Therefore, there should be a small number of segments with the optimum number being between three and five.
4. The decision-making process is also simplified if the state has a small population size, because foreign affairs usually takes on less importance and because the distribution of resources is easier to manage.

5. The existence of external threats may help to unify a society around a common nationalism, and thus increase the potential for cooperation among its component segments. This may precede or follow from the next variable.

6. An overarching sense of national loyalty transcends societal divisions and provides the basis for successful consociationalism.

7. A further important factor is that there should be some degree of socio-economic equality. Though economic inequality is not an insuperable barrier to consociationalism, it is clear that the larger the economic differentiation between segments, the more difficult political power sharing will be.

8. A geographical concentration of segments will aid the development of federalism and decentralization—both important aspects of power sharing in a plural society.

9. Finally, long-standing traditions of accommodation, which settle conflict by consensus and compromise and are rooted in the culture, will increase the likelihood of a successful consociational democracy.

The Case Studies: Favorable or Unfavorable Conditions?

South Africa has come a long way in the decade since Lijphart penned *Power-Sharing in South Africa*. It is perhaps ironic that a number of elements of power sharing (both consociational and consensual) appeared in the first nonracial constitution, when the conditions for consociation were slightly less favorable than Lijphart had initially speculated.[17] First and foremost, the elections of 1994 revealed a society that was not primarily segmented along ethnic lines, even under an electoral system (list PR) that was most likely to facilitate such ethnically defined voting behavior.[18] The black South African electorate did not split into Xhosa, Zulu, Tswana, and Sotho parties, nor was there an exclusively colored or Indian grouping of any consequence. Although whites may have voted overwhelmingly for historically white parties, only the Afrikaner Freedom Front failed to draw support from other ethnic groups.

The first nonracial election revealed three dominant political segments: an alliance of Afrikaners, English-speaking whites, Afrikaans-speaking coloreds, and Indians, who voted for the National Party; the northern and rural portion of KwaZulu-Natal, who voted for Inkatha; and the rest, that is, Xhosa, Tswana, Sotho, Venda, Swazi, Shangaan, Ndebele, and Zulus living in the southern and urban parts of KwaZulu-Natal, who voted for the African National Congress. These three segments were of unequal size, and the ANC had a clear majority (60:20:10, respectively). Nevertheless, because each segment was internally divided, to varying degrees, I have scored South Africa as unfavorable rather than very unfavorable in table 8.2. With respect to the other dimensions, South Africa's rapidly growing population puts it in neither the favorable or unfavorable category. External threats remain inconsequential. There is a growing sense of overarching loyalty to the nation, and socio-economic disparities continue to be great. The geographical concentration of the three segments is more pronounced than Lijphart presumed it would be. An ethos of the politics of accommodation seems today to have taken hold within the political culture. In sum, South Africa's conditions are slightly less conducive to consociationalism because of the existence of nonethnically defined political segments. This finding suggests that South Africa needs power sharing, but not necessarily a consociational-based power sharing resting on the premise that the salient societal divides are ethnic and ascriptive.

The conditions for consociationalism in Namibia and Zimbabwe (both slightly favorable) are roughly equivalent to those in South Africa. Namibia's low population size, small number of geographically concentrated segments, and recent history of accommodation are all positive foundations for consociational structures. However, the numerical dominance of SWAPO and the Ovambo, combined with persisting socioeconomic inequalities, are negatives. Zimbabwe also has a small population, split into only two to three segments. These are tightly concentrated, apart from the whites, and have some degree of overarching national loyalty. On the negative side, the Shona make up three-quarters of the population; socio-economic disparities persist nearly two decades after independence; and the accommodatory efforts of the early 1980s have been sullied by what went before and what went after. The conditions for consociationalism are most favorable in Zambia and Malawi. Indeed, Zambia

TABLE 8.2.   Favorable and Unfavorable Conditions for Consociational Democracy in Malawi, Namibia, South Africa, Zambia, and Zimbabwe

	Malawi	Namibia	South Africa[a]	Zambia	Zimbabwe
No majority segment	1	−2	−1 (2)	1	−1
Segments equal size	1	−2	−2 (1)	1	−2
Small number	2	1	2 (−1)	2	1
Small population size	2	2	0 (1)	2	2
External threats	0	0	0 (0)	0	0
Overarching loyalties	1	1	1 (1)	1	1
Socioeconomic equality	1	−1	−2 (−2)	0	−1
Geographical concentration	2	2	0 (−1)	1	2
Accommodatory traditions	0	1	1 (0)	−1	−1
Total Score	*+10*	*+2*	*−1 (+1)*	*+7*	*+1*

Key: 2 = conditions for consociationalism are very favorable; 1 = favorable; 0 = neither favorable nor unfavorable; −1 = unfavorable; −2 = very unfavorable.

[a]Lijphart's 1985 scorings for South Africa in brackets.

scores only one point less than Switzerland, and by these rankings Malawi is actually more suited to consociationalism than is Switzerland.[19] Zambia scores favorable (or neutral) points on all dimensions, bar its history of accommodatory traditions; Malawi appears to be ripe for consociationalism with three roughly equal, geographically concentrated segments, in which no one region commands a numerical majority. The only problem with consociationalism in Malawi might be that the segments are defined on the basis of region rather than ethnic identity. Although this remains a division based on ascriptive identity and not ideology, it is nevertheless a trait that rests on cross-cutting multiethnic cleavages that could muddy the workings of segmental autonomy.

Challenges to Consociational Theory and Practice

Weakening Opposition. Jung and Shapiro argue that power-sharing systems of government, and more specifically consociationalism, do not allow for a viable institutionalized opposition. True democracy, in their view, depends on such opposition. If the constitution incorporates power-sharing arrangements at the executive level, opposition forces will be marginalized and eventually displaced from political discourse and participation. Building upon Dahl's criteria, that is, that democracy must entail the right to vote, the right to be represented, and the right of an opposition to appeal to voters against the government in both elections and in Parliament—Jung and Shapiro assert that grand coalition governments encourage participation and representation in government rather than opposition. As noted earlier, they (incorrectly) identify the interim South African constitution as being based upon consociational principles. Consociational systems, so the argument goes, emphasize representation in the governing coalition to the "virtual exclusion of opposition."[20] Throwing the rascals out becomes virtually impossible, for elections are only a precursor to the much more important task of building governing coalitions between the contending political elites, and these political elites may find themselves in office despite having suffered electoral setbacks.

Consociational systems are said to undermine the legitimacy, the functionality, and the public interest role of opposing parties, given that they encourage participation in government. Since opposition is not valued, the incentives are structured toward cooperation among the elites rather than presentation of opposing points of view. The voting public is therefore deprived of a real political debate because the political leaders minimize their differences in order to build governing coalitions. As most political parties participate in the governing coalition, there are few incentives to inform the voter of misdeeds, of failures in policy, and of corruption. In this situation, no one dares to criticize the government or its policies, for all are "reluctant to give up [the] influence, perquisites, and patronage that accompanies their positions as part of the government."[21] In

South Africa, not even the president has the capacity to intervene, for his powers are so limited by the constitution that the executive in Parliament completely dominates the agenda-setting and policy-making process. Jung and Shapiro's critique is summarized well in the following passage:

> Facilitating and institutionalizing loyal opposition was not a goal of those who wrote the 1993 constitution. They mandated a government of national unity. They designed a parliamentary and electoral structure that limits effective opposition politics, gives substantial amounts of political power to elites who represent salient minorities, minimizes party competition and conflicts between the executive and the legislature and renders backbenchers impotent. That this is not a recipe for a viable democratic order should be clear from our discussion.[22]

If the South African constitution truly did not allow for opposition, then the public debate in South Africa and other power-sharing democracies would indeed be impoverished. However, in the first five years of South African multi-party democracy precisely the opposite was true. Anyone following the constitutional and policy debates in the new South Africa cannot have failed to have been impressed by the level of public and parliamentary debate concerning issues of democracy, participation, and policy direction.[23] During the period when the NP and IFP were part of the Government of National Unity (GNU), they also, very vociferously, represented an opposition to the ANC in Parliament, at the national, regional, and local levels. Indeed, the opposition in South Africa was every bit as capable of getting its message across as the oppositions in other consociational systems, be they in Belgium, the Netherlands, Switzerland, or Austria. The debates concerning federalism, electoral rules, power sharing, and local government responsibilities provide enough support for the contention that between 1994 and 1996 there was very vocal opposition in South Africa, despite the fact that its leading members were part of the GNU.[24]

Indeed, the ANC noted with some disquiet the National Party's oppositional tactics. In an October 1995 discussion document, the ANC identified the NP's "surreptitious destabilization strategy," which sought to portray the ANC as "incapable of governing; of dealing with crime; improving socio-economic conditions; attracting investment and giving leadership to economic revival."[25] They also claimed that, far from being a mute puppet of the GNU, the NP was using "whatever capacity it has to stall the transformation process and the de-radicalization of South African society." Jung and Shapiro further argue that "no potentially effective parliamentary group exists outside of the cabinet but inside Parliament to oppose government."[26] Although it is true that the ANC is not likely to be defeated in a vote on the floor of the Constituent Assembly, a degree of effective opposition has been mounted by the small Democratic Party that sits outside of the GNU. The seven DP MPs have a disproportionate impact on the standing committees and have been responsible for more than half of the searching questions put down for cabinet ministers. Indeed, in January 1997 President Mandela suggested that the DP join the government of national unity despite the fact that their two percent of the popular vote was insufficient to guarantee them cabinet seats.

Encouraging Secession. Nordlinger argues that segmental autonomy over home affairs and territorial federalism merely encourage groups to seek further autonomy, possibly secession, and thus the eventual break up of the state.[27] Cherry echoes these sentiments and argues that in South Africa the politics of ethnic accommodation merely encouraged spoilers, chiefly Mangosotho Buthelezi of the Inkatha Freedom Party, to extract as many concessions as possible.[28] However, Lijphart rightly points out that such exaggerated divisions are caused by elites unwilling to compromise, and by no means is this solely the domain of a consociational type of government. In consociationalism, as in all other democratic systems, a degree of cooperation between key actors is required. Hence, if this is lacking, the state will flounder.

The Question of Causality. Three challenges to consociationalism rest on the causal relationship between consociationalism and stability. Barry, Steiner, and Obler note that Austria and Switzerland have maintained peace and democracy, are plural in nature, and use consociational forms of governance. However, they contend that their success is due more to post-war economic prosperity than to power sharing. Societal divides will lessen as prosperity increases, regardless of whether the system of government is consociational or majoritarian. Nevertheless, there is evidence to show that Belgium and Canada experienced burgeoning ethnic conflict concurrently with increasing economic well-being.[29] A second criticism of consociational structures proposes that the causal arrows should be reversed, and peace and stability seen as the instigators of consociationalism rather than the other way around. Boynton and Kwon argue that "a stable political system...is a necessary and sufficient condition for accommodation." Therefore, consociationalism cannot be imposed upon a society that was not leaning towards intergroup compromise and power sharing in the first place.[30] Maphai believes that "consociationalism was not the cause of tolerance [in South Africa], but the result. Power-sharing was the mechanism adopted to give expression to the parties' prior readiness to eschew racially exclusive politics in the interest of mutually beneficial outcomes."[31] However, even if these statements are true, it does not negate the advantages of inclusive arrangements for plural societies. They merely expose the multidirectional nature of the causes and consequences of accommodation. For power-sharing institutions to work, political elites must be invested in their success. If power-sharing institutions are withdrawn, then so are the incentives that cultivate those embryonic attempts at accommodation.

Third, Barry contends that accommodation between groups may be viable without using formal and obligating structures. In an analysis of the politics of Northern Ireland, he contends that "if there is a recognition by both sides that some sort of accommodation has to be reached so as to avoid an indefinite continuation in the present communal violence and the disruption of ordinary life, this could be done without any special political arrangements simply by the Protestant majority making conciliatory moves and the Catholic minority responding."[32] Once again, this argument fails to appreciate that the formal rules often provide the main incentives for divided groups to be conciliatory. The behavior of elites is paramount, but without power-sharing structures, accommodatory signals may never be encouraged.

The Dangers of Immobility and Paralysis. A strong practical argument exists against consociationalism, which says that "all four basic principles (of consociationalism) appear to entail a degree of slowness and inefficiency" in the process of governing.[33] Nolutshungu takes the argument further by claiming that it precludes any sort of fundamental change in systems where economic disparities are overwhelming. Therefore, in a country like South Africa, the construct would be "unable to deal with the nature of political demands and configurations" that emerge when the majority of people demand that economic equality be delivered at the same time as political equality.[34] The likely slowing of structural change seems inevitable when we compare consociational bargaining arrangements with the clear-cut decision-making power of cabinets within majoritarian democracies. Perhaps, however, we must look further for a justification of power sharing in efficiency terms. In the short-term, some legislative efficiency may be sacrificed, and in the long-term, majoritarian efficiency in a divided society may exacerbate the already existing tensions into a recipe for disaster. Thus, the trade-off is worthwhile. Moreover, the consociational democracies of Austria, Belgium, the Netherlands, and Switzerland have been no more immobilized or paralyzed than the other majoritarian governments of Western Europe.[35]

The Temporal Nature of Power Sharing. Maphai accepts that power sharing was "an essential precondition of democratization in South Africa," as it guaranteed the continued support from whites, desired by the ANC, and provided a means for monitoring the government for the NP.[36] It provided the arena for jointly crafting the new rules of the political game and it acted as a confidence-building device. But Maphai argues that the institutions needed during a transition to democracy are seldom appropriate for consolidating democracy in the long run. By 1995, both objectives had been largely achieved anyway. Indeed, in its "devaluation of individual political preferences" and "constraints on opposition and alternation in power," Maphai writes that "consociationalism is inherently undemocratic."[37] The cited danger is that over the long run, power sharing arrangements will block advances in a much more important sphere, that of economic development and wealth redistribution. Friedman argues even further that political power sharing is irrelevant when compared to the problems of majority poverty and economic exclusion. "The durability of the postapartheid polity is likely to depend not on strengthening power sharing between political parties but on corporatist accommodation between the majority in the new government, and key constituencies in its own and the minority camp."[38] This view rests on the premise that ethnicity is far less of a threat to stability in South Africa than economic inequality.[39] Perhaps ethnicity has been overplayed as a source of South Africa's ailments, and perhaps economic development and equality are key to any democratic consolidation, but this, in itself, is not a good argument against power sharing in a society where the mutual bonds of trust are nowhere near strong enough to survive the anomalies of majoritarianism. After only five years of democracy, South Africa does not yet possess the tolerant political culture and ethnic integration that might remove the need for governments of national unity.

When Does a Society Need Consociationalism. There are many societies in the world wracked by ethnic violence, religious divides, or regional tensions, which have little hope of recovering without strong institutional structures providing strong incentives for accommodation and reconciliation. Lijphart's 1985 analysis of Lebanon could well be transposed to Bosnia today. "Short of partition, there is really no alternative to consociationalism for a deeply divided country like Lebanon. It is utterly inconceivable that majoritarian democracy would work in Lebanon—or that anyone in his right mind would even propose it. The choice is not between consociational and majoritarian democracy, but between consociational democracy and no democracy at all."[40] However, consociationalism needs to be seen as a stop-gap measure, the lesser of two evils, which keeps the lid on the pressure cooker of a divided society that is about to blow, and perhaps manages to turn down the heat just a little. Perhaps the most powerful criticism is that by entrenching segments and defining all politics in those divisive terms, we actually postpone, or even deny the breakdown of segmental barriers.[41] Indeed, some of the favorable conditions that Lijphart quotes for consociationalism seem to guard against it withering away. The way in which power sharing requires geographically concentrated groups who have autonomy, not only in regional affairs, may ultimately increase the segmental divides. The tension remains: How do we recognize segmental groups, while attempting to diminish their importance? An even greater danger exists of imposing ethnically aware consociational structures on societies where political segments are not clearly or primarily defined along the lines of ethnicity. Nagata argues that in some cases, "the depth of segmental cleavages frequently follows rather than precedes consociational arrangements, thus creating instead of solving problems of pluralism."[42]

The great value of consociationalism is that it offers powerful conflict resolving solutions to those divided societies that show no hope of generating such interethnic political accommodation. It is the solution when all else fails. But if consociational structures are entrenched in plural societies that do show potential for the withering away of ethnic voting, then the very institutions designed to alleviate tensions may merely entrench the perception that all politics must be ethnic politics. Consociationalism provides few incentives for political entrepreneurs to appeal for support beyond their own ethnic bases.

Integrative Consensual Power Sharing

There are important differences, both theoretically and practically, between consociational systems and integrative consensus-oriented systems. Both types contain power-sharing provisions, but are based upon different structures, objectives, and, most importantly, rest on different premises. As noted earlier, consociationalism rests on the premise that society is deeply divided along ethnic lines, what Robert Price calls "politicized ethnicity," segmented into a number of nonconversing and antagonistic cultural groups.[43] Voting affiliation is primarily driven by such ascriptive identities. Though there is little doubt about the importance of consociation for ethnically divided societies, other types of societies may be able to manage socio-political conflicts with consensus-oriented systems in which some of the institutional mechanisms of consociation are practiced, but not all of them are institutionalized. Such consensus systems rest on the premise that society is conflictual and may indeed be divided, but those divisions and voting behavior are not primarily motivated by ascriptive identities. Other cleavages along the lines of class, wealth, regionalism, and clan may be more salient. Institutionally, integrative consensus democracy would call for PR and grand coalitions, but not minority vetoes (based on ethnically defined parties), federalism, and segmental autonomy federalism (based on ethnic groups). Minority cultural rights under a consensus government would be taken care of by a strong individualistic bill of rights. However, and of greatest importance, integrative consensus democracy makes use of institutional mechanisms that encourage cross-cutting ethnic cleavages, while ensuring the fair representation and inclusion of minorities in decision making.

At this point it is useful to recite the distinctions Lijphart himself makes between consociational and consensus democracy—bearing in mind that my specific brand of consensual democracy emphasizes integrative institutions and excludes the more ascriptive facets of consociationalism.[44] He argues that consociationalism and consensus are closely related and have a large area of overlap, but that neither is completely encompassed by the other. Both are antimajoritarian in their ethos, but the four basic principles of consociational democracy are broader than the corresponding consensus traits. First, the power sharing inherent within the grand coalition governments of consociationalism may be reflected in a more informal way in consensual systems (that is, through voluntary oversize coalition governments). Second, for consociational democracy it is the inclusion of all segments, not parties, which is crucial. This again reiterates consociationalism's assumption that ethnic cleavages are the most salient. Third, under consociationalism, federalism may have to be adapted to ensure segmental autonomy for geographically dispersed minorities. Lijphart notes that "when the segments of a plural society are geographically intermixed, segmental autonomy can be instituted in the form of autonomous cultural councils and educational associations."[45] Last, consociationalism's minority veto involves a broader concept than the mere requirement of extraordinary majorities to amend the constitution. This implies veto power within cabinets and on legislative decisions. In sum: The difference between them is that consociationalism is the stronger medicine: although consensus democracy provides many incentives for broad power sharing, consociationalism requires it and prescribes that all significant groups be included in it; similarly, consensus democracy facilitates but consociational democracy demands segmental autonomy.[46]

Three points should be considered regarding integrative consensus democracy. First, if the institutional incentives work as hypothesized, it will allow the space for and, indeed, provide incentives for the growth of multiethnic political parties; but it will not guarantee that such parties flourish. It follows, therefore, that integrative consensus democracy is only an option in plural societies, which shows signs that ethnicity need not endure as the sole driving force of politics. If voters are never likely to look outside of their ascriptive identity to vote for nonethnic parties, then elections will never be anything more than ethnic or racial censuses, and integrative consensualism is redundant. In any society where politics is determined by primordial affiliations, consociationalism is the only viable option.

Second, the rationale of integrative consensus shares much with the logic of Horowitz's vote-pooling schemes, but its institutional prescriptions are at complete variance with those prescribed by integrative majoritarianism—and would produce dramatically different results. Chiefly, integrative consensus rests on the principles of proportionality and coalition government, and elections under integrative majoritarianism would produce nonproportional parliaments and single-party executives. In a plural society that is ripe for consensus government, members of an ethnic group may indeed be more likely to vote for a certain political party, but it is not clear that they do so out of a knee-jerk desire to vote as a communal block for candidates of a similar skin color. Where there is doubt about what drives voting behavior, and the intuition that the electorate is more sophisticated than an ethnic census explanation would give them credit for, then there is space for constitutional mechanisms that encourage cross-cutting cleavages. The goal of integrative consensus government is to proliferate such incentives, while retaining the benefits of inclusionary government (i.e., PR (through preference voting), grand coalition cabinets, and a variety of access points to political power). Table 8.3 illustrates the main similarities and differences between Lijphart's consociationalism and the integrative consensual type I have outlined. The two types share a number of traits, such as proportionality, federalism, bicameralism, and minority vetoes, but differ in the institutional mechanisms they utilize to facilitate such traits. One of the key differences is the choice of electoral system. Whereas consociationalism is nearly always based on a list PR system, integrative consensualism requires the use of preference voting in multimember districts (or the single transferable vote) to encourage party appeals beyond defined ethnic boundaries. Under this system segments of opinion would be represented proportionately in the legislature, but there would be a great incentive for political elites to appeal to the members of other segments, given that second preferences on the ballot paper are of prime importance.[47]

Just as there are few cases of the use of STV in divided societies, to date there have been no fully blown examples of the integrative typology in the real world. Perhaps the bundle of constitutional arrangements that come closest to the typology are the newly constructed arrangements for self-government and multistate consultation in Northern Ireland that were adopted and passed by referendum (in both the North and South) in May 1998. The Northern Irish Assembly elected in July 1998 consists of 108 parliamentarians elected by STV in 17 multimember districts. The size of the constituencies, already small in population, mean that a candidate will need only 2,000–3,000 votes to be elected. Other integrative consensus arrangements include obligatory power sharing in the executive (the First Prime Minister, David Trimble, came from the largest community, and his deputy, Seamus Mallon, came from the minority community), proportional power sharing at all levels of government and in the special commissions set up to deal with particularly culturally contentious issues, and a minority veto over legislation deemed to be relevant to communal interests. However, these institutional mechanisms owe just as much to the theory of consociationalism and the designation of ethnic groups. Parties identify themselves as Catholic/Nationalist or Protestant/Unionist and offices will be shared upon that basis rather than simple party strength. Therefore,

TABLE 8.3.   The Characteristics of Integrative Consensus and Consociational Power-Sharing Types of Democracy

	Integrative Consensus	Shared Traits	Consociationalism
Assumption 1		*A segmented and plural society*	
Assumption 2	Ethnic identities are salient but there is potential for the growth of cross-cutting cleavages		Elections are primarily determined by ethnic affiliations
Institutional Characteristics		*Multiparty system*	
	Grand coalition	*Executive power sharing*	Grand coalition
	Multi-ethnic federations, no cultural federalism	*Federalism and decentralization*	Ethnic segmental autonomy
	Both chambers elected by preference voting in multimember districts	*Strong bicameralism*	Second chamber pays attention to ethnic proportions
	Single transferable vote	*Proportionality*	Both electoral (list PR) and in the bureaucracy
	A supermajority clause for constitutional changes	*Minority veto*	Both a super-majority clause for constitutional changes and minority vetoes in coalition cabinets
		Rigid constitution	

although the Northern Irish peace agreement instituted (or reinstituted) an electoral system aimed to encourage the development of cross-cutting ethnic voting behavior (as integrative consensus democracy would applaud), it mitigated these benefits by entrenching the single aspect of consociationalism that most solidifies ethnic identification (i.e., rewards, the trappings and offices of power, are allocated on the basis of groups rather than party strength per se).

Among the case studies, none exhibits integrative consensus government or full-blown consociationalism. The interim South African constitution was not consociational, contrary to the claims made by both Lijphart[48] and Jung and Shapiro,[49] as it did not contain provisions for segmental autonomy, nor did minorities have a veto (beyond the supermajority clause for constitutional design). Although there was power sharing in the executive and proportional representation in the legislature, these two criteria do not fully satisfy the definition of a consociational system. The best that can be said for the interim constitution is that the constitution was a consensual arrangement. Table 8.4 illustrates that on the majoritarian to consensual continuum this constitution was consensual on both the federal-unitary and executive power-sharing dimensions. The permanent South African constitution moved farther away from consociationalism, although it remained a moderately consensual document. The ending of the government of national unity caused South Africa to move into the intermediate category on the first dimension. Namibia and Zimbabwe (1980–1987) are intermediate on both dimensions. Malawi and Zimbabwe (post-1987) are intermediate on the federal-unitary dimension, but majoritarian on the executive power-sharing dimension, and Zambia falls in the majoritarian box on both dimensions.

The Relevance of Presidentialism

An equally important choice facing a new democracy is that between a presidential or parliamentary system of government. When such a debate is conducted in the context of southern Africa, opinions may too easily be colored by the performance of former African presidents, whether they be democratically elected or not. The political reputation of these presidents, prior to the latest wave of democratization, ranged from poor to atrocious. Nevertheless, all of the main country case studies discussed herein have endured intractable presidential histories, which would presumably make them eager to avoid vesting significant power in the hands of one individual. Despite that experience,

TABLE 8.4.   The Case Studies Classified According to the Two Dimensions of Majoritarian versus Consensus Democracy

	D II		
	Majoritarian	Intermediate	Consensual
Majoritarian	Zambia	Malawi Zimbabwe 2	
Intermediate		Namibia Zimbabwe 1	South Africa (P)
Consensual			South Africa (I)

Key: D I = Dimension I (Executive power sharing, separation of powers, party system, issue dimensions of conflict, and electoral system type); D II = Dimension II (Degree of centralization, uni- or bicameralism, constitutional type); Zimbabwe 1 = 1980–1987; Zimbabwe 2 = post 1987; South Africa (P) = Permanent constitution; South Africa (I) = Interim Constitution.

Source: Calculated from figures in Reynolds 1999, Chapter 4, adapted from Lijphart 1989: 35.

Malawi in 1994 and Zimbabwe in 1985 instigated directly elected presidents. Namibia converted her indirectly elected president into a directly elected one in 1994; and South Africa, by naming the Prime Minister the Executive State President, has created the aura of presidential control if not the practice.

The fundamental tenets of constitutional design for divided societies would deter recommending directly elected presidents for the emerging democracies of southern Africa. Lijphart warns that although "the combination of parliamentarism with proportional representation should be an especially attractive one to newly democratic and democratizing countries," the Latin American experience shows that presidentialism-PR should be particularly avoided.[50] Shugart and Carey list three key criticisms of presidentialism based on the grounds of temporal rigidity, majoritarianism, and dual democratic legitimacy.[51] Of these, the consequences of majoritarianism are by far the most damaging to stability in ethnically divided societies. The winner-take-all nature of a directly elected executive office is in itself enough to discredit calls for presidentialism. For one, in a divided society devoid of a stable democratic history, there is no assurance that the loser, or losers, of a presidential race will accept defeat in what effectively amounts to a zero-sum game. The recent experiences of Angola and Nigeria illustrate that there is little hope for elaborate power-sharing constitutional safeguards if the fragile transition to democracy is shattered at the first hurdle. Ann Reid of the U.S. State Department laid the blame for the collapse of peace plans in Angola, and the subsequent bloody conflict, largely at the door of the presidential election system. Given that "both Dos Santos and Savimbi were vying for the only prize worth having," when Savimbi subsequently lost the election it was inevitable that he would resume his violent struggle.[52] In Nigeria, the all or nothing structure of the 1993 presidential race made it much easier for the military to succeed in annulling the election before the final results had been officially announced: unsuccessful candidates and political factions had no immediate stake in the political outcome, and many readily acquiesced in the annulment in the hope of being able to contest again. Ian Campbell claims, moreover, that Nigerian presidentialism caused a marked increase in electoral corruption in the run-up to the vote. "It was suggested that the problem was the 'size of the jackpot,' with the selection process (for presidential candidates) being seen as an 'investment opportunity' and the presidency as the source of instant wealth."[53]

Another danger of a presidential system is that a directly elected president tends to be pressured into ethnic or regional exclusivity. Such presidents will have a great incentive to offer clientelistic privileges solely to their own ethnic or regional group in order to ensure reelection by maintaining a simple majority or plurality of votes. This particularly threatens democratic stability in Malawi, Namibia, and Zimbabwe. In Malawi, Bakili Muluzi won the 1994 presidential election with 47.2 percent of the vote, delivered on the back of a huge proportion of the votes from his native Southern Region. In the South, which accounts for half the voting population, Muluzi won 78 percent of the votes cast, but in the Central and Northern regions he only polled 27.8 percent and 4.5 percent, respectively. Malawian politics is particularly divided upon regional lines and any constitutional structure that allows one region to be permanently excluded from power will fundamentally destabilize the state as a whole. President Muluzi may well become an inclusive nation-building figure who fairly distributes resources across the country. However, the danger exists that only the personality of the man, not the institutional structure of the office, will ensure that this occurs. The dynamics of Malawi's presidential system invite Muluzi to pamper the south, maintain no more than a third of the votes from the center, and largely ignore the needs and voters of the north.

In Namibia, Dirk Mudge, former leader of the opposition Democratic Turnhalle Alliance (DTA), articulated similar fears of directly electing a president who might emphasize and exaggerate existing ethnic divisions: "Politically, the proposal for a directly elected president is unsound and dangerous, because it denies the existence of a multi-party system. A parliamentary head of state who is mandated by parliament becomes a symbol of unity and conciliation, since in the exercise of his executive powers he needs to follow the wishes of the representatives of the people."[54] In fact, a full 70 percent of Sam Nujoma's national vote of 57.3 percent came from his ethnic base of Ovamboland. In the twenty-two electoral districts outside of Ovamboland, the DTA outpolled SWAPO by 180,787 to 158,946 votes. In the presidential election of December 1994, Sam Nujoma again won on the back of an overwhelming share of the Owambo vote, his 72 percent of the popular vote being strongly concentrated on the Northern Owambo, SWAPO-supporting regions of the country.

The actions of Robert Mugabe in Zimbabwe have clearly shown how a powerful directly elected state president can politically marginalize one ethnic group. During its first seven years in government, Mugabe's Shona-based ZANU (PF) effectively excluded Joshua Nkomo's Ndebele-based PF-ZAPU from political power until 1987, when they signed a unity agreement co-opting three PF-ZAPU leaders into the cabinet in return for acquiescence on the issue of Mugabe's desire for a one-party state. In fact, Zimbabwe's presidential system, combined with the numerical dominance of the Shona, would have allowed Mugabe to maintain his ethnically exclusionary government even without the accord with Nkomo.

If we accept the hypothesis that inclusive rather than exclusionary democracy is what is needed in divided (or plural) societies, then vesting all executive power in the hands of a single individual is clearly detrimental to constructive power-sharing arrangements. Shugart and Carey offer premier-presidentialism as a persuasive alternative to presidentialism. In such systems, the presence of a prime minister tempers the president's "exaggerated sense of mandate." Moreover, the president can dissolve parliament and call new elections when crises emerge, which mitigates the problems of rigid terms. Because of its majoritarianism, however, premier-presidentialism is as inappropriate to the southern African democracies as straightforward presidentialism. As Shugart and Carey note, "[b]ecause the cabinet is subject to parliamentary confidence, it will not be as narrowly representative of the president's interests as will a presidential cabinet, *unless, of course, there is majority support in parliament for the president's narrow interests.*"[55]

When the results of elections in Malawi, Namibia, Zimbabwe, and South Africa are reinterpreted under a hypothetical premier-presidential system, it is clear that such a system would still allow one party to dominate both the executive and legislative branches of government and govern in an ethnically exclusive way. The presence of a statutory multiparty cabinet, such as that which existed in the interim South African constitution, might ease the problem, but as Mainwaring has observed this too is unattractive in practice: "Multiparty presidentialism is more likely to produce immobilizing executive/legislative deadlock than either parliamentary systems or two-party presidentialism."[56] Such deadlock carries with it the danger of popular discontent with the new power-sharing government, which might well overwhelm any executive achievements in the realm of ethnic accommodation.

To engender presidents beholden to nation-building and unifying principles, Horowitz proposes that the president should be elected directly by either the alternative vote (a majority method) or a supermajority requirement. Zambia and Namibia already have majority requirements, although they have provisions for a run-off election if no single candidate achieves an absolute majority on the first ballot. Even so, to date neither country has needed to use it. Lack of credible opposition meant that Nujoma won 74 percent of the vote in Namibia in 1994, and Chiluba won 75 percent in Zambia in 1991 and 69 percent in 1996. Mugabe won consecutive presidential elections (1990 and 1995) with 83 and 92 percent of the popular vote, respectively. The evidence from these countries suggests that absolute majority requirements provide little incentive for presidential candidates to appeal outside of their primary ethnic or regional bases, as successful candidates are in little danger of having to endure second rounds of balloting, nor do they need to appeal for second preferences on an alternative vote ballot paper.

Only in Malawi would the alternative vote have made a difference (Muluzi won with 47 percent), but the three presidential candidates lacked the information that might have encouraged them to make inclusive campaigning appeals. Even if Malawi had used a majority requirement, and Bakili Muluzi had known that he was on the cusp of winning over 50 percent, the need to mobilize his southern regional support would have outweighed the desire to appeal to voters in the center and north. If something along the lines of Nigeria's Second Republic had been used—that is, a winning candidate needed to win both a national plurality and at least one-third of the vote in two-thirds of the regions/provinces—the use of supermajority requirements would have been either an irrelevance or a disaster. Such requirements would have been irrelevant in Zambia, where Chiluba won all of the nine regions by huge majorities in 1991 except for the East where he polled only 24 percent;[57] and in Zimbabwe, where Mugabe won all regions by overwhelming margins in both elections. However, in Malawi, no single candidate achieved such supermajority requirements, nor would one have done so in subsequent repeat elections. Muluzi won only 28 percent of the vote in the center and only 4 percent in the north.[58] This would have thrown the country into a dangerous confusion, a vacuum of power with no national figure available to fulfill the presidential unifying role. Indeed, as Sisk writes, a similar controversy emerged over the results of the 1983 Nigerian Presidential elections, which contributed to the collapse of the Second Republic.[59]

Perhaps the South African practice of electing a parliamentary government headed by a prime minister, and then bestowing upon that leader the title of state president, is the most constructive route to follow. Along with inclusive proportional representation and minority-majority power-sharing arrangements within the cabinet, the country thereby also gains a national figurehead who can serve as a rallying point. President Mandela's early legitimacy was based on his leadership of a majority parliamentary party and an executive branch that represented over 90 percent of the country's voters—a far stronger foundation than the simple plurality of the electorate that usually legitimates a directly elected president.

Applying the Types to Fledgling Democracies in Southern Africa

My analysis of how to determine which institutions are best for a given society places great importance on assessing the degree a society is divided by policized identities and inflexible behavior. Straightforward majoritarian institutions are, on the whole, inappropriate for any plural society in the developing world. Consociational solutions are best for those nations so deeply divided that the space for cross-cutting cleavages does not exist. Integrative consensual arrangements are appropriate for those societies that may have serious divisions, but demonstrate the capacity for interethnic political accommodation and multi-ethnic electoral parties. With this in mind, it is important to try to gauge how much of a role primordial ethnicity plays in electoral politics in the five relevant southern African case studies addressed. With that knowledge, the constitutional engineering prescriptions herein become more tenable.

However, it is not enough to merely ascertain the correlation between ethnicity and voting behavior. We must further assess the causation related to the correlations found.[60] This dispute over democratic legitimacy and the degree of party diversity in essence comes down to the same question that has vexed virtually all political scientists who study the newly democratizing countries of Africa. That is, to what extent do primordial ethnic loyalties determine voting behavior, and if the link is strong, does this in some way taint the legitimacy of the choice? For example, in the case of Namibia, Potgieter argues that "tribal voting"[61] determines elections and has severe and negative implications for the country's democratic consolidation. Potgieter describes "tribal voting" as:

> the phenomenon in traditional societies where voters choices are determined to a large extent by their tribal commitments. The tribal chief or council indicates a particular choice as being the correct one, and members are expected to follow suit. "Ethnic affiliations determine party preference" may be regarded as a general rule in multi-ethnic societies. In such situations the pressure of primordial ties often gains precedence over the requirements of modern competitive elections. In terms of those requirements such voters are not free to make choices of their own. Tribal voting then presents an inherent distortion of the idea of free choice.[62]

Mattes and Gouws note that the ethnic census explanation of election results in southern Africa sees "group based voting as a statement of identity, loyalty and solidarity," and implies that a high correlation between voting behavior and group membership would not exist if voters followed their true interests.[63] Primordial group-based voting therefore retards the ability of integrative institutions to weave their spell, as voters are precluded from their true interests, which, by implication, are not ethnically exclusive interests. Due to the lack of good opinion survey data throughout Africa, assigning reasons for voting behavior to individuals is fraught with speculation and perceived intentions. However, it is possible to match geographical ethnic concentrations to voting behavior, and thus at least gauge the correlations between ethnicity and party support. From these figures, we can tell whether, in Horowitz's terms, southern African political systems are indeed characterized by ethnic parties or racial parties." However, as is the case in Malawi, ascriptive traits may take on alternative forms if conditions allow. Therefore, it is useful to assess whether people living in a region vote together as a block; and this may or may not overlap with the occurrence of ethnic groups voting together as a block.

Table 8.5 outlines the occurrence of ethnic, racial, or regional parties, based on Rose and Unwin's criteria that a party is based on a social group with a shared ascriptive identity if at least two-thirds of its supporters share a given characteristic.[64] Specifically, an ethnic party is one that wins over two-thirds of its total votes from a distinct ethnic group; a racial party is one that wins over two-thirds of its votes from either blacks or whites; and a regional party is one that wins over two-thirds of its votes from a single district or province. Table 8.5 demonstrates that although 80 percent of voters chose racial parties in South Africa, and almost all parties were racially based in Namibia (although this is primarily due to the fact that only 6 percent of the population is white), when it comes to ethnicity the picture is far more complicated. Regional parties were only a serious factor in Malawi. In South Africa, 90 percent of voters chose parties who were not regionally based; in Zimbabwe (1980–1985) the figure ranged between 70 and 79 percent; and in Zambia, Namibia, and Zimbabwe (1990–1995) there were no regional parties.

South Africa

Much has been made of the correlation between race and the vote in the first South African elections of 1994, leading some South African scholars to claim that the election was little more than a racial census that severely threatened the prospects for liberal democracy.[65] Indeed, only the National Party's 20 percent represented a nonracial vote. Nevertheless, it is wrong to dwell on the nebulous concept of racial politics in a country where historical divisions and alliances, political forces and tensions, and constitutional proposals (both good and evil) have been based on the much more nuanced and salient concept of ethnicity. If South Africa's first election was going to be sullied by knee-jerk primordial voting, it would have been ethnic voting, as expected by Horowitz and others during the transition period. As was done by a number of leading South African scholars, we cannot spend years bemoaning the future threat of ethnic voting only to jump horses post-election to bemoan racial voting when the expected ethnic voting does not materialize.[66]

As table 8.5 illustrates, Johnson is wrong to categorize the South African election as a "mere ethnic census."[67] A full 85 percent of the votes went to multi-ethnic political parties. Indeed, only Inkatha (85 percent Zulu), the Freedom Front (83 percent Afrikaans), and the Democratic Party (69 percent English) can legitimately be considered ethnic parties.[68] The ANC's vote was constituted in three equal parts, that is, Xhosa, Tswana, and Zulu (roughly 30 percent each), with the remainder centered among Coloreds, Indians, white Afrikaners, white English speakers, Seswati, Venda, and Shangaan speakers— undoubtedly, a very multiethnic electoral base. Similarly, the National Party's vote was approximately 30 percent Afrikaner, 30 percent Colored, 20 percent English-speaking white, 8 percent Indian, with the rest being Zulu, Tswana, Seswati, and Xhosa. The PAC's vote was just over 55 percent Xhosa, 25 percent Zulu, 10 percent Seswati, 5 percent Venda, and 5 percent colored. These findings are a strong indication that the space for multi-ethnic voting coalitions

TABLE 8.5. Ethnic, Racial, or Regional Parties?

	Ethnic			Racial			Regional		
	Yes	No	% Multi	Yes	No	% Multi	Yes	No	% Multi
South Africa	IFP (Zulu) DP (English) FF (Afrikaner)	ANC NP ACDP PAC	85	ANC (Black) IFP (Black) PAC (Black) DP (White) FF (White)	NP	20	IFP (KwaZulu)	ANC NP PAC DP FF	90
Zambia 91	UNIP (Nyanja)	MMD	74					MMD UNIP	100
Zambia 96		MMD ZDC NP, NLP	85					MMD ZDC NP, NLP	85
Malawi	MCP (Chewa)	UDF AFORD	64				UDF (South) MCP (Center) AFORD (North)		>1
Namibia	SWAPO (Ovambo) UDF (Damara) FCN (Baster) NNF (Herero)	DTA ACN/MAG NPF/DCN	34	SWAPO (Black) DTA (Black) UDF (Black) ACN/MAG (White) FCN (Black)		>1		SWAPO DTA UDF ACN/MAG FCN	100
Zimbabwe 1	ZANU (Shona) ZAPU (Ndebele) UANC (Shona) ZANU-N (Shona)		>5			(Matabeleland) (Manicaland)	ZAPU ZANU-N	ZANU UANC	70[a] 79[b]
Zimbabwe 2	ZANU PF (Shona) ZUM (Shona) ZANU-N (Shona) FORUM (Shona)		>1			(Manicaland)	ZANU-N 1990	ZANU ZUM	99

Key: Zimbabwe 1 = the elections of 1980 and 1985; Zimbabwe 2 = the elections of 1990 and 1995; % multi = the percentage of national votes won by multiracial, or cross-regional, parties. [a]1990; [b]1995, respectively.

and accommodatory elite behavior does exist in South Africa, and the country need not be condemned to governance through closed-door bargains between rigid ethnic segments. The 1994 elections may not have shown much ideological fluidity (Mattes and Gouws note that partisan identification was very high), but they did demonstrate ethnic fluidity and the propensity for cross-cutting voting cleavages.

Namibia

After analyzing the patterns of vote concentration in the first Namibian elections, Potgieter argues that "the Ovambo voted SWAPO; the Damara voted UDF and DTA; the Herero voted strongly DTA, the Nama voted DTA, the whites voted DTA and ACN, while mostly Basters voted FCN." In sum, "the SWAPO victory seems to have been based to a large extent on a massive tribal vote of the Ovambo."[69] It is true that SWAPO fulfill the two-thirds criteria as an Ovambo ethnic party, harvesting 60 percent of their vote from Ovamboland and picking up the vast majority of Ovambo votes elsewhere. Similarly, the UDF were predominantly supported by Damara, the FCN by Basters, and the NNF by Herero. Nonetheless, over one-third of all votes cast went to multiethnic parties (the DTA, ACN, and NPF). In addition, SWAPO only just cleared the two-thirds barrier to be considered an ethnic party: despite its ethnic base, in both 1989 and 1994 SWAPO enjoyed significant non-Ovambo support.[70]

Lindeke, Wanzala, and Tonchi strongly reject the notion that the 1989 election was a reflection of tribal or ethnic processes. They see the results more as a rejection of colonialism, and argue that ethnic identities, far from being inherently antagonistic, can be compatible with a unifying national identity and the building of an inclusive and harmonious multi-ethnic state. They reject Potgieter's ethnic census thesis on two levels: first, that SWAPO's victory was based on some degree of voting support across ethnic groups; and second, that the relative weakness of SWAPO's support outside Ovambo "can be accounted for by the historically uneven access of SWAPO to Namibians in different parts of the country under apartheid structures."[71] They note that SWAPO originated as a "multi-ethnic, issue-orientated organisation." SWAPO eventually became rooted in the Ovambo region because of colonial laws, as well as the labor system. The latter created an Ovambo working class of mine workers, which became organized into the embryonic beginnings of the Ovambo People's Organization (OPO), and subsequently SWAPO. SWAPO was born out of nontribalism, or at least has multi-ethnic roots, and their subsequent leadership, campaigning style, and performance in government all indicate a commitment to national unity and nonracialism.

This in itself does not destroy Potgieter's claim that SWAPO's electoral victory rested on the back of an ethnically exclusive vote. Nevertheless, Lindeke *et al.* prove that Potgieter has, at the very least, exaggerated the numerical basis for his claims. Outside of Ovamboland, SWAPO carried the districts of Kavango, Luderitz, Tsumeb, and Swakopmund. These districts have a substantial Ovambo population, as well as a large number of other minority groups. Lindeke *et al.* argue that the only areas in 1989 where SWAPO can clearly have done poorly were primarily Herero speaking districts—areas where the DTA performed particularly well. A detailed reading of Namibian colonial history reveals that the evidence for "tribal leaders imposing choices on their communal populations...is weak at best," especially when it is noted that the traditional leaders who did cooperate with apartheid structures rapidly lost their support base along with their legitimacy.[72] Lindeke, Wanzala, and Tonchi conclude that SWAPO, as the embodiment of the struggle for independence, was the primary beneficiary of Namibian's desires for the end of South African colonial rule. "Despite the overt and covert attempts by the colonial regime to foster them, ethnic identities were not such an important part of the process."[73]

Zimbabwe

If we follow Masipula Sithole's definition and classify the Shona and Ndebele as nationalities encompassing eight component ethnic groups (the Karanga, Zezuru, Manyika, Korekore, Rozvi, Ndau, Ndebele, and Kalanga), then neither ZANU(PF) nor ZAPU would have qualified as ethnic parties before 1987. Both were broad ethnic coalitions (ZANU(PF)—Karanga, Zezuru, Manyika, Korekore, and Rozvi; and ZAPU—Ndebele and Karanga). Only Ndabaningi Sithole's ZANU-Ndonga might have fulfilled the two-thirds ethnic voting group requirement, given its limited support concentrated among the Ndau in Manicaland. However, the more conventional method of taking the Shona and the Ndebele as the base unit of ethnic analysis results in all main parties in Zimbabwe being classified as ethnic parties. ZANU(PF) won 97 percent of its total vote in the six majority Shona districts in 1980 and 1985; ZAPU won 72 percent of its total vote in Matabeleland in 1980 and 81 percent in 1985. After the 1987 merger between the forces of Nkomo and Mugabe, the new ZANU PF became a majority Shona ethnic party: its electoral base was 80 percent Shona in 1990, and 86 percent Shona in 1995. Even the smaller, less ethnically antagonistic parties could not avoid the ethnic party label. Muzorewa's UANC won 84 percent of its vote from Shonaland in 1980, 87 percent in 1985, and 82 percent in 1990. Tekere's ZUM was 83 percent Shona in 1990, and Dumbutshena's FORUM party was 82 percent Shona in 1995.

Nevertheless, such ethnic imbalances within the minor parties merely reflect the imbalance between Shona and Ndebele in the country as a whole

(75 percent Shona, 19 percent Ndebele). Also, the fact that Ndebele now vote for Mugabe's Shona led ZANU PF, albeit in much lower numbers than they voted for ZAPU, illustrates the potential for Zimbabweans to vote for parties that are not identified as being of their ethnic group. That being said, it must be noted that of the five case studies, Zimbabwe remains the chief example of ethnic voting, where political entrepreneurs seek to mobilize communities around an often hostile and exclusionary notion of ethnic loyalty.

Zambia

The MMD's overwhelming 1991 victory in Zambia was clearly based upon a broad multi-ethnic electoral coalition of the Bemba, Tonga, and Lozi ethnic groups, along with a minority of the Nyanja. They won eight of the nine provinces with over two-thirds of the vote. UNIP were reduced to the status of an ethnic party based on the support of Nyanja in the Eastern region and elsewhere. However, UNIP cannot be classified as a regional party, as only 40 percent of their national vote came from the east, another 12 percent from Lusaka, and 10 percent from the Copperbelt. In 1991, ethnicity appeared to play a relatively subdued role in voting behavior (apart from Kaunda's reservoir of Nyanja support. However, the politicization of divisive ethnicity subsequently became a much more serious problem in Zambia in the lead-up to the second multiparty elections of November 1996. Even so, in the face of a fragmented and ineffective opposition, Chiluba's MMD still managed to cobble together a multi-ethnic and cross-regional support base, even if that vote represented only 20 percent of the electorate and was lead by its Bemba core. The success of UNIP's boycott call in the Eastern province illustrated their continuing strength among the Nyanja and the NP's strong showing in the north and west confirmed their Lozi support, although not enough ethnically based support to qualify as an ethnic party under the two-thirds criteria outlined previously.

Malawi

Malawi demonstrates the clearest example of voters choosing on the basis of where they live, over and above ethnic ties, ideological concerns, or competing individual candidates. In the 1994 election, a full 99.3 percent of the vote went to regional parties, and only the tiny UFMD, MDP, and CSR parties had electoral bases distributed across the whole of Malawi. The UDF won 75 percent of their total vote in the southern region, the MCP took 74 percent of their vote from the center, and 69 percent of AFORD's total vote came from the north. Although most striking in its regional voting homogeneity, Malawi is also the best example of how imagined communal identities and interests can be manipulated, politicized, and ultimately exploited by elite entrepreneurs.

There the vote was not primarily motivated by ethnicity, as each region of Malawi is linguistically heterogeneous and identities are fluid.

Of the three main parties, only Hastings Banda's MCP might be aptly considered an ethnic party as well as a regional party, for his vote was based on support from the Chewa center and those pockets of Chewa (Nyanja speakers) living in the Chikwawa, Mwanza, and Nsanji districts of the south. Even the MCP drew a significant number of votes from Ngoni living in the Central region. In contrast, both AFORD and the UDF were multi-ethnic coalitions, built around one lead ethnicity. Muluzi's UDF gained the support of his native Yao in Mangochi, Machinga (in the south), and Salima (on the center's border with the south), but the balance of his vote came from the Lomwe, Mang'anja, Nyanja, and Sena voters of the southern region.[74] Chihana's AFORD vote was based upon the Tumbuka of the north, but only in two districts do Tumbuka predominate, Rumphi and Mzimba. The rest of AFORD's vote came from the Asukwa, Ngonde, Nyakyasa, and Tonga in the North.[75] As Kaspin notes:

> [O]pposition voters consistently supported the candidate from their
> own region. Not only did non-Tumbuka in the north vote for Aford,
> and non-Yao in the south vote for the UDF, but non-Tumbuka and
> non-Yao groups divided by regional borders tended to support the
> opposition candidates of their own region. For example, Ngoni in
> the north supported Aford, while those closer to the southern region
> supported the UDF. So too, Tonga voters in the north voted for
> Aford, while the contiguous Tonga population in the Center gave
> most of their support to the UDF.[76]

The primacy of regionalism over ethnicity in Malawi was created by centuries of indigenous conflict, colonialism, and missionary activity. In addition, thirty years of Banda's autocratic rule sought to advantage the center through the "Chewaization" of national culture, which was ambivalent to the south and overtly hostile to the people of the north.

Prescriptions for Southern Africa

As outlined earlier, if voting patterns are based on almost unbreakable ascriptive traits, then institutional arrangements should be more consociational than consensual: in such situations, integrative consensus may not be a strong enough dose of power sharing to build confidence between hostile groups. But if voting patterns are more fluid, or rigid but not ethnically rooted, then consociationalism can retard the very real prospects for a decline in the saliency of ethnic/racial divides. Consociationalism, even if it does not institutionalize ethnically/culturally rooted parties, still presumes that they are more likely. Thus, it offers sometimes subtle, sometimes overt, incentives for their persistence. All five case studies, to varying degrees, show signs that their ethnic divides are not primordial but flexible and malleable, and that ethnicity as a political factor has been crafted to serve elite ends. The strongest signs of evolving cross-cutting cleavages are found in South Africa, but they are also clearly present to a lesser extent in Namibia, Malawi, Zambia, and even Zimbabwe. The pertinent question then is, given this opportunistic state of affairs for the constitutional engineer, how do we encourage such integrative tendencies, while retaining the key inclusive confidence building mechanisms that are needed to preserve stability in the short term?

An ideal type might include: 1) an STV electoral system, or some other method allowing for preference voting and proportionality; 2) mandated power-sharing governments that include all significant political parties (à la Switzerland); 3) the practice of rotating the title of President within a parliamentary system;[77] 4) bicameralism with the upper house directly based on regional elections; 5) a written constitution with a strong bill of rights and judicial constitutional review; and 6) a moderately federal and decentralized political system that protects the rights of regional minorities. Indeed, there will be practical and philosophical objections to this system. Preference voting is said to be too complicated for Africans,[78] and governments of national unity are said to cause policy gridlock and weaken the role of parliamentary opposition. However, both of these objections may be surmountable, and the benefits of encouraging both ethnic power sharing and integrative tendencies may well outweigh the negative side-effects.

Notes

[1]Lustick argues that we should recognize another common model of restraining conflict in divided societies, and that is control: a relationship in which the superior power of one segment is mobilized to enforce stability by constraining the political actions and opportunities of another segment or segments (Lustick 1979: 328).

[2]This view is most clearly found in Jung and Shapiro 1995 and Connors 1996.

[3]Sisk notes that although simple majority rule may be the fairest from a theoretical point of view, the scholarly consensus recognizes the principle's limitations in divided societies (Sisk 1996a: 32).

[4]Horowitz 1985: 629.

[5]India can also be seen as a case of qualified majoritarianism as there is a high degree of ethnic balancing in both government and the bureaucracy. See Lijphart 1996.

[6]Sisk 1996a: 41.

[7]For example, in Nigeria in 1979 a winning presidential candidate was required to win a national plurality of the votes and at least 25 percent of the votes in 13 of the 19 states. In 1989, any successful candidate had to win a plurality of the national votes, and not less than one-third of the votes in at least two-thirds of the states. See Sisk 1996a: 55.

[8]Sisk 1996a. Indeed, Horowitz himself implies that his proposals are majoritarian variant in arguing that the task is not to choose between majoritarian and consociational democracy but "to choose between two kinds of majoritarian democracy: a majoritarian democracy that will produce racially or ethnically defined majorities and minorities [pure majoritarianism] or a majoritarian democracy that will produce more fluid, shifting majorities that do not lock ascriptive minorities firmly out of power [integrative majoritarianism]" (Horowitz 1991: 176).

[9]Lijphart 1977: 25.

[10]Riker 1962: 32–3. In two types of societies zero-sum rules clearly do not apply: 1) homogeneous societies with a high degree of consensus where common advantages are taken for granted, and 2) their polar opposites, societies marked by extreme internal antagonisms and hostilities. See Lijphart 1977: 27.

[11]Jean Jacques Rousseau 1950: 107.

[12]Most notably in times of war, as in Britain, and times of internal upheaval, as in West Germany in the 1970s.

[13]Calhoun 1953: 28.

[14]In the first year of the South African government of national unity only three decisions were taken by a majority vote within the multiparty cabinet. All other decisions were reached by consensus.

[15]Lijphart 1977: 42.

[16]Lijphart 1985: 119–26.

[17]Lijphart graded South Africa as having: 1) no majority segment (very favorable); 2) segments of roughly equal size (favorable); 3) more than five segments, but still a manageable number (unfavorable); 4) not too large population (favorable); 5) external threats (neither favorable or unfavorable); 6) a relatively strong loyalty to the nation state (favorable); 7) high socioeconomic inequality (very unfavorable); 8) geographically concentrated, but still interspersed segments (unfavorable); 9) a mixed pattern of accommodatory traditions (neither favorable or unfavorable). In sum, South Africa scored +1

(on a possible −18 to +18 range), leaving conditions for consociationalism on a par with Belgium, Malaysia, and Lebanon, better than Cyprus and worse than Switzerland (Lijphart 1985: 120).

[18]Lijphart said in 1985, "In South Africa it is...highly probable—nay, virtually certain—that the ethnic factor will reassert itself under conditions of free association and open electoral competition. It is highly unlikely that blacks and whites will confront each other as monolithic entities" (Lijphart 1985: 122).

[19]See Lijphart 1985: 120.

[20]*Ibid.*, 273.

[21]*Ibid.*, 277.

[22]*Ibid.*, 277–78.

[23]Welsh 1994b: 17–20.

[24]See Booyson 1995: 30. Booyson argues that in 1995 opposition politics in South Africa was vibrant and not just confined to the parliamentary arena.

[25]African National Congress 1995: 2.

[26]Jung and Shapiro 1995: 277.

[27]Nordlinger 1972: 32.

[28]Cherry 1994: 613.

[29]*Ibid.*, 94.

[30]Boynton and Kwon 1978: 25.

[31]Maphai 1996: 70.

[32]Barry 1975: 411.

[33]Lijphart 1985: 99.

[34]Nolutshungu 1982: 31.

[35]*Ibid.*, 100.

[36]Maphai 1996: 79.

[37]*Ibid.*, 79.

[38]Friedman 1994: 2 (emphasis added).

[39]Cherry 1994.

[40]Lijphart 1985: 13.

[41]Connors argues that in South Africa consociationalism "rather than mitigating ethnic conflict, could only wittingly or unwittingly provide a basis for ethnic mobilization by providing segmental leaders with a permanent platform." 1996: 426.

[42]Nagata 1979: 506.

[43]Price 1995.

[44]The following discussion is drawn from Lijphart 1989: 39–41.

[45]*Ibid.*, 40.

[46]*Ibid.*, 41.

[47]I will not delve into the intricacies of the single transferable vote here. For a much fuller discussion of the appropriateness of STV for South Africa see Reynolds 1993a.

[48]Lijphart 1994c.

[49]Jung and Shapiro 1995.

[50]Lijphart 1991a: 72.

[51]Shugart and Carey 1992: 28–43.

[52]Reid 1993: 2.

[53]Campbell 1994: 182.

[54]Quoted in Cliffe *et al.* 1994: 208.

[55]Shugart and Carey 1992: 49–51 (emphasis added).

[56]Mainwaring 1993: 200.

[57]In 1996, in the face of Kaunda's boycott, Chiluba carried all nine provinces. His lowest vote came in the northwestern province with 50.2 percent of the popular vote.

[58]Banda won 64 percent in the central region, 16 percent in the south and 7 percent in the north. Muluzi won 88 percent in the north, 7 percent in the center and 5 percent in the south.

[59]Sisk 1996a: 55.

[60]Achen notes that "demographics are clues" to voting behavior "not hypotheses" (Achen 1992: 209).

[61]I shall also refer to this theory as the "ethnic census" or "racial census" theory of voting behavior in which ethnic parties are those that derive an overwhelming proportion of their overall support from one ethnic group, or cluster of groups to the exclusion of others. See Horowitz 1985: 295 and the useful discussion of the concept in Mattes and Gouws 1996.

[62]Potgieter 1991: 39.

[63]Mattes and Gouws 1996.

[64]Rose and Unwin 1969: 128.

[65]See Giliomee 1994 and 1995, Schlemmer 1994, Johnson 1996, and Welsh 1994.

[66]Most notably Johnson and Schlemmer.

[67]Johnson 1996: 319.

[68]These figures, and those that follow, are based on the Institute for Multi-Party Democracy's post-election survey, as reported by Mattes and Gouws 1996, and Reynolds 1994: 182–220.

[69]Potgieter 1991: 40.

[70]See Weiland 1995.

[71]Lindeke *et al.* 1992: 121.

[72]*Ibid.*, 129.

[73]*Ibid.*, 136.

[74]Kaspin 1995: 614.

[75]*Ibid.*

[76]*Ibid.*, 614–15.

[77]A combination of the Swiss and South African executive arrangements.

[78]However, see Reynolds 1993 for an objection to this argument.

References

Adam, Heribert. 1995. "The Politics of Ethnic Identity: Comparing South Africa," *Ethnic and Racial Studies*, 18:457–75.

Arendt, Hannah. 1958. *The Human Condition*. Chicago: University of Chicago Press.

Barkan, Joel D. 1995. "Elections in Agrarian Societies," *Journal of Democracy*, 6: 106–16.

Barry, Brian. 1975. "The Consociational Model and its Dangers," *European Journal of Political Research* 3:393–412.

Beetham, David, ed. 1994. *Defining and Measuring Democracy*. London: Sage.

Blondel, Jean. 1968. "Party Systems and Patterns of Government in Western Democracies," *Canadian Journal of Political Science*, 1:180–203.

Booyson, Susan. 1995. "The Changing Face of Opposition Politics in South Africa." Paper presented to the conference on Parliamentary Dynamics, Cape Town, August 11.

Boynton, G. R., and W. H. Kwon. 1978. "An Analysis of Consociational Democracy," *Legislative Studies Quarterly*, 3: 11–25.

Chege, Michael. 1995. "Between Africa's Extremes," *Journal of Democracy*, 6:44–51.

Cherry, Janet. 1994. "Development, Conflict and the Politics of Ethnicity in South Africa's Transition to Democracy," *Third World Quarterly*, 15: 613–31.

Cliffe, Lionel, with Ray Bush, Jenny Lindsay, Brian Mokopakgosi, Donna Pankhurst, and Balefi Tsie. 1994. *The Transition to Independence in Namibia*. Boulder: Lynne Rienner.

Coakley, John. 1992. "The Resolution of Ethnic Conflict: Towards a Typology," *International Political Science Review*, 13:343–58.

Dahl, Robert A. 1989. *Democracy and its Critics*. New Haven:Yale University Press.

Dahl, Robert A. 1971. *Polyarchy: Participation and Opposition*. New Haven: Yale University Press.

Diamond, Larry. 1994. "Rethinking Civil Society: Toward Democratic Consolidation," *Journal of Democracy*, 5:4–17.

Diamond, Larry. 1988a. "Introduction: Roots of Failure, Seeds of Hope." In Diamond, Linz, and Lipset, eds., *Democracy in Developing Countries: Volume 2, Africa*, 1–32. Boulder: Lynne Rienner.

Diamond, Larry, Juan Linz, and Seymour Martin Lipset, eds. 1995. *Politics in Developing Countries: Comparing Experiences with Democracy*. Boulder: Lynne Rienner.

Diamond, Larry and Marc Plattner, eds. 1994. *Nationalism, Ethnic Conflict, and Democracy*. Baltimore: Johns Hopkins University Press.

Diamond, Larry and Marc Plattner, eds. 1993. *The Global Resurgence of Democracy*. Baltimore: Johns Hopkins University Press.

Diamond, Larry, Juan J. Linz, and Seymour M. Lipset, eds. 1988. *Democracy in Developing Countries: Volume 2, Africa*. Boulder: Lynne Rienner.

DiPalma, Guiseppe. 1990. *To Craft Democracies: An Essay in Democratic Transition.* Berkeley: University of California.

Downs, Anthony. 1957. *An Economic Theory of Democracy.* New York: Harper and Row.

Du Toit, Pierre. 1995. *State Building and Democracy in Southern Africa.* Washington, DC: United States Institute of Peace Press.

Du Toit, Pierre. 1989. "Consociational Democracy and Bargaining Power," *Comparative Politics,* 17:419–30.

Eller, Jack David and Coughlan, Reed M. 1993. "The Poverty of Primordialism: The Demystification of Ethnic Attachments," *Ethnic and Racial Studies,* 16:183–201.

Ellmann, Stephen. 1994. "The New South African Constitution and Ethnic Division," *Columbia Human Rights Law Review,* 26:5–44.

Elster, Jon. and Rune Slagstad. eds. 1988. *Constitutionalism and Democracy.* Cambridge: Cambridge University Press.

Friedman, Steven. 1995. "South Africa: Divided in a Special Way." In Diamond, Linz, and Lipset, eds., *Politics in Developing Countries: Comparing Experiences with Democracy,* 531–81. Boulder: Lynne Rienner.

Giliomee, Hermann. 1995. "Democratization in South Africa," *Political Science Quarterly,* 110:83–104.

Gurr, Ted Robert. 1993. *Minorities at Risk.* Washington DC: United States Institute of Peace Press.

Herbst, Jeffrey. 1990. *State Politics in Zimbabwe.* Berkeley: University of California Press.

Horowitz, Donald. 1991. *A Democratic South Africa: Constitutional Engineering in a Divided Society.* Berkeley: University of California Press.

Horowitz, Donald L. 1985. *Ethnic Groups in Conflict.* Berkeley: University of California Press.

Huntington, Samuel P. 1991a. *The Third Wave: Democratization in the Late Twentieth Century.* Norman: University of Oklahoma Press.

Inkeles, Alex. eds. 1991. *On Measuring Democracy: Its Consequences and Concomitants.* New Brunswick: Transaction.

Johnson, R.W. and Lawrence Sclemmer. eds. 1996. *Launching Democracy in South Africa: The First Open Election, April 1994.* New Haven, Yale University Press.

Jung, Courtney and Ian Shapiro. 1995. "South Africa's Negotiated Transition: Democracy, Opposition, and the New Constitutional Order," *Politics and Society,* 23:269–308.

Juteau-Lee, Danielle. 1984. "Ethnic Nationalism: Ethnicity and Politics," *Canadian Review of Studies in Nationalism,* 11:189–200.

Kandeh, Jimmy D. 1992. "Politicization of Ethnic Identities in Sierra Leone," *African Studies Review,* 35:81–99.

Kaplan, Robert D. 1996. *The Ends of the Earth.* New York: Random House.

Kaplan, Robert D. 1994. "The Coming Anarchy," *Atlantic Monthly,* February 44–76.

Kaspin, Deborah. 1995. "The Politics of Ethnicity in Malawi's Democratic Transition," *Journal of Modern African Studies*, 33:595–620.

Knight, Jack. 1992. *Social Institutions and Conflict*. New York: Cambridge University Press.

Koelble, Thomas. 1995. "The New Institutionalism in Political Science and Sociology," *Comparative Politics*, 27:231–43.

Koelble, Thomas and Andrew Reynolds. 1996. "Power-Sharing Democracy in the New South Africa," *Politics and Society*, forthcoming.

Laitin, David. 1986. *Hegemony and Culture: Politics and Religious Change Among the Yoruba*. Chicago: University of Chicago Press.

Lewis, W. Arthur. 1965. *Politics in West Africa*. London: Allen & Unwin.

Lijphart, Arend. 1996. "The Puzzle of Indian Democracy: A Consociational Interpretation," *American Political Science Review*, 90:258–68.

Lijphart, Arend. 1994c. "Prospects for Power Sharing in the New South Africa." In Reynolds, ed., *Election '94 South Africa: An Analysis of the Campaigns, Results and Future Prospects*, 221–231. New York: St. Martin's Press.

Lijphart, Arend. 1991a. "Constitutional Choices for New Democracies," *Journal of Democracy*, 2:72–84.

Lijphart, Arend. 1985. *Power-Sharing in South Africa*. Berkeley: Institute for International Studies, University of California, Berkeley.

Lijphart, Arend. 1984. *Democracies*. New Haven: Yale University Press.

Lijphart, Arend. 1977. *Democracy in Plural Societies*. New Haven: Yale University Press.

Lijphart, Arend. 1971. "Comparative Politics and the Comparative Method," *American Political Science Review*, 65:682–93.

Linz, Juan and Alfred Stepan. 1996. "Toward Consolidated Democracies," *Journal of Democracy*, 7:14–33.

Lustick, Ian. 1979. "Stability in Deeply Divided Societies: Consociationalism versus Control," *World Politics*, 31:325–44.

Magagna, Victor. 1988. "Representing Efficiency: Corporatism and Democratic Theory," *Review of Politics*, 50:420–44.

Mandela, Nelson Rolihlahla. 1994. *Long Walk to Freedom*. Boston: Little Brown.

Maphai, Vincent. 1996. "The New South Africa: A Season for Power-Sharing," *Journal of Democracy*, 7:67–81.

March, James and Johan Olsen. 1984. "The New Institutionalism: Organizational Factors in Political Life," *American Political Science Review*, 78:734–49.

Montville, Joseph V., ed. 1990. *Conflict and Peacemaking in Multi-ethnic Societies*. Lexington, MA: Lexington Books.

Moyo, Jonathan. 1992. *Voting for Democracy: A Study of Electoral Politics in Zimbabwe*. Harare: University of Zimbabwe Publications.

Murphy, Walter. 1993. "Constitutions, Constitutionalism, and Democracy." In Greenberg, Katz, Oliviero, and Wheatley, eds., *Constitutionalism and Democracy: Transitions in the Contemporary World*, 3–25. New York: Oxford University Press.

Nagata, Judith. 1979. "Review of Lijphart's *Democracy in Plural Societies*," *International Journal*, 34:505–6.

Nolutshungu, Samuel C. 1993. "Constitutionalism in Africa: Some Conclusions." In Greenberg, Katz, Oliviero, and Wheatley, eds., *Constitutionalism and Democracy: Transitions in the Contemporary World*, 366–78. New York: Oxford University Press.

Nordlinger, Eric. 1972. *Conflict Regulation in Divided Societies*. Cambridge: Center for International Affairs, Harvard University.

North, Douglas, 1990. *Institutions, Institutional Change and Economic Performance*. Cambridge: Cambridge University Press.

O'Donnell, Guillermo, 1994. "Delegative Democracy," *Journal of Democracy*, 5:55–69.

O'Donnell, Guillermo, and Philippe Schmitter. 1986. *Transitions to Democracy: Tentative Conclusions About Uncertain Democracies*. Baltimore: Johns Hopkins University Press.

Pitkin, Hanna F. 1969. *Representation*. New York: Atherton Press.

Pitkin, Hanna F. 1967. *The Concept of Representation*. Berkeley: University of California Press.

Price, Robert M. 1997. "Race and Reconciliation in the New South Africa," *Politics and Society*, 25:149–78.

Price, Robert M. 1995. "Civic versus Ethnic: Ethnicity and Political Community in Post-Apartheid South Africa," unpublished paper.

Przeworski, Adam. 1991. *Democracy and the Market: Political and Economic Reforms in Eastern Europe and Latin America*. New York: Cambridge University Press.

Przeworski, Adam. 1988. "Democracy as a Contingent Outcome of Conflicts." In Jon Elster and Rune Slagstad, eds., *Constitutionalism and Democracy*, 59–80. New York: University of Cambridge Press.

Putnam, Robert D. with Robert Leonardi and Raffaella Y. Nanetti. 1993. *Making Democracy Work: Civic Traditions in Modern Italy*. Princeton: Princeton University Press.

Rabushka, Alvin and Kenneth Shepsle. 1972. *Politics in Plural Societies: A Theory of Political Instability*. Columbus: Charles Merrill.

Rae, Douglas W. and Michael Taylor. 1970. *The Analysis of Political Cleavages*. New Haven: Yale University Press.

Rawls, John. 1971. *A Theory of Justice*. Cambridge: Harvard University Press.

Reynolds, Andrew. 1999. *Electoral Systems and Democratization in Southern Africa*. Oxford: Oxford University Press.

Reynolds, Andrew. 1995a. "Constitutional Engineering in Southern Africa," *Journal of Democracy*, 6: 86–100.

Reynolds, Andrew. 1995b. "The Case for Proportionality," *Journal of Democracy*, 6:117–124.

Reynolds, Andrew, ed. 1994. *Election '94 South Africa: The Campaigns, Results and Future Prospects*. New York: St. Martin's Press.

Reynolds, Andrew. 1993. *Voting for a New South Africa*. Cape Town: Maskew Miller Longman.

Reynolds, Andrew and Timothy D. Sisk. 1998. "Elections, Electoral Systems, and Conflict Management." In Sisk and Reynolds, eds., *Elections and Conflict Management in Africa*. Washington DC: United States Institute of Peace Press.

Rose, Richard, and Derek Unwin. 1969. "Social Cohesion, Political Parties and Strains in Regimes," *Comparative Political Studies*, 7:7–67.

Rousseau, Jean-Jacques. Translation 1985. *The Government of Poland*. Indianapolis: Hacket.

Sartori, Giovanni. 1994. *Comparative Constitutional Engineering: An Inquiry Into Structures, Incentives, and Outcomes*. New York: Columbia University Press.

Schmitter, Phillippe C. 1995. "Consolidation." In Lipset, ed., *The Encyclopedia of Democracy*, 295–99. Washington DC: Congressional Quarterly Press.

Shapiro, Ian. 1993. "Democratic Innovation: South Africa in Comparative Context," *World Politics*, 46:121–50.

Sisk, Timothy D. 1996. *Power Sharing and International Medation in Ethnic Conflicts*. Washington DC: United States Institute of Peace Press.

Sisk, Timothy D. 1995. *Democratization in South Africa: The Elusive Social Contract*. Princeton: Princeton University Press.

Sisk, Timothy D. and Andrew Reynolds, eds., 1998. *Elections and Conflict Management in Africa*. Washington DC: United States Institute of Peace Press.

Sithole, Masipula. 1995. "Ethnicity and Democratization in Zimbabwe: From Confrontation to Accommodation." In Glickman, ed., *Ethnicity and Democracy in Africa*, 121–60. Atlanta: African Studies Association Press.

Sylvester, Christine. 1991. *Zimbabwe: The Terrain of Contradictory Development*. Boulder: Westview Press.

Young, Crawford M. 1976. *The Politics of Cultural Pluralism*. Madison: University of Wisconsin Press.

CHAPTER 9

Global Economics, Local Politics: Lijphart's Theory of Consensus Democracy and the Politics of Inclusion

Markus M. L. Crepaz and Vicki Birchfield

Does the international economy define the limits of domestic politics in this "global age"? What role, if any, do different political institutions play as waves of internationalization reach the shores of national politics? If the once coveted principle of sovereignty erodes as a result of globalization, who will address the demands of marginalized and dislocated citizens? Where is the locus of legitimate government if that very government is paralyzed by international market forces? We believe these to be some of the most central questions facing policymakers, scholars, business people, and ordinary citizens alike as what is called globalization impinges on the processes whereby private desires are turned into actual policies.

We contend that variations in political institutions systematically mediate the pressures of globalization. Arend Lijphart, in his seminal study *Democracies* and his extension *Patterns of Democracy* (Lijphart, 1984, 1999), outlined two forms of channeling political power. One is called majoritarian democracy and the second he termed consensus democracy. Here we make three propositions as to how these two forms of democracy mediate the forces of globalization: (1) Consensus governments have institutional incentives to behave more responsibly than majoritarian governments; that is, they should absorb the pressures of globalization more slowly and cautiously being as much concerned with the losers as the winners of globalization. (2) Consensus governments should enjoy higher legitimacy than majoritarian governments based on the principles of inclusion rather than exclusion, which is typical of majoritarian governments. (3) Consensus governments should be characterized by higher public investments in both human and physical infrastructure, directly and positively affecting productivity rates and economic growth.

Based on the principles of "new growth theory," consensual systems should have a higher capacity than majoritarian systems to prepare society for the ever growing challenges ahead through investments in infrastructure, education, and the environment.

The contemporary debate over the impact of globalization on domestic politics provides a compelling backdrop against which to explore how Arend Lijphart's work fits into what Almond (1990) refers to as the "international-national connection." Our central argument revolves around domestic constitutional structures and the way in which these structures refract and mediate the "pressures" of globalization. We contend that whatever happens in the international arena, it will be filtered through domestic institutions. As long as institutions differ, different outcomes will ensue. As long as politicians' survival depends on the support of geographically determined constituencies we should heed Tip O'Neill's insight that "All Politics is Local" no matter how much globalization is taking place. In this age of globalization, what may change is the notion of "local" insofar as it may not only refer to districts or regions, but also to territorially defined nations.

Since the process of globalization represents a crucial part of our essay, we will first define globalization, outline what magnitude it has reached, and diagnose how much influence such forces yield over domestic politics. Secondly, after introducing consensus and majoritarian democracy, we will address each of the three propositions outlined previously; that is, we will investigate how and why consensual governments should behave more responsibly, create greater legitimacy, and promote higher public investment than majoritarian governments. Lastly, in our conclusion, we will offer an assessment of the capacity of different constitutional structures to deal with the challenges of globalization in such a way as to ensure economic efficiency and yet maintain a sense of "fairness" in the distribution of opportunity and equality consistent with the fundamental principles of democracy.

Globalization: The Inchoate Nature of a Concept

Precisely what is meant by globalization? Given that this line of research is becoming the latest new growth industry within the Academy, it is necessary to delimit the concept for purposes of clarity and tractability. First, it is worth noting that as early as 1978, Peter Gourevitch alerted our attention to the rather dubious distinction between international relations and domestic politics, and implored scholars to bring into their analyses the interaction of the two. In the conclusion of his seminal article, he asserts: "International relations and domestic politics are therefore so interrelated that they should be analyzed simultaneously, as wholes" (Gourevitch 1978: 911).

By globalization we mean no more and no less than did Gourevitch when he elaborated the idea of the "second image reversed," which is also explicitly stated as the broad framework of the Keohane and Milner (1996: 6) volume, entitled *Internationalization and Domestic Politics*. Keohane and Milner (1996: 4) define internationalization as "the process generated by underlying shifts in transaction costs that produce observable flows of goods, services, and capital." We restrict our conceptualization of globalization to this definition, which is concerned more with the economic parameters of the globalization process than with the broader cultural dimensions.

According to many observers of globalization, cross-border flows of trade, foreign direct investments, and particularly finance capital, have increased to such magnitudes that the nation-state loses its ability to respond meaningfully to citizen's demands through the crafting of policies. Globalization, so the argument goes, is the death knell of the state since its *Diktat* will leave no room for any policies not designed to maximize economic efficiency, such as welfare policies, national styles of regulation, industrial policies, or nation-specific workplace arrangements. Sympathizers of globalization argue that international market forces will clear all such obstacles away in order to make room for the ultimate goal: hegemony of international capitalism, sometimes also referred to as "neoliberal convergence."

According to this logic, the state is withering away, but not exactly in the manner predicted by Marx. Rather, the state has been likened to "...an old tree, still sprouting new leaves and branches and apparently still alive, but actually hollow in the middle, inactive and ineffectual in the really basic matters of security and money for which it was designed" (Strange 1995: 304). Not long ago we were told that the state has to "be brought back in" (Skocpol 1985), and now we are supposed to throw it back out already?[1]

It is astonishing to observe the enthusiasm with which students of international relations absorb and produce literature on globalization and the fervor with which they present it, as if globalization was a novel development.[2] For comparativists, the impact of the international system on domestic politics has always played a major part in their scholarship (Hintze 1975; Gerschenkron 1963; Katzenstein 1978, 1985; Cameron 1978; Rogowski 1987; Gourevitch 1978; Almond, 1989). Most of this literature argues that as a result of exposure to international business cycles, nations developed specific ways to deal with these challenges. Practically all of these nation-specific corporatist arrangements were fostered either during the Great Depression or during WWII.[3] Consequently, international challenges did not weaken the respective states; if anything, they have learned to adjust dynamically to these international challenges in such a way as to ensure economic efficiency with a minimum of social dislocation. "For the small European states, a reactive, flexible, and incremental policy of industrial adjustment occurs together with an astonishing capacity to adjust politically to the consequences of economic change. The small European states adapt domestically to economic change imposed by an international economy that they cannot hope to control" (Katzenstein 1985: 200).[4]

Obviously, there is a glaring contradiction, leading to diverging hypotheses between those who argue that increased exposure to the international economy will hollow out the state, destroy idiosyncratic state-society relationships such as social democratic corporatism, where "deliberative democracy may suffer" (Schmidt 1995: 77), leading to "erosion of state capacity" (Cerny 1994: 334), in short, leading to a situation where the state is becoming "defective" (Strange 1995: 55).[5] If this school of thought is correct, indeed we should expect a cross-national convergence of policies, of state-society relations, of national styles of regulation, of lifestyles, and of popular cultures, centering on the requirements of international economic forces. On the other hand, if there is any truth to the massive literature on how small states adjust to challenges in the international economy, we should expect not a weakening, but a strengthening of the importance of extant and new institutions and a variety of nation-specific policies.

How do we know that globalization is actually taking place? A typical indicator of this process is the increase in trade that has risen significantly more strongly than growth of GDP. From 1960 to 1990, among the OECD economies (the richest 24 industrial economies), the ratio of exports to GDP doubled from 9.5 percent in 1960 to 20.5 percent in 1990. World merchandise trade grew about one and a half times the rate of growth of world GDP from 1965 to 1990 (Wade 1996). These developments mean that an increasing proportion of production from each national economy is for foreign markets, making the competitiveness of a country dependent on how well its firms can compete against imports and how competitive the firms' products are in comparison with those produced by firms in other countries.

A second driving force in the globalization process has been the rapid growth of foreign direct investment (FDI) through transnational corporations (TNCs). After the mid-1980s there was an explosive growth of FDI by roughly 400 percent over six years, far greater than previous growth and three times faster than the growth of trade. Much of the FDIs took place in the service sector involving the integration of banking and other services in the global economy (Cable 1995).

Thirdly, as a result in modern communication methods and national financial deregulation, finance capital has undergone the most drastic of all changes since the early 1970s. Removal of national controls over interest rates and the lifting of traditional barriers to entry into banking and other financial services have led to foreign exchange trading in the world's financial centers to the tune of a trillion dollars a day, a multiple of fifty times or more of the daily amount of world trade and greater than the total stock of foreign exchange reserves held by all governments, heralding what Vincent Cable (1995: 26) calls "the end of geography."

Advances in technology, such as jet aircraft, containerization, motorways, telecommunications, digital systems, satellite technology, the Internet, fiber, optics, have dramatically reduced transportation and transaction costs, making products that were hitherto not tradable, ready to be exchanged in the global marketplace. Such products include perishable and seasonal fashion items, components of integrated production processes, and information itself, such as management consultancy, films, records and compact discs, television news, telecommunications services, software systems, design, and programming. Finally, institutions such as the WTO (formerly the GATT), the European Union (EU), and NAFTA are working relentlessly to remove political obstacles that could stand in the way of letting the world market deal its "invisible hand."[6]

These structural processes, so the globalization argument goes, will lead to an erosion of policy-making capacity and policy-implementation effectiveness of national governments, where under certain conditions, "government per se will essentially become privatized, losing much of its public character. The world will be a neofeudal one, in which overlapping and democratically unaccountable private regimes, regional arrangements, transnational market structures, 'global cities', nongovernmental organizations (NGOs), quasi-autonomous NGOs and international quasi-autonomous NGOs, with rump governments—the extreme form of the residual state—attempting to ride free on global/local trends for short term competitive interests" (Cerny 1995: 625).

For comparativists, these are certainly disconcerting trends insofar as it appears that if indeed globalization has these proclaimed effects, there will soon be no variation among countries left to be analyzed and explained. Although there are certainly dramatic changes taking place in the world economy today, we feel compelled to put these claims of globalization into perspective. It is intriguing to observe the most recent development of a "backlash" literature (Krugman 1995; Boyer and Drache 1996; Hirst and Thompson 1996; Berger and Dore 1996) to these, at times, somewhat ahistorical accounts of globalization. We will briefly deal with two issues: First, is globalization as new as it appears? Second, given these intimidating numbers on trade, foreign direct investments, and finance capital mentioned previously, what is their significance?

Paul Krugman (1995: 330) calls it a "late twentieth-century conceit that we invented the global economy just yesterday" and provides for anyone interested in putting down a date for the beginning of "globalization" the year 1869 "in which both the Suez Canal and the Union Pacific Railroad were completed."[7] Indeed, world markets achieved an impressive degree of integration during the second half of the nineteenth century. In fact, shortly before WWI in

1913, world merchandise exports as percentage of GDP had reached such impressive levels that, after significant drops in the interwar period and also after 1950, it took the OECD countries until the late 1970s to reach similar levels of world trade! The trade share, measured as the average of exports and imports, as a share of GDP in the United Kingdom was 27.7 percent in 1913; this level dropped to 13.1 percent in 1950, increased to 16.6 percent in 1970, and reached 21.1 percent in 1987, still significantly short of the 27.7 percent the United Kingdom had achieved in 1913. The United States had a slightly larger trade share in 1970 than in 1913, but Germany in 1970 was also below its level reached in 1913 (Krugman 1995). Vincent Cable (1995: 24) argues that "the main achievement of the postwar international economic order has been to restore the degree of 'globalization' to a level close to that which existed in 1913." According to the advocates of globalization, this interconnectedness should have made the nation-state obsolete sometime at the beginning of the twentieth century. In fact, only one year after the highest degree of globalization had hitherto been achieved in 1913, history witnessed the most bloody and brutal rise of nationalism yet in the form of WWI, just the opposite of what globalization theorists would predict! The state was, as it were, alive and kicking!

How significant are these most recent, dramatic increases in trade, financial mobility, and foreign direct investments? Are countries indeed converging towards the blissful automaticity of international markets devoid of any regulatory mechanisms? Are national characteristics such as workplace arrangements, management methods, cultural behaviors, national styles of regulation, nation-specific identities, systems of interest representations, formal and informal political institutions, and idiosyncratic political behavior bound to become extinct as a result of the silent compulsion of the market?

Hirst and Thompson (1996: 2) in their recent book entitled *Globalization in Question,* find that genuinely transnational companies (TNCs) appear to be relatively rare. Most companies are still nationally based and trade internationally on the basis of a major national location of production and sales. They find no major tendency towards the growth of truly international companies. Regarding FDIs, they find that capital mobility is not producing a massive shift of investment and employment from the advanced to the developing countries. In fact, FDIs are highly concentrated among the advanced industrial economies. Furthermore, trade, investment, and financial flows are heavily concentrated in the "triad" of Europe, Japan, and the United States.

Other observers are not only dampening the enthusiasm on the globalization of financial markets but are actually wondering whether these developments are not reversible. Helleiner (1996: 204), in an essay entitled "Post-Globalization" argues that because the globalization trend has been dependent on state support and encouragement from its beginnings in the 1960s, it is possible that states withdraw their support for free financial markets. In fact, despite a high degree of international capital mobility, the degree of international diversification of investments is surprisingly low. For example, in December of 1989, U.S. investors held 94 percent of their stock market wealth in their home country stock, Japanese investors held 98 percent of their stocks at home, and investors in the United Kingdom held 82 percent in home stocks (Epstein 1996: 213). Further empirical evidence has been offered by Swank (1997), who finds that increased capital mobility has not diminished the autonomy of states to pursue their preferred policy goals. Instead, the author argues that business taxation has shifted from "market regulating" to "market conforming" policy rules while still preserving the revenue-generating capacity of the state.

Also, a closer look at trade reveals that trade shares in percentage of GDP are still quite small in all but the smallest countries. Exports account for 12 percent of GDP or less for the United States, Japan, and single-unit Europe, and the Asian and Latin American averages are well below 10 percent. Wade (1996: 66) claims that "this means that 90 percent or more of these economies consists of production for the domestic market and that 90 percent of consumption is produced at home." In addition, the widely claimed impact of "footloose" and stateless corporations in undermining the nation-state seems largely exaggerated. Most transnational corporations (TNCs) hold the bulk of their assets and employees in their home country making them quite susceptible to pressure and persuasion from the home country government. General Motors in 1989 had about 70 percent of its employees and over 70 percent of its assets in the United States. Among the Japanese TNCs, Honda, the most internationalized of Japanese auto makers, had 63 percent of both assets and workers at home and only 22 percent of its total manufacturing workers worldwide in the U.S. Honda, Nissan, and Toyota produce 70 to 90 percent of worldwide output at home (Wade 1996: 79).

One of the least mobile of production factors is labor. Only the most destitute and the most professional are the ones who are willing to settle in foreign countries. Clearly, the majority of the labor pool does not fit into that category. If convergence is to be taken seriously, what should occur is a "diffusion of best practice;" that is, a system of production that proves to be the most efficient in one country and, through a process of diffusion, should be absorbed by other countries. Wilhelm Streeck put the "diffusion of best practice model" to the test by examining lean production in the German automobile industry. He finds that lean production principles based on broad rather than specialized skills and company specific skills rather than portable skills between companies is consistent with Japanese culture but would not transfer to German automobile plants because of the different cultural occupational ethos of the German workforce. For these reasons, Streeck argues, "convergence of institutional arrangements on international best practice is unlikely" (Streeck 1996: 168).

This last argument against convergence emphasizes a very important element that distinguishes separate countries—an element that the literature on globalization has consistently overlooked. This element is simply national differences in political culture. Culture can dramatically affect economic adjustment to economic crises and, thus, can become a resource for some countries or paralyze others. The degree to which populations of different countries accept or refuse, for instance, rationing of strategic goods such as gasoline, can either make a country more or less powerful when negotiating with other nations. Keohane and Nye, in *Power and Interdependence* (1977) made a long forgotten distinction between "sensitivity dependence" and "vulnerability dependence." The former simply refers to the ability of a country's prices of a scarce good to adjust over time. More interesting is their discussion of "vulnerability" dependence, which is defined as the ability of a country as a whole to adjust to costs imposed by the international economy. Vulnerability dependence is sociopolitical as it refers to behavior and, thus, is deeply rooted in national character. Depending on national character, outside costs may be absorbed with either minor or major social upheavals. For instance, during the 1973/74 oil shock, the Austrian government simply created another month of winter school holidays for its teachers and pupils, and more importantly, imposed that motorists choose one day of not using their car. A sticker, indicating the weekday in which the car was not to be used, had to be displayed on the windshield of the car for police to enforce that law. The Austrian population accepted these decrees without much grumbling. Such a solution to a worldwide economic emergency would be unthinkable in the United States. The point is, that in case of severe economic costs imposed from the outside, different behaviors, deeply rooted in national character, can either assist the state to creatively adjust to hard times or to suffer from governmental instability, industrial disputes, or wider civil unrest. This "cultural capital" may prove to be an important national resource, particularly in economically hard times. Assessing the potential for neoliberal convergence, Peter Gourevitch (1996: 258) is doubtful for it to take place since among many other factors, he argues that "Cultural traditions are powerful: countries have different traditions in networking, personal relationships, conceptions of authority, models of organizations and individuals."

This discussion on the limits of globalization indicate that the purported demise of the nation-state is exaggerated, although we readily admit that changes in the international economy have taken place that have put pressures on the policy-making capacity of national governments. However, different countries will deal with these pressures in distinct ways depending on their political culture, styles of regulation, workplace arrangements, work ethos, and formal constitutional structures, all of which are deeply rooted in the specific histories of the respective nations. For the rest of this paper we will focus only on formal political structures, such as presidentialism vs. parliamentarism, single-member district system vs. proportional representation, single-party, bare-majority cabinets or various forms of coalitions governments, and other formal political institutions.

Our general argument is that whatever degree of international pressure is brought to bear on domestic societies, it will be reacted to differently, depending upon extant political institutions through which they are refracted. "Globalization" is the independent variable, different political institutions are our intervening variables, and policy preferences of relevant social and political actors and various policies themselves are the dependent variables. Thus, we fundamentally agree with Keohane and Milner (1996: 4) that "the effects of internationalization are mediated through domestic political institutions."

Globalization and Political Institutions: The Politics of Inclusion

In 1968, Arend Lijphart in his *Politics of Accommodation: Pluralism and Democracy in the Netherlands,* long before "neoinstitutionalism" became en vogue among political scientists, had systematically studied the effects of different institutions on fragmented societies, coining the acclaimed concept of "consociational democracy." His central insight is that fragmented societies can, by establishing a particular set of institutional rules such as grand coalitions, mutual vetoes, a proportional representation electoral system, and segmental autonomy and federalism, achieve stability and democracy in plural societies (Lijphart 1977).

The tremendous influence of Lijphart's scholarship derives from its potential applicability to actual political conflicts be they ethnic, racial, linguistic, socio-economic, regional, or religious. His insights readily lend themselves to "electoral engineering," and thus, unlike most other political science research, becomes something like an "applied science." Given a particular cleavage structure in a society; that is, whether it is cross-cutting or reinforcing, different constitutions can have dramatically different effects on how nations deal with ethnic, religious, or racial conflict. Not unlike an architect who can build aggression into his physical structures, so can some constitutions, written in such a way that minorities are consistently excluded from political power, lead to upheaval and civil war. There is no simple causal arrow going from type of constitution to the incidence of civil war , but constitutions—the formal flow of political power—mediate very strongly the success or failure of political movements. Those who are constantly excluded from power, because the constitution is majoritarian in nature, may be inclined to resort to violent means to achieve their political ends, whereas in the case of consensual political institutions, where minorities are included in the governing process, there is more of a stake in cooperating with the political system than if they were excluded from formal power.

Arend Lijphart made the crucial distinction between consensus and majoritarian governments in a book entitled *Democracies* (1984), which has already become a classic text for those interested in the different forms of contemporary democratic systems. The difference between majoritarianism and consensualism is powerfully captured in Lijphart's answer to the question: "Who will do the governing and to whose interests should the government be responsive when the people are in disagreement and have divergent preferences? One answer is: the majority of the people....The alternative answer to the dilemma is: as many people as possible" (Lijphart 1984: 4).

Consensual political institutions consisted originally of five items (Lijphart 1984): oversized cabinets, balance between executive and legislative relations, multiparty systems, multiple issue dimensions, and a proportional representation electoral system. In later research in collaboration with Crepaz (Lijphart and Crepaz 1991; Crepaz and Lijphart 1995), corporatism was added as an additional factor of consensus democracy. Majoritarian systems, on the other hand, are characterized by single-party, bare-majority cabinets or minimal winning coalitions, executive dominance, two-party systems, partisan issue dimensions based solely on the socio-economic cleavage, a plurality or majority electoral system, and interest group pluralism.

The essence of consensus democracy is the political inclusion of otherwise unrepresented groups mostly achieved through proportional representation (PR), multiparty systems, and power-sharing grand coalitions, parliamentarism and corporatist systems of interest representation.[8] PR will most likely lead to the representation of more than two parties in the legislature, which will in most cases necessitate the formation of multiparty coalitions (Duverger 1954).[9] Parliamentary first-past-the-post systems, on the other hand, tend to create single-party, bare-majority cabinets with manufactured majorities in the various legislatures but not with majorities in popular votes. Thus, whether a country has mostly consensual or majoritarian institutions, significantly affects the way citizens' preferences are translated into political outcomes. Do these differences in political institutions systematically and predictably shape politics as the challenges of globalization impinge on democratic countries? We will attempt to answer this difficult question in the next section by introducing three propositions.

Proposition One: Consensus Democracy Fosters Responsibility

As stated earlier, we argue that the institutions of consensus democracy engender higher responsibility than majoritarian systems. We define responsibility simply as the capacity of government to minimize redistributive policies favoring particular groups; that is, a responsible government is one that does not respond disproportionately to the interests of well-defined, small "pressure groups." In other words, consensus governments should have a higher capacity to create diffuse benefits at diffuse costs, whereas majoritarian systems tend to create concentrated benefits at diffuse costs.

In list-PR systems, party elders play a tremendous role in advancing or hindering the careers of members of Parliament as it is within their power to rank various candidates. This system also engenders tremendous party loyalty, as opposed to the more individualized and personal relationship between the representative and his/her constituency found in single-member district systems. In PR systems, the representatives and their constituencies are rather removed from each other, thus there is less direct accountability on a district basis; putting it differently, the MP enjoys significant autonomy from his/her voters as a result of their insulation and, therefore, may escape the temptations of parochialism.

Thus, precisely because MPs in PR systems are more sheltered from their constituencies than in SMD systems, we propose that this institutional feature should have direct effects when it comes to the degree representatives have to decide on how much they should absorb or resist pressures of globalization. Because Parliamentary-PR systems have a higher capacity to respond to diffuse national interests, such systems should respond to pressures for globalization more slowly since MPs are more insulated from special interest groups and the interests of wider sectors of society; that is, those who stand to lose from globalization have to be taken into consideration as well (Rogowski, 1987). More recent empirical analyses tend to support our proposition. Mansfield and Busch (1995) found, among other factors, that nontariff barriers are highest when the electoral system is PR and when domestic institutional systems (large districts) protect policymakers from district-specific interests.

Parliamentary-PR systems insulate MPs from the pressures of their constituency, allowing them to take a national view, rather than responding to sectoral and district-specific temptations to sell out to the highest bidder, which tends to occur in presidential-SMD systems, which may either want protection from globalization or jump headlong into it, as the case may be. Parliamentary-PR systems allow a more programmatic, goal-oriented approach to policy making since the strong party discipline circumvents the often observed collective action problems found in more independent districts where each representative is elected based on what he/she does for the district even if the cumulative outcome has adverse consequences for the nation as a whole. In presidential systems with single-member district electoral rules such as the United States, national policy making is hampered by parochialism and susceptibility to the temptations and pressures of district-specific sectoral interest groups. Thus, "incoherent national policies are often the result" (Olson 1982: 50).

The more inclusive, consensual, and encompassing political institutions are, the more they thwart sector-specific pressures towards globalization, whereas exclusive, majoritarian political systems tend to come under strong influence from either the winners of globalization to liberalize or from the

losers of globalization to prevent neoliberal convergence. Whatever the outcome, policies are a hodgepodge of interests of sectoral pressure groups and
"exposed" representatives, each trying to maximize their immediate interests,
with the interest groups protecting their business opportunities and the representatives attempting to maximize their chances for re-election.[10]

On the other hand, as the number of political groups that gain access to governmental decision making increases, and thus, as governments begin to encompass wider sectors of society, they will, for electoral reasons, have to become
more responsive to all interests, which manifests itself in a slower, more deliberative style of policy making. Empirical evidence tends to support this thesis.
Schwartz (1994) investigated four countries, Australia, Denmark, New Zealand,
and Sweden, with respect to their ability to reorganize their welfare states in light
of globalization and finds that New Zealand reacted most strongly to change,
followed by Australia, then Sweden, and lastly, Denmark. The constitutional
structures of Sweden and Denmark allowed only cautious and incremental
change. Clearly, New Zealand[11] and Australia fall into the majoritarian camp and
Sweden and Denmark fall into the consensus camp.

The concept of consensus democracy, based on inclusion and maximum
input in the decision making process, is consistent with Olson's concept of
"encompassing organizations," which have a higher capacity to "internalize the
externalities of collective action." The rationale behind Olson's argument is
that the more encompassing parties become, the more their interest and the
"general interest" converge, and thus, the more dysfunctional it becomes to
unload the externalities of one party's action onto members of another party.
Thus, as a result of their wider encompassment these institutional systems have
the capacity to "internalize the externalities" of their collective action.
Therefore, they tend to behave more responsibly by minimizing redistributive
policies favoring particular groups, and supporting policies that are more likely
to approximate the "general interest." In societies, where encompassing interest groups are dominant, those interests will "internalize much of the cost of
inefficient policies and accordingly have an incentive to redistribute income to
themselves with the least possible social cost, and to give some weight to economic growth and to the interests of society as a whole" (Olson 1982: 92).

It is precisely consensual political institutions that create encompassing
organizations, often with the need to form coalition governments. These coalition governments encompass more members of society than majoritarian political systems, which are often quite narrow, exclusionary, and in most cases do
not represent a majority of the people, though they may carry legislative
majorities.[12] Crepaz (1996) found strong evidence that the more encompassing
institutional structures are, the more responsibly governments behave, in the
sense that these policies do not bluntly redistribute from members supporting
opposition parties to members of the ruling governmental coalition. The mean

popular cabinet support, defined as the percentage of voters to vote for parties that are carrying governmental responsibilities for the years between 1945 and 1987, was 45 percent in parliamentary-plurality systems, such as Australia, Canada, New Zealand, and Great Britain, and it was over 56 percent in Parliamentary-PR systems. Thus, in terms of voters supporting governments, Parliamentary-PR systems are clearly more encompassing (Crepaz 1996).

Proposition Two: Consensus Democracy Engenders Legitimacy

The principle of consensus democracy is about deliberation based on shared responsibility without the option of hiding behind institutional vetoes and shifting responsibility to the "problems of divided government." Consensus democracy engenders higher legitimacy than majoritarian systems because many voices are heard, many options are entertained, a greater range of information is taken into consideration and eventually policy decisions are jointly made and, equally important, responsibility for these policies is carried jointly. The essence of higher legitimacy in consensual governments, thus, lies not so much in the substantive policies themselves, but by the process in which they were created. Quite simply, widespread participation in policy decisions will be more widely accepted, strengthening the legitimacy of government.

The concept of consensus democracy is clearly about dispersion of political power in such a way as to allow greater access to the political system. The conventional wisdom holds that the more power is dispersed, the more difficult it is to change the status quo (Immergut 1992; Huber, Ragin, and Stephens 1993; Maioni 1992; Tsebelis 1995; Garrett and Lange 1996). However, just simply counting the number of veto points and claiming that a higher number will make it more difficult to change things is too simplistic. After all, consensus democracy is certainly about dispersal of power, but in such a way as to include as many people as possible in an accommodative manner, not in a manner of institutionalized competition as is argued by those who favor institutional veto points. Thus, an important distinction has to be made between competitive veto points and collective veto points.

Competitive veto points occur when different political actors operate through separate institutions with mutual veto powers, such as federalism, strong bicameralism, and presidential government. These institutions, based on their mutual veto powers, have a tremendous capacity to restrain government. These are also the same institutions that have the greatest tendency to lead to deadlock, immobilism, and even to shutdowns of whole governments as witnessed by the United States at the end of 1995 and the beginning of 1996. Competitive veto points lead to what Goodin (1996: 340) calls, "least common denominator politics."

Collective veto points, on the other hand, emerge from institutions where the different political actors operate in the same body and whose members interact with each other on a face-to-face basis. Typical examples of collective veto points are proportional electoral systems, multiparty legislatures, multiparty governments, and parliamentary regimes. These are veto points that entail collective agency and shared responsibility. In such an environment, the pressure to produce responsive policies is much greater, and partisan politics is also more muted (Schmidt 1996). In such systems, compromise and extended negotiation will result in more goal-oriented policy making as opposed to the more process-oriented policy making that is typical for institutions with competitive veto points. Indeed, institutions with collective veto points should indicate a higher responsiveness to the desires of the voters than institutions with competitive veto points. Goodin (1996: 340) sees in such collective veto points institutions that favor the "highest common concerns."

Huber and Powell (1994) discovered a similar mechanism of Parliamentary-PR systems. In their path-breaking article entitled "Congruence between Citizens and Policymakers in Two Visions of Liberal Democracy" they found, contrary to their expectations, that there is a higher congruence of policies between policymakers and the median citizen in their "proportionate influence model" as opposed to their "majority control" model.[13]

The Huber and Powell finding means that their proportionate influence model, which is empirically quite similar to our consensus measure and substantively similar to our "collective veto points" concept, is closer to the desires of the median voter than the majority model. In other words, policies that are created in an institutional arena of PR, multiparty legislators, and multiparty governments, are more responsive than the policies created in majoritarian, single-party, bare-majority, SMD systems. Government distance, thus, is a function of the constitutional set up of various countries— the more inclusionary, accessible, and accommodative the constitution, the more responsive government is to the median voter; conversely, the more exclusionary, inaccessible, and competitive the constitution, the less responsive government is to the median voter. The cause is institutional, the effect is government distance. The literature on consensus systems, Olson's concept of encompassing organizations, Huber and Powell's "proportionate influence model," the logic of corporatism, and Goodin's concept of the "the highest common concern"—all these conceptual understandings of the workings of political institutions are highly intertwined and lead to predictable effects, namely that "...institutions which respond to a single, unified, nationwide constituency are presumably more likely to take an all-encompassing, highest-common-concern view of matters" (Goodin 1996: 340).

The more political power is dispersed, that is, the more a country employs consensual political structures that allow inclusion and access of many groups of society to political power mostly through PR electoral rules, the higher the representativeness and capacity of such governments to respond to policy issues such as how and to what extent to react to the forces of globalization. The wider encompassment of different groups ensures that losers of globalization have a stake in the viability of government. If the pressures of globalization on governments increase, consensus governments should remain more stable and maintain higher policy control domestically, and should make such countries more predictable internationally. In majoritarian systems, no matter whether institutions favor either the winners or losers of globalization, government instability, policy instability, increased industrial disputes, or even rebellion could ensue as significant societal strata are systematically excluded from effectively engaging in politics.

The Chiapas rebellion on New Year's day of 1994 is a fitting example of the dangers of internationalization without inclusion. Labor strikes in France at the end of 1995, which were aimed at reversing the French government's efforts to bring its budget in line with the Maastricht criteria, plunged the country into one of its worst crises since the May events of 1968. Again in France, part of the overwhelming victory of the Socialists in the general election in June of 1997 indicate that citizens resent the idea of being governed by "Brussels bureaucrats" to whom they feel no ideological connection and from whom they do not expect any help. Adding to the sense of frustration, French politicians, in responding to political protests over the erosion of the Common Agricultural Policy (CAP), argued that their hands were tied by agreements with the European Union and the WTO. This type of blame shifting represents a major break between the principles representativeness and accountability. Voters will respond by voting for anti-EU parties leading to a slowdown if not a reversal of neoliberal convergence.[14] In the same vein, the recent violent clashes between ordinary citizens and WTO delegates in Seattle is another powerful manifestation of the systemic contradictions between global economic opportunity and local democratic accountability.

Should the erosion of democracy occur as a result of globalization, it should be less severe in consensus systems as compared to majoritarian systems as such institutional features cushion the effects of globalization and reduce social dislocation. Most recent evidence indicates that losers in consensual systems are more satisfied with the political system and its process than in majoritarian systems. Anderson and Guillory (1997: 78) find that "...the more consensual the democracy, the more likely it is that losers are satisfied with the functioning of democracy...." The explanation for their finding of a higher satisfaction with government among losers (those who have not voted for the governing party or parties) is that "... losers are more likely to be satisfied with the way democracy works, despite their minority status, if there are mechanisms for procedural justice in the democratic process and opportunities for input into the decisions made by the government" (Anderson and Guillory 1997: 79).

The concepts of sharing power, of inclusion and accommodation, central to consensual arrangements, become the guarantor of the legitimacy of government. This particular understanding of legitimacy becomes even more important as globalization forces countries to reevaluate long-standing social institutions that once represented the pride of nations such as social security, national health plans, paid vacations, support for elderly, unemployment insurance, and retraining programs. These are the very institutions that helped to achieve social harmony amidst turbulent economic circumstances. The potential effects of globalization are twofold: it tends to undermine these very long-standing institutions of the welfare state and, secondly, it leads to social fragmentation by creating new fissures in society such as those between economic sectors like agriculture and manufacturing, skilled and unskilled labor, degree of mobility, dependence on the state for income supplements, or simply put, those who prosper in a globalized economy and those who do not, or skilled and unskilled labor. Dani Rodrik, a neoclassical economist recognizes these dangers quite clearly; thus, he asserts that a balance between openness and domestic needs has to be found and he strongly argues for increasing social insurance as globalization increases (Rodrik 1997).

Ultimately, the content of policies—whether a country pursues globalization or not—is less important than the way in which that decision has been achieved. The deliberative mechanism inherent in consensus democracy becomes the procedural guarantor of legitimacy of a government facing the challenges of globalization.

Proposition Three: Consensus Democracy Promotes Public Investment

Consensual political institutions should have a higher affinity with state-led infrastructure provision than majoritarian institutions for the following reasons: broad, inclusive political institutions are supported by a wider range of groups of citizens than in majoritarian systems (Crepaz 1996). Consequently, minority groups, disadvantaged groups, those whose livelihoods depend on public works, and those with limited mobility, will use consensual institutions to ensure that such public projects will in fact be undertaken.

Recently, neoclassical economists have wondered why it is that growth rates do not converge among industrialized democracies. Some economists have argued that variations in growth patterns are linked to the degree of public investment in physical and educational infrastructure actually increasing productivity and competitiveness by providing public goods that are undersupplied by market forces (Aschauer 1990; Lucas 1988; Romer 1986, 1990). This form of "endogenous growth," so the argument goes, solves collective action problems facing individual entrepreneurs and provides a wide array of goods and services that contribute positively to economic growth by increasing the productivity of private capital. Aschauer (1990: 4) claims that the reduction of public investment in the United States over the last 25 years has halved the growth of productivity, depressed the rate of profits on nonfinancial corporate capital, and has reduced private investment in plants and equipment. New growth theory is not inconsistent with big government and strong political influence in the provision of public goods. Garrett (1996) finds that, contrary to what neoclassical wisdom would predict, left labor power and fiscal expansion based on deficit spending has increased with greater internationalization rather than decreased.

Our hypothesized relationship between the degree of consensus democracy and public investment finds considerable empirical support in figure 9.1.

Figure 9.1 clearly shows that consensus democracy and public investment are positively related. Countries with consensual institutions such as Switzerland, Finland, and the Netherlands display high levels of public investment, whereas majoritarian countries such as Canada, Australia, and the United States display lower levels of public investments. As hypothesized, there is an elective affinity between consensus democracy and the instruments of new growth theory. If the promises of new growth theory are borne out, consensus governments should be in a better position than majoritarian ones to generate support for increased public investments leading to superior productivity. Hence, in the era of global capitalism, consensual political institutions in and of themselves may provide the real comparative advantage over other economies embedded in majoritarian constitutional systems.

In addition, in order for policies to be successful, such as investment in infrastructure both in physical and human capital, such policies need to be consistently pursued over a longer time horizon. A parliamentary-PR system not only provides access of various political interests but also tends to include these interests in multiparty executive cabinets fused to the legislature, ensuring representativeness on the one hand, and effectiveness on the other. This allows Parliamentary-PR systems to steer a more stable and long-term policy path. Despite occasional reshuffling of coalition partners, the general policy path is hardly ever dramatically changed. Diamond (1993: 99) argues convincingly that "Whatever the exact shape of a country's policy, it can only work if it is pursued consistently and pragmatically."[15]

The eminent British political scientist S.E. Finer (1975: 30–31) makes a similar argument when he says that economic development requires not so much a "strong hand as a steady one." Gamble and Walkland (1983) attribute the limited effectiveness of British economic policy to Britain's adversarial governmental system, which does not allow a steady policy path to emerge as a result of abrupt alternations of polarized parties in power. Policy moves in

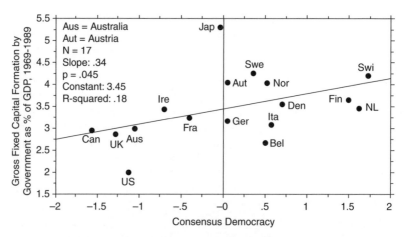

Fig. 9.1.   The relationship between consensus democracy and average gross fixed capital formation by government as percentage of GDP, 1969–1990.

Source: Data on gross fixed capital formation are from Boix (1997: 821). Data on Consensus Democracy are from Lijphart and Crepaz (1991: 245). The p-value is based on a one-tailed test.

fits and starts; what one government built up is dismantled by the next. The time horizon is too short for *any policy*, independent of partisan coloration, to take root.

Referring to the parliamentary party style in the British House of Commons, Finer (1980: 10) states "... the goal of the opposition is simply expressed: it is, and is seen to be, the *alternative government*. As such it does everything in its power to turn the government out and put itself in its place. There is an old Spanish proverb that expresses this role exactly: *Dejame tu para ponermi yo*—'Get out so that I can get in.' ...[T]he opposition and the government parties are zero-sum competitive. ...In short, the entire tradition of politics in the House is *adversary*."[16]

Finer's argument is that the electorate itself is fairly moderate, but, as a function of a majoritarian institutional structure, the electorate becomes artificially polarized. As a result, the electorate "...tends to have policies rammed down its throat with which it does not agree" (Robertson, 1984: 217). An example is the poll tax. Without much reflection and debate Thatcher decided to levy a flat tax on every British citizen. Even conservatives were outraged and in the spring of 1990 mass protest against the poll tax erupted into rioting in central London, producing extensive property damage and looting.

The more voices are heard, the more options will be entertained, and a greater range of information will be taken into consideration ensuring a steady, long term, and responsive policy style. In addition, widespread participation in policy decisions will be more widely accepted. Although it is true that multiparty coalition governments are shorter lived than bare majority cabinets (Lijphart 1984) this need not adversely affect regime performance. The relative difference in change of public policy is larger in two-party systems when parties alternatively become governing parties than in multiparty systems where one or two minor coalition parties are exchanged with other small parties.

To be successful, many policies need to be pursued over a lengthy period of time. In two party systems, where governmental responsibility alternates regularly between two parties with varying views on how to solve economic, political, or other problems, policy tends to get interrupted, reversed, modified, reviewed, etc. In other words, as governmental responsibilities alternate between two parties, stability, predictability, and steadiness of policy suffers. The more adversarial the policy style, the less steady and predictable policy is; conversely, the more consensual the policy style, the more steady and predictable it is.[17] We thus propose that if the predictions of the "new growth theory" are borne out, consensual systems should be better equipped than majoritarian systems in undertaking and escorting over a longer period of time the massive public investments necessary to remain internationally competitive.

Conclusion

Globalization inevitably creates opportunities as well as risks; the key difference in the way the two are distributed among a given population will be largely determined by political institutions. Our assessment of the impact of the forces of globalization against the insights of Lijphart's two models of democracy reinforces the critiques leveled against the literature treating all states as virtually equal in their exposure to and capacity of accommodating or resisting globalization. We argue that nationally specific constitutional structures and institutions will interact with the international economy in distinctive ways and that consensus democracies will have a greater capacity to ensure that domestic societies remain the most significant site of authority as well as social change.

The extent to which sovereignty and accountability become eroded due to globalization is contingent upon the very institutional foundations of those concepts in the first place. We submit that consensus democracies by virtue of what we have termed the "politics of inclusion" have a stronger propensity to foster responsibility, engender legitimacy, and promote public investment. All of these factors fundamentally will qualify the changes a society undergoes in this increasingly globalized world.

A careful reconsideration of Lijphart's work allowed us to elucidate the specific ways in which consensus democracies exhibit a higher capacity to deal with the repercussions of international economic integration in both a more equitable and a more efficient manner than majoritarian democracies. We posited that consensual systems will experience less economic dislocation and social and political unrest resulting from globalization than we would expect to transpire in majoritarian systems. The main argument here derives from the observation that in consensual systems, particularly those with Parliamentary-PR institutions, a greater degree of programmatic and nationwide policy making occurs. Thus, more deliberation and careful discussion of the consequences of global markets may prevent rash policy decisions that would tend to promote short-term profits to the sacrifice of long-term social stability and prosperity. Conversely, given the pure economic rewards of globalization accruing to the few and the powerful who are equipped with higher skills, greater access to capital and ease of mobility, a more sectoral, short-term policy approach would be preferred, and this type of approach is endemic to majoritarian systems where narrowly based interests are able to dominate the political process.

If democratic governance truly rests upon the notion of consent, then how consent is determined and expressed becomes critical in establishing the degree of legitimacy people attach to their governments and political systems. We argued that legitimacy is higher in consensual systems than in majoritarian systems. Winners and losers in consensual systems are merely differentiated by which party had a clearer electoral mandate as often the losers still have an essential role to play in the formal political process, unlike their counterparts in majoritarian systems who often get completely shut out as a consequence of the winner-take-all approach to politics. In an era that has been described as a challenge to big government and the welfare state because of increased pressures of international markets, new and more numerous losers are emerging. If these groups have a more vocal role in politics and a more credible sense of efficacy consistent with our argument about legitimacy of consensus governments, then it certainly follows that less dislocation will take place in such societies. If there is no conscious, deliberate effort on the part of government to respond proactively to the challenges of an increasingly competitive international market by encouraging new skills and broad-based implementation of new technologies, then only the most well-positioned and privileged will be the winners. In political systems where winners and losers are not so easily distinguished, we expect this also to be the case for the benefits and detriments of globalization. Thus, there will be far fewer left on the margins of society as a result of economic forces because the marginalized are also an integral part of governing in consensus democracies, whereas in majoritarian systems, both in terms of governing and as the recipients of the gale winds of economics, they are perpetually on the margins of society.

Our aim in this essay has been to reaffirm the "primacy of the political" in the face of global economic challenges and to draw out how variations in domestic politics, consistent with Lijphart's typology of democracies, may put this primacy on firmer theoretical and empirical grounds. Neither economic forces nor democratic politics take place in a vacuum devoid of the constraints and possibilities created by the other. What we believe to be the most critical factor in assessing the impact of globalization is the degree to which policies—whether they be in favor of, or resisting, further globalization—are based on mass support. Our contention is that consensual political institutions provide the mechanisms whereby more inclusive participation ensures that no matter what policy direction these countries take, it will rest upon the widest consent possible, which is, after all, the essence of democracy.

Notes

[1]It is paradoxical that during a period in which political science discovered the importance of institutions, that is, mechanisms designed to enable markets to overcome market failures such as monopolies, public goods, moral hazard, adverse selection, externalities, and asymmetrical information, to claim that states and other structures of governance should best move out of the way to allow markets free reign. Markets and market outcomes do not just happen automatically, based on some natural order (despite Adam Smith's claim to the opposite); instead, at least according to the French Régulation School, they need to be embedded in a system of governance, both in order to enable markets to function in the first place, and also to protect citizens from some of the consequences of markets such as poverty, environmental degradation, strikes and industrial disputes, and other manifestations of unfettered market forces. Marx warned us long ago that markets left alone will develop into oligopolies and monopolies, thereby undermining the logic of capitalism. Paradoxically, the state is needed to ensure the functioning of "free markets."

[2]Although within that very group there are some who refer to the process of globalization as "globaloney."

[3]In Norway, the Basic Agreement was created in 1932. In Switzerland, the Peace Agreement was fostered in 1937. The famous Swedish Saltsjøbaden Agreement was made in 1938, and Belgium's Social Solidarity Pact came into existence in 1945. Denmark led all of these small countries by establishing the Kanslergade Agreement in early 1932.

[4]The gist of the corporatism literature argued distinctly that small states cannot hide behind high tariff barriers, that they have to liberalize their economies since they are price takers rather than price makers. Certainly, neoliberal convergence should not be much of a challenge for the small states that have lived with open economies since the end of WWII. Thinking this line of

thought consequently to its end, we should expect larger states to be more worried about globalization than smaller states since they have remained relatively more closed than smaller states.

[5]Strange (1995) goes so far as to say that globalization threatens to render, not just the study of international relations and comparative politics, but much of Western social science obsolete.

[6]There are many observers, of course, who do not share the idea that markets represent anything like an invisible hand or that markets are natural or spontaneous. Keynes, for example, clearly realized that some economic crises may require state intervention to restore the confidence of investors and consumers. Others, such as Polanyi (1957) have strongly argued that markets only function if they are embedded in a set of agreed or imposed rules. Similarly the Paris-based Régulation School of Political Economy also claims that, to be efficient, markets work best when the state is a strong regulator (Boyer 1996).

[7]Even before 1869 there were questions raised by those deeply concerned about the impact of global markets arguing that "Separate individuals have become more and more enslaved under a power alien to them,...a power which has become more and more enormous and, in the last instance, turns out to be the world market." These words were uttered by one Karl Marx in 1845–1846 as he penned *The German Ideology* (as quoted in Tucker 1978: 163).

[8]These are the most relevant constitutional features although the last one, multiple issue dimensions, is certainly consistent with the logic of inclusion and access to the political system found in consensual systems.

[9]There are, however, countries in which, despite PR electoral rules, the number of parties remained rather low, such as Austria which, until the early 1980s had a very stable two and a half party system despite PR. The reasons for this unusual outcome lie in the political culture of Austria, often described as "Lagermentalität" (camp mentality) or pillarization, or what Stein Rokkan (1977) once called "Verzuiling."

[10]The overall outcome is anarchical and devoid of any conscious direction. Whatever the outcome—liberalization or protectionism—in presidential-SMD systems, "...the whole is an accident in aggregation. Only the pieces are important" (Moe and Caldwell 1994). This is, of course, a very similar critique that Theodore Lowi lodged against pluralism in general when he claimed that "In a pluralistic government there is, therefore, no substance. Neither is there procedure. There is only process." (Lowi 1969: 63)

[11]The time period of Schwartz's investigation ranges from roughly the early 1950s to the early 1990s. Since then, of course, New Zealand shifted to a PR system in 1993 which, most likely, will make the politics in this country more consensual than has hitherto been the case.

[12]A typical example is the British case where none of the two leading parties commanded a majority in popular votes since 1935 although they alternately commanded legislative majorities, which is, of course, a result of the first-past-the-post electoral system.

[13]The institutional items that constituted the proportionate influence model were the effective number of parties, the proportionality of the electoral system, and the degree of opposition committee influence. The majority control system was made up of the identifiability of future governments, the past government status, single party or a pre-election coalition wins majority, and also the degree of opposition committee influence.

[14]Manfred Bienefeld (1996: 434) argues that a return to stronger nation-states is actually inevitable. "The only question is what form these states will take and whether the restoration of national sovereignty can be achieved before globalization drags the world into a dark age of chaotic instability and conflict. Globalization is essentially a negative phenomenon, destroying the sovereignty and cohesion of nation-states, and thereby depriving markets of the social and political guidance without which they cannot function effectively."

[15]But Diamond (1993: 102) also warns that: "With the fragmentation of the party system [as a result of PR], voters may keep getting virtually the same coalition governments, with minor shifts in cabinet portfolios, no matter how the vote may change among parties. Thus, it becomes difficult truly to change policy, and to 'throw the rascals out.' This may *enhance stability of policy* even as it leads to frequent changes in government (as in Italy), but at the cost of denying voters clear electoral choice." Although Diamond's warnings are certainly in order, he chose a particularly suspect case, namely Italy, to make his point. Yet, even Italy's widely perceived governmental chaos is not that disorderly, and economically, Italy is certainly outperforming the stalwart Westminster system. There are a host of highly successful countries, such as Germany, Austria, the Low and the Nordic Countries, which have employed Parliamentary-PR systems without seriously undermining issues of representativeness.

[16]Even the face-to-face seating arrangement in the British House of Commons suggests an adversarial style of confrontation as opposed to many other Parliaments in which the various members of political parties are seated in a half circle.

[17]Gamble and Walkland (1983: x) have argued that this adversary political style has negatively affected British economic policies. "The rituals of the two party adversary system have contributed to the political failure to reverse or arrest relative economic decline." Their argument is that the British majoritarian political system does not provide sufficient steadiness in order to steer the economy along a stable, continuous path. "The [British] government pursued these sound policies...but just as they were bearing fruit there was a general election which it lost, and its adversary then returned to office with its own new radical manifesto. So the cycle began again. The main casualty was business confidence and the main consequence a deteriorating economic performance" (1983: 25).

References

Almond A. Gabriel. 1989. Review Article: "The International-National Connection," *British Journal of Political Science*, 19:237–59.

Anderson, Christopher, J. and Christine A. Guillory. 1997. "Political Institutions and Satisfaction with Democracy: A Cross National Analysis of Consensus and Majoritarian Systems," *American Political Science Review*, 91:66–81.

Aschauer, David. A. 1990. *Public Investment and Private Sector Growth. The Economic Benefits of Reducing America's 'Third Deficit'.* Washington, DC: Economic Policy Institute.

Berger, Suzanne and Ronald Dore, eds. 1996. *National Diversity and Global Capitalism.* Ithaca: Cornell University Press.

Bienefeld, Manfred. 1996. "Is a strong national economy a utopian goal at the end of the twentieth century?" In Boyer, Robert and Daniel Drache, eds., *States against Markets. The Limits of Globalization,* 415–40. London: Routledge.

Boix, Charles. 1997. "Political Parties and the Supply Side of the Economy: The Provision of Physical and Human Capital in Advanced Economies, 1960–1990," *American Journal of Political Science,* 41:814–45.

Boyer, Robert. 1996. "State and Market: A New Engagement for the Twenty First Century." In Boyer, Robert and Daniel Drache, eds., *States against Markets. The Limits of Globalization,* 84–116. London: Routledge.

Boyer, Robert and Daniel Drache, eds. 1996. *States against Markets. The Limits of Globalization.* London: Routledge.

Cable, Vincent. 1995. "The Diminished Nation State: A Study in the Loss of Economic Power." *Daedalus,* 124:23–54.

Cameron, David, R. 1978. "The Expansion of the Public Economy: A Comparative Analysis." In *American Political Science Review*, 72:1243–61.

Cerny, Philip, G. 1994. "The dynamics of financial globalization: Technology, market structure, and policy response," *Policy Sciences,* 27:319–42.

Cerny, Philip. G. 1995. "Globalization and the changing logic of collective action," *International Organization,* 49:595–625.

Crepaz, Markus, M. L. 1996. "Consensus versus Majoritarian Democracy: Political Institutions and their Impact in Macroeconomic Performance and Industrial Disputes," *Comparative Political Studies,* 29:4–26.

Crepaz, Markus, M. L. and Arend Lijphart. 1995. "Linking and Integrating Corporatism and Consensus Democracy: Theory, Concepts, and Evidence," *British Journal of Political Science,* 25:281–88.

Diamond, Larry. 1993. "Three Paradoxes of Democracy." In Larry Diamond and Mark F. Plattner, eds., *The global resurgence of democracy,* 95–107. Baltimore: Johns Hopkins University Press.

Duverger, Maurice. 1954. *Political Parties: Their Organization and Activity in the Modern State.* New York: Wiley.

Epstein, Gerald. 1996. "International Capital Mobility and the Scope for National Economic Management." In Boyer, Robert and Daniel Drache, eds. *States against Markets. The Limits of Globalization,* 211–26. London: Routledge.

Finer, Samuel, E. 1975. *Adversary Politics and Electoral Reform.* London: Wigram.

Finer, Samuel, E. 1980. *The Changing British Party System, 1945–1979.* Washington DC: American Enterprise Institute.

Gamble, A. M. and S. A. Walkland. 1984. *The British Party System, 1945–1979.* Washington, DC: American Enterprise Institute.

Garrett, Geoffrey. 1996. "Capital Mobility, Trade, and the Domestic Politics of Economic Policy." In Keohane, Robert, O. and Helen V. Milner, eds., *Internationalization and Domestic Politics,* 79–107. Cambridge: Cambridge University Press.

Garrett, Geoffrey and Peter Lange. 1996. "Internationalization, Institutions, and Political Change." In Keohane, Robert, O. and Helen V. Milner, eds., *Internationalization and Domestic Politics,* 48–78. Cambridge: Cambridge University Press.

Gerschenkron, Alexander. 1963. "Economic Backwardness in Historical Perspective." In *Economic Backwardness in Historical Perspective.* Cambridge: Harvard University Press.

Goodin, Robert, E. 1996. "Institutionalizing the Public Interest: The Defense of Deadlock and Beyond," *American Political Science Review,* 90:331–43.

Gourevitch, Peter. 1978. "The Second Image Reversed: The International Sources of Domestic Politics," *International Organization,* 32:881–912.

Gourevitch, Peter. 1996. "The Macropolitics of Microinstitutional Differences in the Analysis of Comparative Capitalism." In Berger, Suzanne and Ronald Dore, eds., *National Diversity and Global Capitalism,* 239–62. Ithaca: Cornell University Press.

Helleiner, Eric. 1996. "Post-Globalization: Is the financial liberalization trend likely to be reversed?" In Boyer, Robert and Daniel Drache, eds., *States against Markets. The Limits of Globalization,* 193–210. London: Routledge.

Hintze, Otto. 1975. "Military Organization and the Organization of the State." In Gilbert, Felix, ed., *The Historical Essays of Otto Hintze.* New York: Oxford University Press.

Hirst, Paul and Thompson, Grahame. 1996. *Globalization in Question. The International Economy and the Possibilities of Governance.* Cambridge: Polity Press.

Huber, John D. and Bingham G. Powell, Jr. 1994. "Congruence between Citizens and Policymakers in Two Visions of Liberal Democracy," *World Politics,* 46:291–326.

Huber, Evelyne, Charles, Ragin, and Stephens, John D. 1993. "Social Democracy, Christian Democracy, Constitutional Structure, and the Welfare State," *American Journal of Sociology,* 99:711–49.

Immergut, Ellen. 1992. *The Political Construction of Interests: National Health Insurance Politics in Switzerland, France and Sweden, 1930–1970.* New York: Cambridge University Press.

Katzenstein, Peter, ed. 1978. *Between Power and Plenty: Foreign Economic Policies of Advanced Industrial Countries.* Madison: University of Wisconsin Press.

Katzenstein, Peter. 1985. *Small States in World Markets.* Ithaca: Cornell University Press.

Keohane, Robert, O. and Joseph, Nye, Jr. 1977. *Power and Interdependence: World Politics in Transition.* Boston: Little Brown.

Keohane, Robert, O. and Helen V. Milner, eds. 1996. *Internationalization and Domestic Politics* Cambridge: Cambridge University Press.

Krugman, Paul. 1995. "Growing World Trade: Causes and Consequences," *Brookings Papers on Economic Activity,* 327–77.

Lijphart, Arend. 1968. *Politics of Accommodation: Pluralism and Democracy in the Netherlands.* Berkeley: University of California Press.

Lijphart, Arend. 1977. *Democracy in Plural Societies. A Comparative Exploration.* New Haven: Yale University Press.

Lijphart, Arend. 1984. *Democracies. Patterns of Majoritarian and Consensus Government in Twenty-One Countries.* New Haven: Yale University Press.

Lijphart, Arend. 1999. *Patterns of Democracy. Government Forms and Perfomance in Thirty-Six Countries.* New Haven: Yale University Press.

Lijphart, Arend and Markus M. L. Crepaz. 1991. "Corporatism and consensus democracy in eighteen countries: conceptual and empirical linkages," *British Journal of Political Science,* 21:235–46.

Lowi, Theodore. 1969. *The End of Liberalism: Ideology, Policy, and the Crisis of Public Authority.* New York: Norton.

Lucas, Robert. E. 1988. "On the Mechanics of Economic Development," *Journal of Monetary Economics,* 22:3–42.

Maioni, Antonia. 1992. "Explaining Differences in Welfare State Development: A Comparative Study of Health Insurance in Canada and the United States," Ph.D. dissertation, Northwestern University, Department of Political Science.

Mansfield, Edward, D. and Marc L. Busch. 1995. "The political economy of nontariff barriers: a cross national analysis," *International Organization,* 49:723–49.

Moe, Terry, M. and Caldwell, Michael. 1994. "The Institutional Foundations of Democratic Government: A Comparison of Presidential and Parliamentary Systems," *Journal of Institutional and Theoretical Economics,* 170:171–95.

Olson, Mancur. 1982. *The rise and decline of nations. Economic growth, stagflation, and social rigidities.* New Haven: Yale University Press.

Polanyi, Karl. 1957. *The Great Transformation.* Boston: Beacon Hill.

Robertson, David. 1984. "Adversary Politics, Public Opinion and Electoral Cleavages." In Dennis Kavanagh and Gillian Peele, eds., *Comparative Government and Politics. Essays in honour of S. E. Finer,* 214–41. Boulder: Westview Press.

Rodrik, Dani. 1997. *Has Globalization Gone Too Far?* Washington, DC: Institute for International Economics.

Rogowski, Ronald. 1987. "Trade and the Variety of Democratic Institutions," *International Organization,* 41:203–15.

Rokkan, Stein. 1977. "Towards a General Concept of Verzuiling," *Political Studies,* 25:563–70.

Romer, Paul. 1986. "Increasing Returns and Long-Run Growth," *Journal of Political Economy,* 94:1002–37.

Romer, Paul. 1986. "Endogenous Technological Change," *Journal of Political Economy,* 98:71–102.

Schwartz, Herman. 1994. "Small States in Big Trouble. State Reorganization in Australia, Denmark, New Zealand, and Sweden in the 1980s,"*World Politics,* 46: 527–55.

Schmidt, Manfred. 1996. "When Parties Matter: A Review of the possibilities and limits of partisan influence on public policy," *European Journal of Political Research,* 30:155–83.

Schmidt, Vivian, A. 1995. "The New World Order, Incorporated: The Rise of Business and the Decline of the Nation State," *Daedalus,* 124:75–106.

Skocpol, Theda. 1985. "Bringing the State Back In: Strategies of Analysis in Current Research." In Peter B. Evans, Dietrich Rueschemeyer, and Theda Skocpol, eds., *Bringing the State Back In.* Cambridge: Cambridge University Press.

Strange, Susan. 1995. "The Limits of Politics," *Government and Opposition,* 291–311.

Streeck, Wolfgang. 1996. "Lean Production in the German Automobile Industry: A Test Case for Convergence Theory." In Berger, Suzanne and Ronald Dore, eds., *National Diversity and Global Capitalism,* 138–70. Ithaca: Cornell University Press.

Swank, Duane. 1997. "Funding the Welfare State: Globalization and the Taxation of Business in Advanced Market Economies." *Political Studies,* forthcoming.

Tsebelis, George. 1995. "Decision Making in Political Systems: Veto Players in Presidentialism, Parliamentarism, Multicameralism and Multipartyism," *British Journal of Political Science,* 25:289–325.

Tucker, Robert. 1978. *The Marx-Engels Reader.* New York: W. W. Norton and Company, second edition.

Wade, Robert. 1996. "Globalization and its Limits: Reports of the Death of the National Economy are Greatly Exaggerated." In Berger, Suzanne and Ronald Dore, eds., *National Diversity and Global Capitalism,* 60–88. Ithaca: Cornell University Press.

CHAPTER 10

Varieties of Nonmajoritarian Democracy

Arend Lijphart

I am delighted and very grateful to receive the great honor that this volume represents and also very pleased to have received the invitation to contribute a final chapter to the volume myself—an invitation that was indirectly suggested by my good friend and former UC San Diego colleague, the late Henry W. Ehrmann, as David Wilsford explains in his introduction. It has also been a pure delight to read all of the preceding chapters as they arrived on my desk, with their incisive commentaries on ideas pioneered or partly pioneered in my work, their further analyses of these ideas, and creative suggestions for additional conceptual and theoretical development.

Three major themes unite the chapters in this book. First, all authors emphasize that there is more to democracy than just the majoritarian kind and that the contrast between majoritarian and nonmajoritarian democracy is one of great importance and magnitude. The second common theme is that there is not just one alternative to majoritarian democracy, but rather alternatives (in the plural)—that is, a variety of nonmajoritarian democratic systems and models: consociational and consensus democracy, degrees and subtypes within the main consociational and consensus types, and the different dimensions and ingredients of the two main types. Third, the chapters emphasize the consequences of the different forms of democracy, both in terms of democratic quality and in terms of public policy outcomes, with generally positive conclusions about what nonmajoritarian democracies can accomplish. Let me comment on each of these three themes in turn—with a special emphasis on the second.

Democracy and Majority Rule

There is a paradox in political science about how democracy is treated. On the one hand, political scientists tend to differentiate among a large number of different types and subtypes of democracy. In their article on democracy "with adjectives," David Collier and Steven Levitsky (1997: 431) count "hundreds of subtypes" that have been used. A recent example of a classification of democracies into a large number of types is Richard S. Katz's (1997: 280–96) analysis of binary, Downsian, Ostrogorskian, legislative, socialist, Tory, Benthamite, Schumpeterian, Madisonian, polyarchal, consociational, and communitarian democracy.

On the other hand, political scientists tend to revert to thinking in terms of just one type—the majoritarian type—when they define democracy in terms of its bare essentials as a decision-making system, that is, democracy without adjectives. A good example is the alternation-in-office criterion that Adam Przeworski and his collaborators (1996) use to determine which political systems qualify as democracies. This criterion implies a government-versus-opposition pattern, in which one large party holds office and another large party is in the opposition but can replace the governing party at the next election. According to this criterion, Switzerland, normally regarded as one of the world's most democratic countries, would not be counted as a democracy on account of its semipermanent grand coalition of governing parties since 1959. An even clearer example is the "two-turnover test" that Samuel P. Huntington (1991: 266–67) proposes to determine whether a democracy is stable or consolidated, because the term turnover means not just a slight change in government, such as one party entering or leaving an existing coalition, but the opposition becoming the government: "By this test, a democracy may be viewed as consolidated if the party or group that takes power in the initial election at the time of transition loses a subsequent election and turns over power to those election winners, and if those election winners then peacefully turn over power to the winners of a later election."

An explicit argument along these lines is Stephanie Lawson's (1993: 192–193) statement "that political opposition is the sine qua non of contemporary democracy in mass polities and that its institutionalization in some form or another is required before a regime can be called 'democratic' with any real meaning"—again relegating a country like Switzerland to the non-democracies. And a classic example is the following statement by Alexis de Tocqueville: "The very essence of democratic government consists in the absolute sovereignty of the majority" (cited in Dahl 1956: 35).

Nonpolitical scientists also tend to equate democracy with majority rule. Striking examples are comments prompted by developments in South Africa—a case discussed at length by Thomas Koelble and Andrew Reynolds in this volume—from spokesmen at the two extreme ends of the political spectrum: conservative columnist William Safire and the late Joe Slovo, leader of South Africa's Communist Party. Safire (1986) argued that the democratic rule of "one person, one vote...means majority rule." Slovo was quoted as saying: "We should stop playing with words. We know only one kind of democracy and that is majority rule" (New York Times News Service 1990).

Most people—both political scientists and nonpolitical scientists, and probably including the authors of the preceding apodictic pronouncements—would hasten to add that majority rule does not mean absolute and unrestrained majority rule. Even when they do not explicitly add that majority rule must be limited by minority rights, it is likely that they mean to make this reservation implicitly. However, limited and restrained majority rule still means majority rule, albeit with certain reservations and qualifications. And the concept of majoritarian democracy with restraints differs fundamentally from the conception of two alternative approaches to democracy. Bingham Powell captures the essence of the contrast very well when he emphasizes that the two constitutional designs have sharply divergent visions, based on divergent underlying logics. In fact, as he points out, this divergence prevents us from judging their records on such a basic democratic principle as democratic responsiveness, because it is impossible to find neutral standards that are not deeply embedded in the divergent conceptions and assumptions of the two visions themselves.

If there is one main contribution to political science that I think I can be credited with is that I have tirelessly—perhaps even tiresomely!—promoted the idea that nonmajoritarianism consists not just of a series of peripheral reservations that can be attached to majoritarian democracy but that it represents a comprehensive alternative model and philosophy of democratic government. Having made this claim, modesty requires me to add at once that I have certainly not been the only scholar, and not even the first scholar, to promote this idea. Robert A. Dahl's (1956) distinction between populist and Madisonian democracy, Jane Mansbridge's (1980) distinction between adversary and unitary democracy, and William H. Riker's (1982) *Liberalism Against Populism* (to cite his book title) represent similar contrasts between two alternative visions. And Powell's (1982) *Contemporary Democracies,* in which he distinguishes between majoritarian and representational democracies, was published two years before my *Democracies* (Lijphart 1984).

Let me also add that I may have been the most tireless champion of consociational theory, but not its only or first champion either. Both my case study of consociationalism in the Netherlands and my first comparative article on this subject were published in 1968 (Lijphart 1968a, 1968b), a year after Gerhard Lehmbruch's (1967) study of *Proporzdemokratie* (proportional democracy) in Austria and Switzerland. My nominee for the first modern consociational theorist is the late Nobel Prize-winning economist Sir Arthur Lewis. In his short book *Politics in West Africa,* published in 1965, Lewis argued that majority rule had been a disaster for the plural societies of West Africa, and he proposed an alternative form of democracy that would be workable; he did not attach a name to his alternative but it clearly was the consociational alternative.

Consociational Democracy and Consensus Democracy

In the preceding section, I repeatedly speak of majoritarian democracy and the nonmajoritarian alternative. I must now shift from the singular "alternative" to the plural "alternatives." All of the chapters in this volume recognize and, in most cases, strongly urge the notion that there are numerous forms and degrees of nonmajoritarian democracy. Let me first discuss the two kinds of nonmajoritarianism on which much of my work has focused: consociational democracy (which I have also referred to by its less polysyllabic and more easily pronounceable synonym "power-sharing democracy") and consensus democracy. In my writings, I usually have dealt with one or the other concept and—unlike, in particular, Andrew Reynolds in this volume—I have rarely used them jointly or in juxtaposition.

The two concepts are obviously closely related, but there are important differences as well. In *Democracy in Plural Societies* (Lijphart 1977) and elsewhere, I have defined consociational democracy in terms of four basic characteristics (grand coalition, segmental autonomy, proportionality, and minority veto), but in *Democracies* (Lijphart 1984), I defined consensus democracy in terms of eight characteristics (oversized coalitions, executive-legislative balance of power, a multiparty system, multiple issue dimensions, electoral proportionality, federalism and decentralization, bicameralism, and a rigid constitution protected by judicial review). These two lists of characteristics overlap considerably, but there is not a single instance in which characteristics from the two lists coincide completely. How the two concepts came to be defined so differently can be explained by their intellectual history—the kind of step-by-step, serendipitous process that Rein Taagepera correctly detects in the development of my *Democracies* and that he argues is typical of scientific progress.

I discovered consociationalism by examining the cases of stable democracy in deeply divided societies. These were deviant cases for political science theory as it had developed until the 1960s, which held that such divided societies were too conflictual to be able to sustain democracy. By examining the four main European cases of divided societies but stable democracy—my native country of the Netherlands, Belgium, Switzerland, and Austria—and later also Lebanon and Malaysia, I found that the key explanation consisted of the cooperative and coalescent, instead of majoritarian and competitive, behavior of the political elites that turned the potentially unstable political systems into stable ones. In the same way, I also discovered the four essential practices of consociational democracy mentioned earlier. In short, in *Democracy in Plural Societies* and in several articles leading up to this book, my modus operandi was deviant case analysis and generalization on the basis of empirical spadework.

My original plan for *Democracies* was to build onto the consociational-majoritarian contrast of *Democracy in Plural Societies* and to achieve the three further aims of 1) using the contrast as the organizational framework for the analysis of all democracies, not just those in deeply divided societies; 2) making the consociational and majoritarian features as precise and measurable as possible; and 3) starting out with the characteristics of majoritarian democracy and defining each of the consociational traits as the opposite of the corresponding majoritarian trait. As far as the third point is concerned, what had struck me is that, if the basic majoritarian principle is defined as concentration of power in the hands of the majority, the institutional characteristics of majoritarian democracy can be logically and easily derived from this principle. The eight majoritarian features that I formulated in this way then logically led to eight contrasting nonmajoritarian features; for instance, the opposite of single-party, bare-majority cabinets is multiparty oversized cabinets; the opposite of two-party systems is multipartism; and so on. I originally continued to use the label consociational for this nonmajoritarian alternative in my thinking and even in some writings like my edited book on Belgian politics (Lijphart 1981), as Rein Taagepera points out. However, I shifted to the term "consensus democracy" when I became convinced that the new concept deviated too much from the original consociational idea.

The substantive differences between consociational and consensus democracy are summarized in Andrew Reynolds's chapter and need not be repeated here. However, one aspect to which I do want to pay attention is that, in spite of these differences, the two concepts are sufficiently similar that we would expect a particular democracy that is consociational to also be a consensual system (as well as a system with what Bingham Powell calls a proportional constitutional design). But there are two important cases where major discrepancies and disagreements exist: Austria, which I describe as consociational in *Democracy in Plural Societies* but as majoritarian (on the first dimension) in *Democracies*, and South Africa, which I have described as consociational, but which Andrew Reynolds regards as consensual but not consociational and Thomas Koelble as only partly and potentially consensual.

Shortly after I had finished the book manuscript of *Democracies*, but before the book was published, I met Gerhard Lehmbruch and showed him my two-dimensional conceptual map with the location of each of my democracies on it. I have mentioned Lehmbruch before as one of the first consociational theorists with a special interest in the Austrian and Swiss cases. When he saw the location of Austria in one corner of the map—majoritarian with regard to its cabinets and party system, although consensual on the second, federal-unitary dimension—he told me bluntly that the majoritarian classification of Austria was totally wrong even for the period after the heydays of the consociational Grosse Koalition from 1945 to 1966. My only response at that time was that I was also unhappy about this discrepancy, but that unfortunately my measurements did not give me a choice.

Since then, however, I have come to the conclusion that, when this kind of discrepancy between expert judgment and hard measurements occurs, it is necessary to take a second look at our measurements. Two adjustments are clearly needed in the Austrian case. One mistake was that I operationalized bare-majority cabinets versus broad coalition cabinets as what coalition theorists call "minimal winning" and "oversized" cabinets, respectively. Minimal winning cabinets are either single-party majority cabinets or coalition cabinets in which all parties are needed to command a parliamentary majority; that is, the loss of even the smallest cabinet partner means that the cabinet becomes a minority cabinet. Oversized cabinets are coalition cabinets that have unnecessary parties in them. According to these definitions, the Austrian grand coalitions of the country's two largest parties that together had an overwhelming majority in parliament—never less than 87 percent of the seats in the years from 1949 to 1966—were still "minimal winning" coalitions in this period because neither party had a parliamentary majority. Here common sense has to override definitional rigor, and such broad coalitions—probably any coalition based on more than 80 percent of parliamentary seats—should be counted as oversized.[1]

The second adjustment consists of adding a crucial variable to the first dimension, on which Austria wrongly ended up on the majoritarian side: the interest group system. One glaring omission from *Democracies* was that I included all of the major institutional variables except interest groups—especially glaring because the political science literature on interest groups has been dominated by the contrast between interest group pluralism and corporatism (also often referred to as societal or neocorporatism). Pluralism means free-for-all competition among interest groups, whereas corporatism means a coordinated system and concertation among the peak organizations and the government. This contrast is conceptually so similar to the majoritarian-consensus contrast that it cries out for inclusion. As Markus Crepaz and Vicki Birchfield mention in their chapter, corporatism was successfully added as a sixth element of the first dimension—in an article coauthored by Markus Crepaz and myself (1991). Experts disagree on how corporatist or pluralist some countries are, but there is no dissensus on where Austria belongs: it is usually regarded as the world's most strongly corporatist system. With this addition and with the reclassification of the grand coalitions as oversized, Austria moves to the consensual side of the spectrum, where Lehmbruch believed, and I agree, it belonged in the first place. This means that there is no longer a discrepancy between a consociational and a majoritarian Austria.

The South African Case

The disagreement with regard to South Africa cannot be resolved so easily, although I do not think that, in the final analysis, much disagreement between Thomas Koelble, Andrew Reynolds, and myself remains. Koelble emphasizes both the limitations and the uncertainties with regard to the consensual nature of South Africa's new democratic system. Reynolds argues that the 1994 interim constitution was not consociational but that it could be considered consensual, and that the permanent constitution, adopted in 1996, moved farther away from consociationalism and that it also moved from a consensual arrangement to one intermediate between consensus and majoritarianism, particularly after the National Party left the Government of National Unity in mid-1996. My own interpretation, written immediately after the 1994 election, was that the interim constitution represented a fully consociational arrangement (Lijphart 1994a). I agree that developments since then have weakened consociationalism, but I would argue that the current system is still more consociational than majoritarian and considerably more consensual than majoritarian, especially on the first dimension.

We agree on four important points. First, the trend in South Africa has been away from nonmajoritarian rule in the direction of majoritarianism. Second, the two forms of nonmajoritarianism—consociation and consensus—have moved in tandem. This means that the kind of discrepancy that arose in the classification of Austria, noted earlier, is not a problem here. Third, political systems cannot be judged solely by what their constitutions prescribe. How political actors behave within—and sometimes beyond and against—constitutions is the crucial factor; constitutions have to be, in Koelble's words, "contextualized." As a matter of fact, my conclusion about the consociational nature of the system set up in 1994, particularly the question of group autonomy, was partly based on extra-constitutional grounds, such as statements by President Nelson Mandela. The most important element of cultural autonomy in consociational democracies is usually the right of each group to establish and run its own religious or linguistic schools. One of Mandela's pronouncements held out the promise that such minority schools would not only be permitted, as guaranteed by the constitution, but would continue to be subsidized by the government. The latter now seems to be much less clear and certain.

Fourth, we agree that there is a great deal of uncertainty about how South African politics will develop, and our slightly different interpretations can be attributed to a large extent to the fact that they are based on only five years of South African democracy. The new constitution was formally adopted in 1996 but did not enter into force until 1999. In *Democracies*, I included only those 21 democracies that had been continuously democratic from the late 1940s until 1980, not only because I wanted to be sure these were firmly established democracies, but also because I wanted to measure these democratic systems over a long period of time. For instance, there are few democracies that always have either minimal winning or oversized government coalitions; this means that we have to examine them for a long time in order to find out what the usual pattern of government formation is. Another example is executive-legislative balance of power, which I measured in terms of how long executives last—based on the assumption that durable executives predominate over their legislatures and that shorter cabinet duration indicates greater legislative influence; obviously, the measurement of cabinet durability requires analysis over many years, preferably decades.

In the South African case, the 1994 and 1999 elections were conducted according to the world's most proportional PR methods, but will future elections remain as proportional? The departure of the National Party from the Government of National Unity in 1996 spelled the end of a grand coalition, but the Inkatha Freedom Party remained a cabinet partner and hence the cabinet was still an oversized one. This oversized coalition was continued in 1999, but will the ANC eventually opt to rule by itself in a minimal winning cabinet? So far, cabinet durability has not been great; in the first five years, there were two different cabinets, a three-party grand coalition followed by a two-party oversized coalition. The two-party coalition was renewed in 1999, but it may well be followed by a long stretch of one-party ANC cabinets. The permanent constitution appears to be at least partly federal with a new upper house patterned after the German model, but will this federal—or semi-federal—chamber and the provincial governments have significant powers in practice in the longer run? The new constitutional court has so far behaved in an independent and activist fashion, but will it continue to do so?

In contrast with all of the preceding variables that make South Africa look quite consensual in its first three years of democracy, the party system as it emerged from the 1994 elections looks much more majoritarian than consensual. Thomas Koelble calls it a one-party dominant system. The measure that I use in *Democracies* is the effective number of political parties, originally proposed by Markku Laakso and Rein Taagepera (1979), which takes into account both the number and the relative sizes of the political parties. The effective number of parties in a pure two-party system with two roughly equal parties is about 2.0; it is 3.0 for a system with three equal parties; and it is about 2.5 for a system with two strong parties and one considerably weaker party as in the German two-and-a-half party system. When this formula is applied to the seats won by the parties in the 1994 and 1999 elections—in which the ANC captured 252 and 266, respectively, of the 400 seats—the effective number is 2.2 parties in both cases. This is much more like a majoritarian party system—the number for the United Kingdom in the 1945–1980 period was 2.1 parties—than like the party systems with about 5.0 effective parties in consensual Switzerland, Finland, and the Netherlands.

The question that arises here is whether the measure provides a valid picture for party systems with large parties that are highly uncohesive and heterogeneous, like the main American parties, the Congress party in India, and the faction-ridden Italian Christian Democrats, Japanese Liberal Democrats, and Colombian Liberals and Conservatives. Should some adjustment be made in these cases, for instance, by counting intraparty factions as well as parties? If so, this should probably also be done for the heterogeneous ANC—described by Koelble as an alliance of disparate groups—resulting in a higher value for the effective number of parties. Here, too, observation over a longer period is needed in order to get a correct assessment of the degree of ANC unity and cohesion.

Let me make one final comment on the distinction drawn by Andrew Reynolds between consociational and consensus systems of power sharing in which the former is ethnically based and the latter is not. His observation that consociational democracies tend to be based on ethnic groups as the main building blocks (in the broadest sense of ethnicity, including religious-cultural differences) is essentially correct. In fact, ethnic groups are often explicitly named in constitutions or other basic laws or pacts as the constituent elements of the power-sharing system, as currently in Belgium and Lebanon, and also in the 1960 constitution of Cyprus. Moreover, even when the constitution does not explicitly name them, ethnic groups often become the main players in the consociational game, as in Switzerland, India, and Malaysia. The reason is that ethnic groups tend to be strong and tenacious, and that the framers of consociational systems have recognized this fact as an objective reality—in perfect agreement with the argument presented by Milton Esman in his chapter in this volume. It is a reality that constitution-makers and political scientists can ignore only at their own and their countries' peril.

At the same time, my thinking about possible solutions for the problem of South Africa from the 1970s on taught me that the optimal consociational system is one that does not predetermine that its constituent segments have to be ethnic groups. The special characteristic of South Africa was that, on the one hand, it was clearly a deeply divided society, but that, on the other hand, many people, especially those in the ANC, rejected the very notion of ethnicity; moreover, for those willing to think in ethnic terms, it was difficult to specify which ethnic or racial groups qualified as basic units. I also became more aware of the fact that, while ethnic groups tend to be strong and tenacious, they can also be fluid; as Esman emphasizes, ethnic groups are not static entities. For all of these reasons, I searched for consociational rules that would allow ethnic groups to become the main actors in consociational systems without predetermining this outcome.

In my 1985 book *Power-Sharing in South Africa*, I recommended two methods for the self-determination, instead of predetermination, of the segments in a consociational system. One is proportional representation, which allows any group, ethnic or nonethnic, to gain political representation if it so desires and if it receives sufficient support from its voters. The other is segmental autonomy on a voluntary basis; for instance, any group that wishes to have and run its own schools can organize to do so, and to receive full state support. There are several historical precedents for this self-determinative approach, notably the 1917 consociational settlement in the Netherlands. An additional advantage is that such a system is much more flexible than a predetermined system and allows for the gradual adjustment to changes in the sizes of and relations between groups and in the strength of ethnic sentiments. In short, although I believe that consociationalism offers the best chances for a workable democracy in ethnically divided societies, I also believe that the optimal consociational system is one that permits the self-determination rather than predetermination of the constituent segments.

Degrees and Dimensions

Beyond the two categories of consociation and consensus, all of the authors think in terms of degrees and varieties in nonmajoritarian democratic systems. In particular, Jack Nagel proposes a spectrum of democratic systems—a spectrum that he tries to expand—and Milton Esman argues that the core necessity in power-sharing systems is symbolic recognition and some measure of participation implemented by a range of methods, the specifics of which are not as important as the basic commitment to share power. But in all of the other chapters, too, the authors in one way or another think in terms of a continuum within nonmajoritarianism.

This has also been the approach in my own work. In *Democracy in Plural Societies*, for instance, I describe my prime consociational cases in terms of four characteristics that can be found in all of them, but not necessarily to the same degree and with the same strength. And in addition to the fully consociational cases, I discuss the two semiconsociational cases of Canada and Israel. As stated earlier, one important aim of *Democracies* was to go beyond *Democracy in Plural Societies* by measuring the degrees of consensus and majority rule as precisely as possible on the assumption that, at least in principle, democratic systems can range from zero percent to 100 percent consensus.

Another aspect of the variety of nonmajoritarian forms is that different dimensions of nonmajoritarianism can be discerned. Rein Taagepera diagnoses the step-by-step and rather haphazard procedure by which I arrived at this conclusion in *Democracies* very well. I started out thinking in terms of a single dimension of majoritarianism vs consensus and with the working hypothesis that, in line with this one-dimensional assumption, all eight individual characteristics would correlate with each other. It was indeed not until the last chapter that my factor analysis showed that there were not one but, very clearly, two separate dimensions. I simply referred to these two dimensions as the first and second dimensions but, in later writings, I shifted to the more descriptive labels of executives-parties and federal-unitary dimensions. The first groups together five characteristics of the party and electoral systems and of the arrangement of executive power; the second has to do with the three variables of government centralization, constitutional flexibility, and bicameralism vs unicameralism.

In retrospect, it is difficult for me to understand that I did not recognize these two separate dimensions at a much earlier stage. For one thing, in my work on consociational democracy I had already described grand coalition and segmental autonomy as the two principal characteristics (with proportionality and the minority veto as secondary traits), and I had described them as based on complementary but clearly different principles: participation in the making of joint decisions vs exclusive decision-making in the group's own concerns. More importantly, the old-institutional theorists of federalism had already pointed out the connections among my three characteristics of the federal-unitary dimension a long time ago: the obvious purpose of federalism is to promote and guarantee decentralized government, and for this guarantee to work it is important that there be a powerful federal chamber in a bicameral legislature plus a constitution that cannot be amended easily and that is protected by the neutral arbiter of a supreme or constitutional court (Wheare 1946, Friedrich 1974). I could have cited their work as suggesting a separate federal-unitary dimension in my first chapter, and then found confirmation of this hypothesis in my concluding chapter. That would have been more elegant—but less representative of how my research actually proceeded.

As indicated earlier, Markus Crepaz and I added the variable of interest group pluralism or corporatism to the analysis of majoritarianism vs consensus. Our hypothesis was that this new variable would be part of the first or executives-parties dimension instead of the second, federal-unitary dimension, because it is a phenomenon at the national level instead of one having to do with national-subnational relations; another way of expressing this difference would be to call the first dimension the horizontal and the second the vertical dimension. Our hypothesis found strong empirical confirmation: pluralism-corporatism is highly correlated with the executives-parties dimension—which now should probably be called the executives-parties-interest-groups dimension, except that this is too much of a mouthful!

A second new variable that I have entered into the comparative analysis of democracies in recent work is the independence of central banks: independent central banks represent a dispersal of power and hence fit the consensus model, whereas central banks that are dependent on the government, and especially on the executive branch, represent concentrated power and fit the majoritarian model. My original assumption was that, since central banks, like the major interest groups, operate mainly at the national level, the degree of central bank independence would be part of the executives-parties dimension. The alternative possibilities were that it might be part of the second dimension or that it might not correlate with either of the two dimensions.

To my surprise—serendipity at work once again!—central bank independence turned out not to fit the first dimension at all, but it did fit the federal-unitary dimension very comfortably. My tentative explanation is that the horizontal-vertical contrast may not be the critical consideration after all, and that the better distinction may be the difference between collective and shared responsibility on the one hand and divided responsibilities on the other, suggested by Robert E. Goodin (1996: 331). These are both forms of diffusion of power, but the executives-parties dimension with its multiparty face-to-face interactions within cabinets, legislatures, and legislative committees has a close fit with the collective-responsibility form. In contrast, the old second-dimension variables as well as the role of central banks fit the format of dispersal of power by means of institutional separation. If this is the correct perspective, a good case can be made for a renaming of the second dimension, too. However, I must confess a preference for the nicely concrete contrast between executives-parties and federal-unitary dimensions instead of the much more abstract collective responsibility versus divided responsibilities dimensions, although the latter may be a better characterization of the two dimensions at a deeper theoretical level.

Another surprise is that all of the institutional characteristics that I have examined cluster in just two dimensions: do these two dimensions exhaust the entire institutional realm? Bernard Grofman suggests that there may be as many as four additional dimensions. One of these is the weight of direct democracy in different systems. I studied one small, but important, part of this variable in *Democracies* in the form of the frequency of referendums, and I found that it did not correlate with either of my two main dimensions—which means that it indeed formed a separate third dimension by itself. But I find it difficult to predict how the more inclusive variable of direct democracy, properly defined and operationalized, would behave in empirical analysis. It may be necessary to first disaggregate referendums because these have both majoritarian and consensual characteristics as well as both first-dimension and second-dimension consensus characteristics. Conventionally, we tend to think of the referendum as more majoritarian than consensual; in fact, referendums are often regarded as even more majoritarian than representative majoritarian government, because elected legislatures offer at least some opportunities for minorities to present and discuss their case and to engage in bargaining and logrolling. In the words of David Butler and Austin Ranney (1978: 36), "because they cannot measure intensities of beliefs or work things out through discussion and discovery, referendums are bound to be more dangerous than representative assemblies to minority rights."

On the other hand, when the referendum is combined with the popular initiative, as in Switzerland, it gives even very small minorities a chance to press a claim against legislative majorities. Even if the effort does not succeed, it forces the majority to spend its energy and money on a referendum campaign. The potential calling of a referendum by a minority is therefore a strong incentive for the majority to heed minority views and a strong incentive to form broad coalitions. Franz Lehner (1984: 30) has argued that, in Switzerland, "any coalition with a predictable and safe chance of winning has to include all parties and organizations that may be capable of calling for a successful referendum." This aspect of referendums reinforces consensus on the executives-parties dimension. Referendums are also often required for the adoption of constitutional amendments and hence serve as instruments to make constitutions more rigid, that is, less easy to amend—a second-dimension consensus characteristic. When we look at all of the referendums held at the national level, it is striking that most of these have been held in one country—consensual Switzerland—and that many of the others have been part of the process of constitutional amendment.

The other three potential dimensions proposed by Bernard Grofman all sound plausible and promising. It seems quite possible to me that if judicial power can be separated into two realms, federal-state relations and individual claims against the state at either level, the latter may not cluster with the federal-unitary dimension. Similarly, the nature of citizenship and the question of individual versus group rights do not appear to be linked a priori with either of my two main dimensions and may therefore well constitute separate dimensions, as Grofman suggests. In principle, these variables can all be operationalized and all three of the Grofman hypotheses deserve to be tested empirically.

So far in this section, I have dealt with varieties of nonmajoritarian democracy. The other side of the coin has to do with varieties of majoritarian government, and several authors analyze this side of the coin, too. Andrew Reynolds proposes three forms of majoritarian democracy by first distinguishing between unadulterated majoritarianism—the pure Westminster model—and majoritarianism qualified by proportionality and minority rights, and then adding the kind of system that has been advocated by Donald L. Horowitz (1991). Reynolds attaches the suitable label of integrative majoritarianism to the Horowitzian model. Horowitz's proposal is designed for the government of ethnically plural societies, which gives it a clear affinity to consociational and consensus forms of democracy. However, I believe that

Reynolds is correct in classifying this model not as a form of consensus but of majority rule: minority interests and rights are supposed to be protected not by direct minority inclusion in decision-making but by making majorities more moderate. Bernard Grofman distinguishes between two forms of majoritarian democracy, one of which is what Jack Nagel calls pluralitarian democracy—a subject to which I shall return next.

Two authors even venture into nondemocratic territory. Milton Esman argues that power sharing is not necessarily synonymous with consociational or power-sharing democracy, and that it is also possible in authoritarian systems. The many examples he cites, including the major historical examples of the Ottoman and Austro-Hungarian empires, are highly persuasive. From the constitutional designer's point of view, I would say that in deeply divided societies consociational democracy is preferable to consociational oligarchy, but that consociational oligarchy is much to be preferred to nonconsociational oligarchy.

Jack Nagel proposes an intriguing one-dimensional spectrum that smoothly moves from consensus to majoritarian forms of democracy and then further to elite rule and dictatorship. This perspective is reinforced when we look at some of the separate elements that distinguish majoritarian from consensus democracy. For instance, with regard to party systems, there is a spectrum from multipartism (consensus democracy), to two-party systems (majoritarianism), to one-party rule (authoritarianism). Another such continuum is from executive-legislative balance of power (consensus), to executive dominance (majoritarianism), to absolute executive power (authoritarianism). However, the order is partly reversed for the interest group system: interest group pluralism (majoritarianism), societal corporatism (consensus), state corporatism (authoritarianism).

The Individual Ingredients of Power Sharing

In addition to all of the different kinds, degrees, and dimensions of nonmajoritarian democracies discussed previously, these democracies may also differ in their different combinations of the separate ingredients of power sharing. For instance, some consociational democracies may be especially strong with regard to grand coalitions (Switzerland) and others may have unusually strong minority veto provisions (Belgium). Similarly, the two dimensions of consensus vs majoritarianism are made up of separate elements and, though these elements are correlated to a high degree, a particular country may be more or less strong with regard to the different elements. An example here is that the United States is clearly on the majoritarian side of the executives-parties dimension (concentrated executive power, two-party system, plurality elections) in spite of also having a powerful legislature and, in fact, as high a degree of executive-legislative balance as occurs in any democracy.

I have already commented on several of these elements at some length: minimal winning vs oversized governments (especially in the context of Austria and South Africa), the interest group system, and central banks as well as the other three elements in the federal-unitary dimension. However, there are two other important elements that are discussed in the previous chapters but that I have not covered yet: first, proportional representation (PR) and its links with other consensus variables and, second, the question of "fusion of power" in executive-legislative relations.

Jack Nagel rightly emphasizes that the abolition of plurality voting and the introduction of PR in New Zealand did not simultaneously introduce full consensus democracy—and should not have been expected to do so. Electoral proportionality correlates with the other elements of the executives-parties dimension, but the relationship is actually not all that strong. In my factor analysis in *Democracies*, the effective number of parties has the strongest correlation (.99) with the first factor representing the executives-parties dimension, and the correlation coefficient for electoral disproportionality is only .42. The other three coefficients are all considerably higher: .85, .75, and .72. On the other hand, the electoral system is causally linked both to the party system and, indirectly, to cabinet formation. PR generally leads to an increase in the number of parties and decreases the likelihood that one party will win a majority of legislative seats. This was especially relevant in the New Zealand case where, under plurality voting, legislative majorities were created for parties that won less than 44 percent of the vote on average since 1972. PR systems differ with regard to their degree of proportionality, but only an unusually disproportional PR system would convert 44 percent of the votes into a majority of seats. Multiparty systems are also more likely than two-party systems to be systems with more issue dimensions dividing the parties.

Furthermore, if there is no majority party in the legislature, there cannot be a one-party majority cabinet. But indeed, as Nagel points out, there are still two options that differ from the consensus norm of an oversized cabinet: a minority cabinet and a coalition cabinet that is minimal winning. I think that a minimal winning coalition cabinet should be regarded as more consensual than a minimal winning one-party cabinet—in retrospect, I wish that I had used the one-party vs coalition contrast as an additional criterion for measuring the variable of executive power sharing in *Democracies*—but a minimal winning coalition is obviously less consensual than an oversized coalition. There may be a further relationship between coalition cabinets and less cabinet predominance over the legislature, but it probably goes too far to regard this as another indirect effect of PR. If the interest group system is also taken into consideration, there is no logical link between PR and corporatism at all, of course. It is also good to remember the example of Malta, which has PR elections but a Westminster-style government in all other respects.

Both Thomas Koelble and Jack Nagel mention the distinction between fusion and separation of powers as one of the differences between majoritarian and consensus democracies. Fusion of power means a parliamentary system of government, and separation of power normally means a presidential system, although it can also be used to describe the Swiss system of an executive elected by, but not responsible to, the legislature. I introduced this distinction in the first chapter of *Democracies*, but I now think that this was a mistake. My main excuse is that I was tempted into this error by my choice of the United Kingdom and Switzerland as the exemplars of the two models. The distinction that I really wanted to make was between executive dominance and executive-legislative balance. This distinction is logically independent of the parliamentary-presidential contrast and, to the extent that there is an empirical connection, it is the reverse of what I imply in the first chapter of *Democracies*.

First of all, executive dominance can be found in both parliamentary and presidential systems. Lord Hailsham's (1978: 127) characterization of the British parliamentary system as an "elective dictatorship" is frequently quoted; it is similar to the label of "delegative democracy" that Guillermo O'Donnell (1994) has attached to Latin American presidential systems with all-powerful presidents and that could also be applied to France (except in periods of so-called cohabitation). On the other side, the United States and Costa Rica are presidential systems with relatively weak presidents, and most continental European parliamentary systems have cabinets that are considerably less dictatorial than the British. What is more important is that although U.S.-style presidentialism means executive-legislative balance, other features of presidential government promote majoritarian characteristics: concentration of executive power in the hands of not just one party, but one person; the fact that presidential elections favor the largest parties and hence tend to reduce the number of parties; and the inherent disproportionality of presidential elections in which the winning candidate wins "all of the seats"—that is, the one seat at stake—and the loser loses completely. This is one important reason why presidentialism is unsuitable for deeply divided societies, as Andrew Reynolds discusses in his chapter.

Does Type of Democracy Make a Difference?

Finally, let me turn to the "so what?" question: Does the type of democracy that a country has, or the degree to which a democracy is majoritarian or consensual, make a difference in how well the democratic system performs? Three concerns dominate the chapters in this book: the consequences of the type of democracy on 1) the maintenance of peace and the survival of democracy in deeply divided societies; 2) how well different governments handle the day-to-day problems of macro-economic management; and 3) how responsive governments are to the outcome of elections.

As far as the first question is concerned, it is indeed hard to see, as Milton Esman emphasizes, how a positive future for the world's most deeply divided societies can be visualized except through some variation on the theme of power sharing. I find it striking that even in those cases where consociational democracy was tried but failed—Lebanon, Cyprus, and Northern Ireland—the response to failure has not been to give up on power sharing, but to recognize that it is still the only alternative—and to keep trying to introduce it. Lebanon's consociational system ended in civil war in 1975, but when democracy was restored by the Taif Accord in 1989, most of the old consociational system was also resurrected with only minor improvements—far fewer repairs than I would have liked to see. But the important fact is that the Lebanese realized that they did not have a choice between majoritarian and power-sharing forms, and that their only realistic choice was among different kinds of power sharing.

Power sharing was instituted in Cyprus upon independence in 1960, but it never worked well and was ended by the 1963 civil war. It appeared to be permanently doomed by the Turkish invasion in 1974 and the subsequent de facto partition of the island into Greek Cypriot and Turkish Cypriot states. Nevertheless, the main proposals for a unified Cyprus, notably those by U.N. Secretaries-General Javier Pérez de Cuéllar and Boutros Boutros-Ghali, all resemble the basic consociational features of the old 1960 constitution. Similarly, the brief experiment with power sharing in Northern Ireland in 1974 failed, but this has not deterred the British government from insisting that such a system is the only possible and acceptable solution; the peace agreement that was finally reached in 1998 is unmistakably and thoroughly consociational.[2]

As far as macro-economic management is concerned, Markus Crepaz (1996) has found strong links between consensus democracy and the successful handling of unemployment, inflation, and industrial disputes; and he found that economic growth was about the same in the two types of democracies. In my own research (Lijphart 1994b), I have found similar relationships but not strong enough to be statistically significant. The slight difference in our results can be attributed to our different methods, different definitions, and different time periods. In their chapter in this volume, Markus Crepaz and Vicki Birchfield persuasively extend the logic of this conclusion to the new challenge of globalization: consensus democracies can be expected to respond more efficiently and responsibly to the new pressures while maintaining legitimacy and fairness.

Bingham Powell's main emphasis is on democratic quality and especially the crucial question of democratic responsiveness. One striking conclusion that I mentioned earlier is that he finds the ideals of the alternative constitutional designs to be so different that it is very difficult to measure their performance according to the same standard. Where there does seem to be common ground—notably with regard to the desirability in both visions that the party or preelection coalition winning the largest number of votes would form the government after the election and would last until the next election—the majoritarian designs appear to have at least a slight advantage. Even here, however, I think that there is no perfect unanimity on what responsiveness means. I, for one, am not greatly bothered by the formation of a new coalition between elections as long as the parties forming the new coalition have majority support and continue to support the same policies to which they committed themselves at the time of the election. But I know that this is a pattern that many democrats dislike, and the negative reaction to it has led to the unwritten rule in both German and the Netherlands in recent years that major coalition shifts cannot be made without new elections. This is obviously also a rule that could be made into a formal constitutional requirement.

One aspect of responsiveness—the extent to which the party or parties forming the cabinet are supported by popular majorities—examined by Powell is also prominently discussed by Jack Nagel, Bernard Grofman, and, in earlier work, by Markus Crepaz. In his *Considerations on Representative Government*, John Stuart Mill (1861) already worried that when majority rule is used twice—first in the conversion of popular votes to legislative seats and second as a decision rule in the legislature—it runs the risk of turning into undemocratic minority rule. If the election is by absolute majority, parliamentary decisions may be made that are supported by only slightly more than 25 percent of the voters; if the election is by plurality, this percentage can be even lower. Mill's main reason for advocating PR was that it could better safeguard majority rule. Grofman follows Mill's lead when he argues that PR is a more truly majoritarian institution than plurality. Crepaz (1996) develops a measure of popular cabinet support and shows that it is positively linked with consensus democracy. And on Nagel's spectrum of democratic systems, PR is likely to lead to truly majoritarian democracy and possibly to super-majoritarian or consensus democracy, whereas plurality elections are likely to fall short of majority rule and provide only pluralitarian democracy.

Bingham Powell mentions one important qualification to these conclusions. What this discussion assumes is that cabinets will be formed by parties that together have a majority in the legislature. But it is also possible, both in plurality and PR systems, that minority governments form. In fact, especially in the Scandinavian PR countries, such minority cabinets are quite common. These obviously cannot claim popular majority support. However, there is still a big difference between such minority cabinets that, in PR systems, are dependent on and carefully watched by a majority in parliament on the one hand and majority cabinets based on mere plurality support in majoritarian democracies on the other.

The case for PR is strengthened when we measure popular cabinet support not just in terms of the support of the actual voters but of all eligible voters. According to the latter criterion, popular cabinet support by majorities is harder to achieve in both systems, but PR systems have the advantage of stimulating higher levels of voter turnout—by as much as 10 percentage points as several studies have found (e.g., Blais and Carty 1990).

Overall, the chapters of this book point to the conclusion that nonmajoritarian democracy in its various forms and shapes is clearly preferable to the majoritarian or pluralitarian alternative. This is a conclusion that I wholeheartedly endorse.

Notes

[1]My book *Patterns of Democracy* makes this adjustment for the Austrian grand coalitions and for similar broadly based, although technically minimal winning, coalitions in a few other countries. It also makes several other improvements discussed later in this chapter, such as the addition of the interest group system as an element of the executives-parties dimension (Lijphart 1999).

[2]The main provisions of the agreement correspond closely to the British government's proposals in the so-called *Framework Document on Northern Ireland*, published in early 1995 (see Lijphart 1996).

References

Blais, André, and R. K. Carty. 1990. "Does Proportional Representation Foster Voter Turnout?" *European Journal of Political Research*, 18, 2 (March): 167–81.

Butler, David, and Austin Ranney. 1978. *Referendums: A Comparative Study of Practice and Theory*. Washington DC: American Enterprise Institute.

Collier, David, and Steven Levitsky. 1997. "Democracy with Adjectives: Conceptual Innovation in Comparative Research," *World Politics* 49, 3 (April): 430–51.

Crepaz, Markus M. L. 1996. "Political Institutions and Their Impact on Macroeconomic Performance and Industrial Disputes," *Comparative Political Studies* 29, 1 (February): 4–26.

Dahl, Robert A. 1956. *A Preface to Democratic Theory*. Chicago: University of Chicago Press.

Friedrich, Carl J. 1974. *Limited Government: A Comparison*. Englewood Cliffs, NJ: Prentice-Hall.

Goodin, Robert E. 1996. "Institutionalizing the Public Interest: The Defense of Deadlock and Beyond," *American Political Science Review* 90, 2 (June): 331–43.

Hailsham, Lord. 1978. *The Dilemma of Democracy: Diagnosis and Prescription*. London: Collins.

Horowitz, Donald L. 1991. *A Democratic South Africa? Constitutional Engineering in a Divided Society*. Berkeley: University of California Press.

Huntington, Samuel P. 1991. *The Third Wave: Democratization in the Late Twentieth Century*. Norman: University of Oklahoma Press.

Katz, Richard S. 1997. *Democracy and Elections*. New York: Oxford University Press.

Laakso, Markku, and Rein Taagepera. 1979. "'Effective' Number of Parties: A Measure with Application to West Europe," *Comparative Political Studies* 12, 1 (April): 3–27.

Lawson, Stephanie. 1993. "Conceptual Issues in the Comparative Study of Regime Change and Democratization," *Comparative Politics* 25, 2 (January): 183–205.

Lehmbruch, Gerhard. 1967. *Proporzdemokratie: Politisches System und politische Kultur in der Schweiz und in Österreich*. Tübingen: Mohr.

Lehner, Franz. 1984. "Consociational Democracy in Switzerland: A Political-Economic Explanation and Some Empirical Evidence," *European Journal of Political Research* 12, 1 (March): 25–42.

Lewis, W. Arthur. 1965. *Politics in West Africa*. London: Allen and Unwin.

Lijphart, Arend. 1968a. *The Politics of Accommodation: Pluralism and Democracy in the Netherlands*. Berkeley: University of California Press.

Lijphart, Arend. 1968b. "Typologies of Democratic Systems," *Comparative Political Studies* 1, 1 (April): 3–44.

Lijphart, Arend. 1977. *Democracy in Plural Societies: A Comparative Exploration*. New Haven: Yale University Press.

Lijphart, Arend, ed. 1981. *Conflict and Coexistence in Belgium: The Dynamics of a Culturally Divided Society*. Berkeley: Institute of International Studies, University of California.

Lijphart, Arend. 1984. *Democracies: Patterns of Majoritarian and Consensus Government in Twenty-One Countries*. New Haven: Yale University Press.

Lijphart, Arend. 1985. *Power-Sharing in South Africa*. Berkeley: Institute of International Studies, University of California.

Lijphart, Arend. 1994a. "Prospects for Power-Sharing in the New South Africa." In Andrew Reynolds, ed., *Election '94 South Africa: The Campaigns, Results and Future Prospects*. New York: St. Martin's Press.

Lijphart, Arend. 1994b. "Democracies: Forms, Performance, and Constitutional Engineering," *European Journal of Political Research* 25, 1 (January): 1–17.

Lijphart, Arend. 1996. "The Framework Document on Northern Ireland and the Theory of Power-Sharing," *Government and Opposition* 31, 3 (Summer): 267–74.

Lijphart, Arend. 1999. *Patterns of Democracy: Government Forms and Performance in Thirty-Six Countries*. New Haven: Yale University Press.

Lijphart, Arend, and Markus M. L. Crepaz. 1991. "Corporatism and Consensus Democracy in Eighteen Countries: Conceptual and Empirical Linkages," *British Journal of Political Science* 21, 2 (April): 235–46.

Mansbridge, Jane. 1980. *Beyond Adversary Democracy*. New York: Basic Books.

Mill, John Stuart. 1861. *Considerations on Representative Government*. London: Parker and Bourn.

New York Times News Service. 1990. "Mandela Assails Guarantees for S. Africa Whites," *San Diego Union*, May 7.

O'Donnell, Guillermo. 1994. "Delegative Democracy," *Journal of Democracy* 5, 1 (January): 55–69.

Powell, G. Bingham, Jr. 1982. *Contemporary Democracies: Participation, Stability, and Violence*. Cambridge, MA: Harvard University Press.

Przeworski, Adam, Michael Alvarez, José Antonio Cheibub, and Fernando Limongi. 1996. "What Makes Democracies Endure?" *Journal of Democracy* 7, 1 (January): 39–55.

Riker, William H. 1982. *Liberalism Against Populism: A Confrontation Between the Theory of Democracy and the Theory of Social Choice*. San Francisco: Freeman.

Safire, William. 1986. "The Suzman Plan," *New York Times*, August 7.

Wheare, K. C. 1946. *Federal Government*. Oxford: Oxford University Press.

Index